Muskoka Originals

Artistry and Inspiration
on the Muskoka Autumn Studio Tour

Muskoka Originals

Artistry and Inspiration
on the Muskoka Autumn Studio Tour

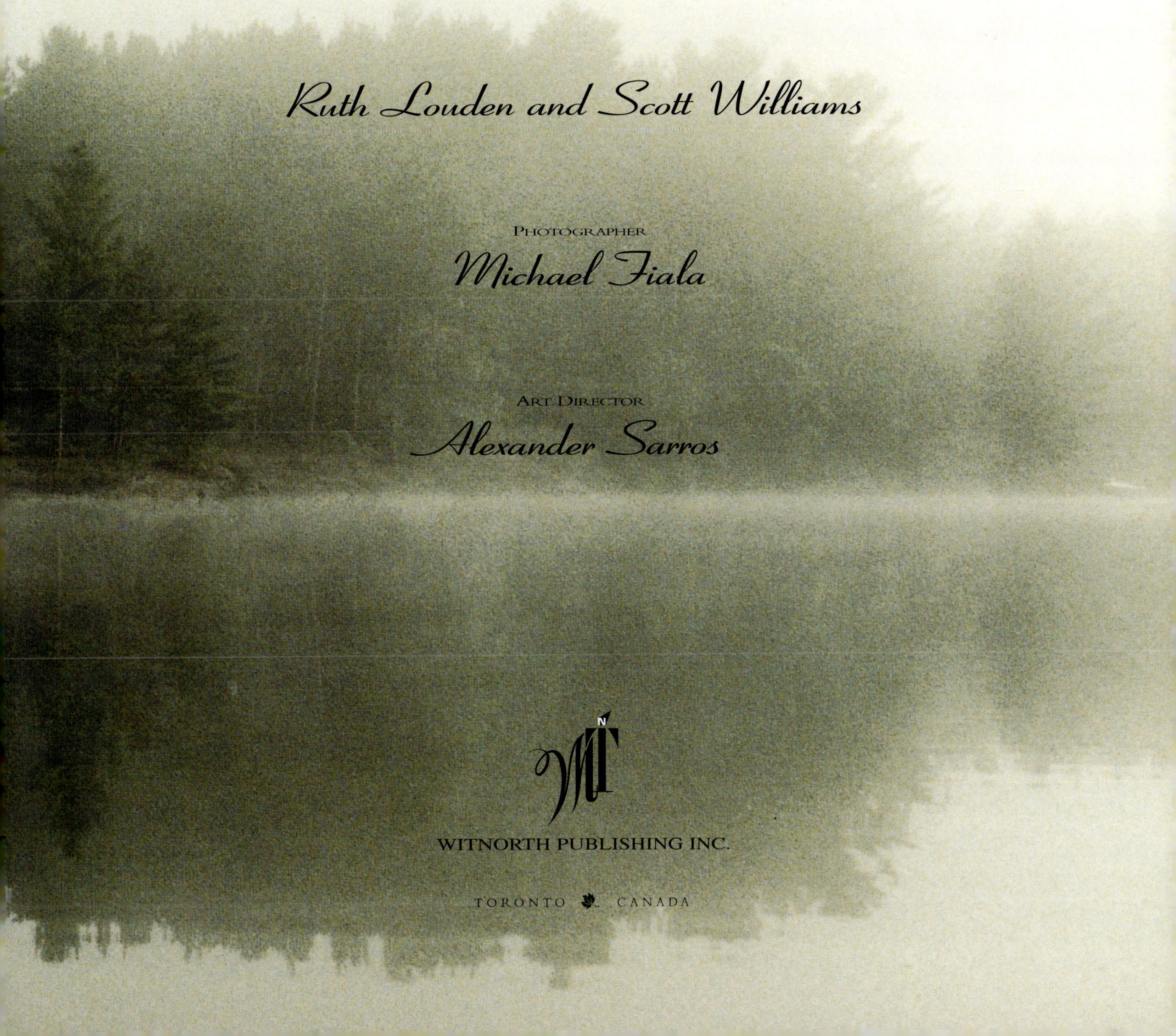

Ruth Louden and Scott Williams

PHOTOGRAPHER
Michael Fiala

ART DIRECTOR
Alexander Sarros

WITNORTH PUBLISHING INC.

TORONTO CANADA

Published in 1998 by:
Witnorth Publishing Inc.
47 Colborne Street, Suite 300
Toronto, Canada M5E 1P8
Telephone: (416) 947-9358
Fax: (416) 947-1722
E-mail: wit@globalserve.net

Canadian Cataloguing in Publication Data

Louden, Ruth
Muskoka Originals/Ruth Louden and Scott Williams

ISBN-0-9683235-0-2

1. Art - Canada
2. Crafts
3. Biography
I. Williams, Scott II. Title

Distributed in Canada by:
Hushion House
36 Northline Road
Toronto, Ontario M4B 3E2
Telephone: (416) 285-6100
Fax: (416) 285-1777
E-mail: jaddison@hushion.com

Title Page Photograph: *Muskoka Inkblot*, Goozie Kerr
Designer: Shelna Kathleen Brace
Colour Separations and Film: Transmedia Graphics Inc., Mississauga
Printed on 100 lb. Bravo Gloss, Island Paper Mills, New Westminster, B.C.
Printed in Canada by Friesens

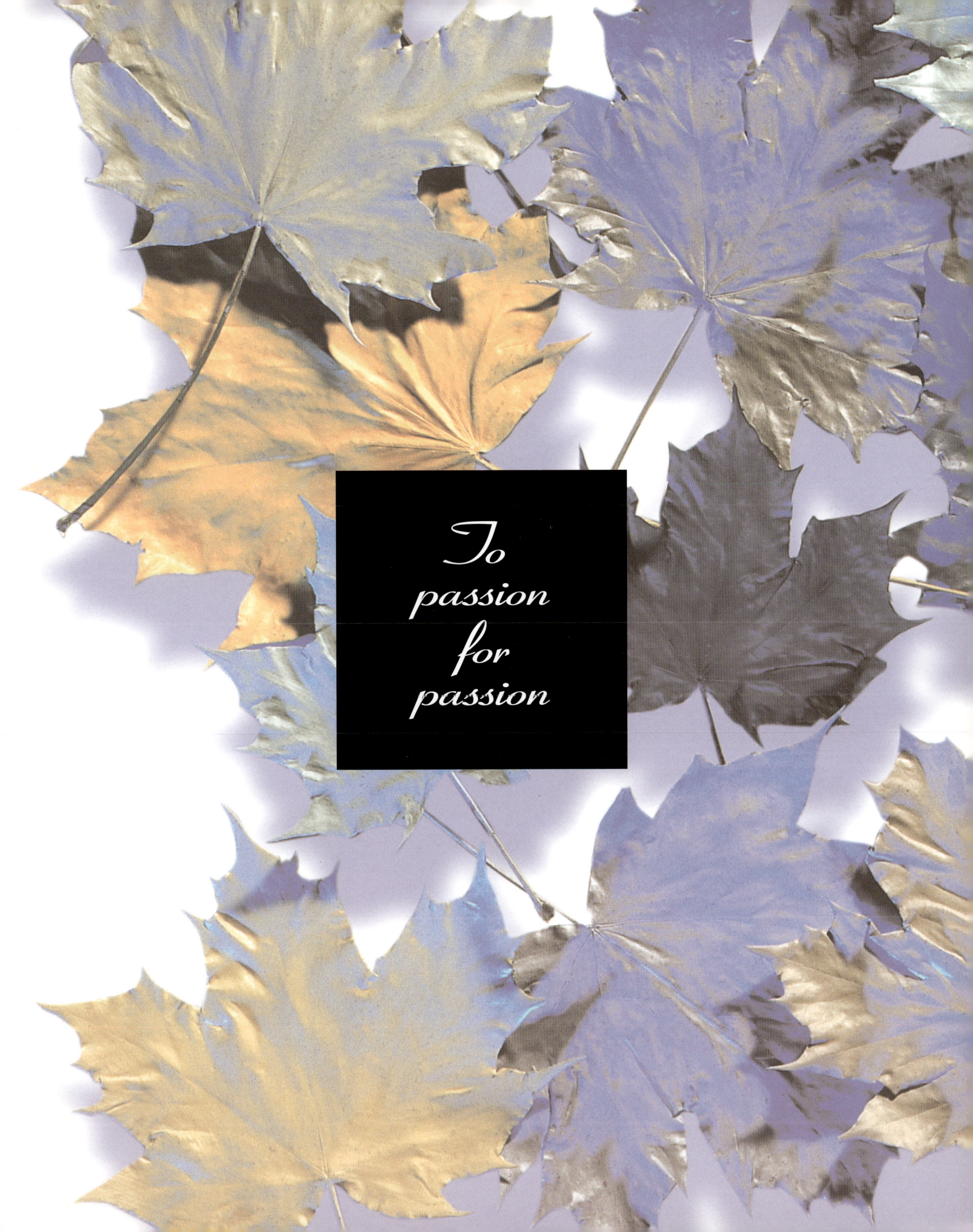

To
passion
for
passion

Acknowledgements

This book, without a doubt, is a true symbol of spirit and synergy among an impromptu and inventive assembly of associates, artisans and artists.

We could not have attempted to capture the artistry and inspiration of the 1998 Muskoka Autumn Studio Tour without the trust and good will of its 22 members.

We could not have transformed an abstraction into an absolute without tremendous support from Shelna Brace Graphics, TransMedia Graphics, Hushion House and Friesens Corporation, all of whom responded graciously to challenging budgets, impossible schedules, and occasional indecision.

And, lastly, we could not have pushed ourselves that extra inch without support from each other, family members young and old, friends, mentors and significant others. Their input and advice, though not always heeded, were welcome and immeasurably valuable. Take note Rita, Peter, Mark, Harry and Christina.

Contents

Nurturing Nature

I learned this, at least, by my experiment, that if one advances confidently
in the direction of his dreams, and endeavours to live the life which he has imagined,
he will meet with a success unexpected in common hours.
— Henry David Thoreau

Muskoka Originals undertook its journey with two objectives. The first was to capture moments of artistry in the life and work of a select group of artists and craftspeople. The second, to inspire those who leaf through these pages to strive for artistry in their own lives, in whatever form that may be.

The journey takes place on the Muskoka Autumn Studio Tour. It's Ontario's original studio tour, begun in 1979. Today, it's an annual rite of fall among Ontario's fabled Muskoka lakes.

Membership on the tour has changed over the years, but a common theme unites those present and past: their choice to make a living at something heartfelt and meaningful, and to fully integrate it into their lives. Their work may help define them, but they aren't defined by their work.

Muskoka Originals visits the 22 artists and craftspeople who are members in 1998, the studio tour's 20th anniversary. Just before our tour begins, Muskoka writer Mel Malton spins us through the area and its history, an archetypal story of man confronting nature, then learning to live in harmony with it.

Then the tour proper begins. Along the way you'll meet six potters, two cabinet makers, a bronze sculptor, a woodcarver, two artist blacksmiths, three painters, two jewellers, a printmaker, three glass blowers and a stained glass artist.

Michael Fiala's luminous photography reveals the outer expression of these people's creative inner lives. Their work is striking, glorious; it's also subtle and, in some instances, subversive. But make no mistake. It's the work of individuals, not icons. Their personal stories reveal days light and dark; their anecdotes recount successes, failures, and lessons learned while on their journeys of the heart.

At the centre of Muskoka Originals is the theme of right livelihood. It suggests that within all of us lies a natural order, a compass that guides us to our right place in life. The more we align our lives and work according to the guidance from this internal compass, the greater will be our happiness and ultimate success. The singer must sing, the healer must heal, the teacher must teach.

The artist's path, though not the only path to right livelihood, is a clear and compelling example. Finding right livelihood requires both creativity and originality, the hallmarks of artistry. To express creativity, an artist must translate an idea into concrete form. An artist must do. To do well, an artist must employ his or her innate wisdom rather than rely solely on the wisdom of others.

This is a challenge. Communications technology has wired us to the world, but most of us have inadvertently tuned out our inner voice. We look elsewhere for answers, when they're already in our heart.

Artists of our own lives, we awaken each morning to a palette of colour, a set of tools, a universe of subjects. We have infinite choice. Our internal compass is as unique as our thumbprint. Not everyone is or should be a potter, a glass blower, a painter, but we can all aspire to artistry in the creation of our lives, to combine in artful ways choices that are meaningful and heartfelt.

Muskoka Mystique

by H. Mel Malton

In the hearts and minds of the first Muskoka settlers, the abundant wilderness was a bargain. All they had to do was survive. Seemingly limitless, the region that came to be known as Muskoka was a vast, untamed expanse of land, thick with potential lumber, its forests alive with game and fur-bearing creatures, its waters teeming with fish. Rivers and streams fringed with dense bush connected hundreds of deep, cold lakes. Majestic waterfalls thundered into breathtaking rock chasms, and splendid vistas presented themselves at every turn.

Before the area was opened up for white settlement, much of it had been Indian hunting and fishing territory – a collection of destinations reached by canoe, criss-crossed by portage routes, mapped in memory, but never considered home base.

In 1815, the land that lay north of Lake Simcoe was bought by the government for $20,000 from the original inhabitants, destined originally to become a reserve. In 1858, a colonization road was begun from Washago, heading north. Ten years later, the Free Grant Act offered any settler 18 years of age and over an opportunity to select 100 acres in any surveyed township. The head of a family could choose 200 acres. Within five years of taking up a grant, the settler was to have cleared and cultivated at least 15 acres of land, and built a house at least 16 by 20 feet, in which he had resided continuously and consecutively, not being away for more than six months at a time. If these conditions were met, a patent would be issued and the settler would hold his or her estate in fee simple.

In 1874, mapmaker W.E. Hamilton noted optimistically that "on the north, there seems to be no bar to our ultimate advancement till we reach a climate too cold or high in latitude for agriculture."

Muskoka, all 10,000 squares miles of it (described grandly by Hamilton as "the territorial heritage of our people") was to be cultivated. Neither governments nor settlers took into account the rock, until they attempted to till the soil. A hard, undeniable fact, the rock – called gneiss to the initiated, and something else entirely by would-be farmers – heaved up every spring through the thin topsoil like demon grain, taking the edge off the harrow and reducing grown men to tears. The rock towered on the banks of the rivers, porous and damp, harbouring the roots of trees and sprouting lichens thick as hair.

Many settlers persevered, scratching out a meagre living for the first few years, dragging boulders to the edge of the hay field and building walls with their mineral harvest. Some productive farms remain, but they must be tended, always, or the forest threatens to reclaim them, tree roots reaching hungrily for the greying walls of the barn.

With the failure of the agricultural experiment came the success of other ventures. Stands of white pine were there for the taking, translatable wealth for the brave and strong. Lumbering companies thrived, offering employment and stability. In a short time, villages matured into towns, shanties became frame houses and Muskoka started booming.

With the growth of the Muskoka settlements came a pleasant discovery that the unforgiving land, though nearly impossible to cultivate, had an attraction of its own. It was beautiful.

"To the artistic eye of the traveller who hungers after tidbits of forest vistas... Muskoka is a thing of beauty and a joy not soon to be forgotten," proclaims an early brochure. "Take a rest cure in a canoe!"

Residents discovered that a timid knock on the door was often followed by a request for accommodation. As ploughshares were beaten into inn signs, tourism – now Muskoka's prime industry – was born. Resorts sprouted like cattails on the shorelines of the lakes. As hundreds and then thousands of weary city folk arrived by train and steamer, grand resorts rose up out of the trees. In addition to clean air and birdsong, guests who were so inclined could also enjoy a glittering social season of picnics, promenades, black tie dinners, and dances in lakeside pavilions.

Wealthy industrialists from southern Ontario and the United States also bought waterfront property and built palatial summer homes, weaving themselves into the fabric of Muskoka. The raw material of rock and water was gradually fashioned into a linked bracelet of lakes, studded with jewels.

As the era of servants gave way to the age of the automobile, grand homes gave way to family cottages dotting the waterways like ducks. Muskoka became a playland for everyone.

One constant through change and growth was the green and fragrant forest. The tenacity of the forest may have plagued the farmers, but it helped the land recover from clear cutters. Early photographs show bald land, shorn of old-growth forest, unlovely stubble surrounding crude buildings, stumps uprooted by exhausted horses and desperate men. New growth rooted quickly. Some sections remained intact, and bit by bit people began designating key tracts as untouchable. Those who had first tried to conquer now tried to preserve.

Muskoka Notes

Bordered by Georgian Bay to the west, the Severn River to the south and Algonquin Park to the northeast, Muskoka covers about 4,000 square kilometres. The area is one sixth lakes and rivers. Much of what remains is Canadian Shield, or in other words, rock.

Highway 11, a north/south corridor, bisects Muskoka. Flanking the highway are the area's three largest communities, Gravenhurst, Bracebridge and Huntsville. They account for two thirds of Muskoka's permanent population. This group is growing steadily, from 32,000 in 1972 to 50,000 in 1997, and a projected 67,000 by the year 2011. Statistics show that the permanent population is greyer than the rest of the province, in part from an influx of retirees from the south.

More startling to the casual observer is the annual flood of seasonal visitors. In summer the resident population almost doubles. Another 600,000 people breeze through on short visits.

John Campbell and James Bain were Muskoka's first tourists. They arrived in 1860, long before the first village was incorporated, and ate Muskoka's first tourist meal at Mrs. Robinson's place (later known as the Three Flowers Inn). Presumably, they paid in cash. Campbell and Bain eventually established The Muskoka Club, a group of like-minded fellows who wished to explore the wild beauties of the region by canoe.

Under a bell-jar labelled "natural heritage," the wilderness continues to flourish. Thousands of acres of forest are alive with the kind of creatures found here a century ago, the waters still home to fish and fowl, the human hand invisible.

The heart of this Muskoka beats quietly, inviting its visitors to enter and be refreshed, asking nothing but to be experienced. The creative spirit thrives in this stillness, which is why artists first came, and why many have stayed for good.

From pioneer pencil-sketches to day-trippers' polaroids, the urge to preserve the moment has continued to generate art and artifacts, to encourage the birth of studios and galleries, and to enrich the lives of those who pass this way.

The artists and artisans who live and work here create Muskoka originals, but are originals themselves – taking in what is offered and giving form to the beauty that surrounds them.

This is a moment in their story.

The Muskoka Autumn Studio Tour – Bracebridge, Ontario, 1979

"We were a bunch of struggling artists in the middle of nowhere," says Richard Green, sculptor. In 1979, he lived on 60 acres on High Falls Road north of Bracebridge, working quietly in a small studio built into a hillside.

He had come to Muskoka for the solitude, but discovered that the peace of his piece of paradise had its price. "You could fire a cat down Main Street after Labour Day."

While the market for artists' work was active in the summer, the welcoming carpet was rolled up when the leaves turned colour.

"People were just coming up to close their cottages down," Green says. Artists barely knew one another, each working alone, relying on Toronto galleries, struggling to make a living.

Green shared his idea for a studio tour in the autumn with a few fellow artists. Nothing big, nothing terribly public. A small nugget of a notion, designed to lure known art buyers into the workplaces of the people who produced it. The most successful among those first 10 studio tour members maintained mailing lists, carefully compiled, guarded, perhaps. These lists were pooled, and after a few meetings, an unpretentious flyer went out announcing the first Muskoka Autumn Studio Tour – a 2-day event in September 1979, from 9:00 a.m. to 6:00 p.m.

"This was an ending for me of my own isolation," Green says. "It was a way for people to see and experience the artists. You had to show how you did your work."

Summoned, they came. The concept of watching an artist in action was relatively new, and the invitation held a fascination for some that went beyond a mere interest in the artistic process. Green remembers walking into a back room during one tour to find a woman quietly examining the contents of his closet, leafing through his suits like the pages of a book.

"I just wanted to see how you live," she explained.

Twenty years later, the original 10 has grown to include many of Muskoka's best known artists and artisans, with studios from one end of the region to the other. The tour isn't just a visit, it's a journey.

For the artist, the solitude of living and working in "cottage country" is no longer a constant. Every autumn, when the hillsides blaze with orange and gold, thousands of tourists and residents make their annual pilgrimage to the studios and homes of those who make art.

For many of us, it's a holiday. We witness clay rising from the wheel under a potter's hands, we peer over the painter's shoulder as colour is stroked onto canvas, and we marvel as life is breathed into a bubble of molten glass. We ask questions, gain insight and often buy art that we feel we had some part in making.

A connection has been made and for a moment we are given a peep into a private world. It's an enormously compelling place.

More Facts About Muskoka

The smallest railroad in the world used to run in Muskoka – the Portage Railroad in Lake of Bays. A project was launched in 1997 to re-establish the rail line in downtown Huntsville. The original steam engine, the Portage Flyer, will run on a new track from Muskoka Pioneer Village to Fairy Lake, where passengers will board the Bigwin ferry, also refurbished, a lakeside tour. Guides may or may not inform passengers of the following:

- The first newspaper published in Muskoka was the Northern Advocate, in Bracebridge in 1870
- In 1887, prospectors discovered gold, in nugget-form, in Gravenhurst.
- Huntsville's entire Main Street was ravaged by fire in 1894.
- NHL Hall of Famer Ace Bailey was born in Bracebridge.
- Norman Bethune was born in Gravenhurst.
- Seven miles north of Huntsville, American lawyer Clifton Dyer erected a memorial to his wife, Betsy. The 13-metre column of Muskoka stone is a tourist attraction.
- Canadian marathon swimmer Cindy Nicholas trained at Windermere.
- The great blue heron nests annually on Eleanor Island, in Gravenhurst.
- Six types of turtles reside in the Muskoka area.
- When the Port Carling lift bridge was raised for the first time in 1973, the pavement slid off into the water.

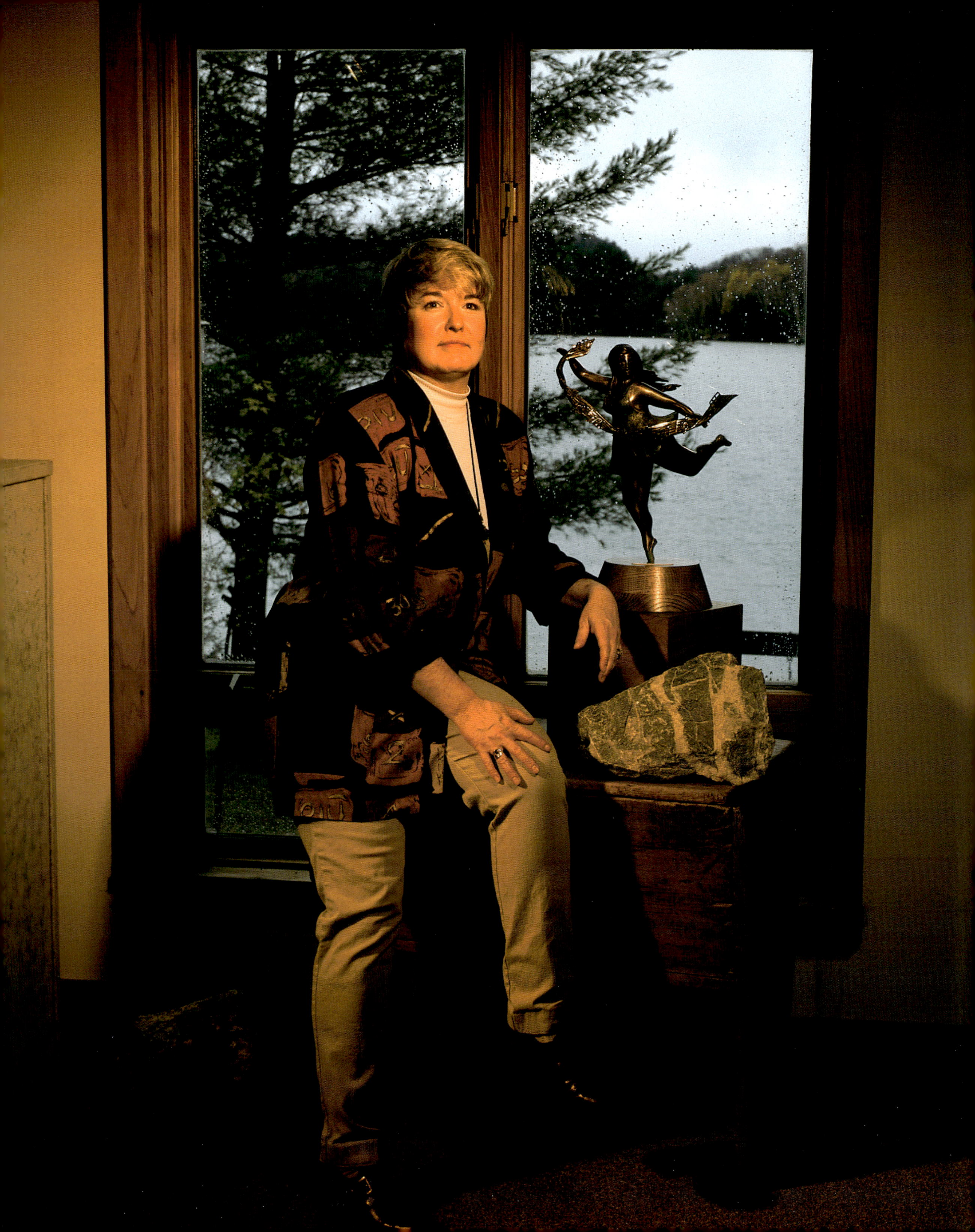

BRENDA WAINMAN GOULET

Nothing before / Nothing after / In faith my footsteps fall / on a seeming void / and find the rock beneath. – John Whittier

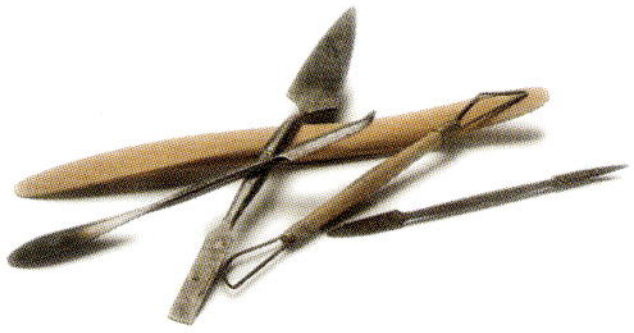

The Rock Beneath

The windows of Brenda Wainman Goulet's living room draw your eyes out across Walker Lake. An afternoon breeze chips the water's surface into brilliant shards of white, but peripheral shapes and colours draw you back inside. The room is full of life, bursts of colour on canvas, still lives, landscapes, and sculpture. One in particular dominates, an Indian rock drawing reinterpreted in bronze. It's a native spirit, hands raised, feet poised to step forward, the mouth an "O." This is Brenda's favourite piece, and it's not for sale.

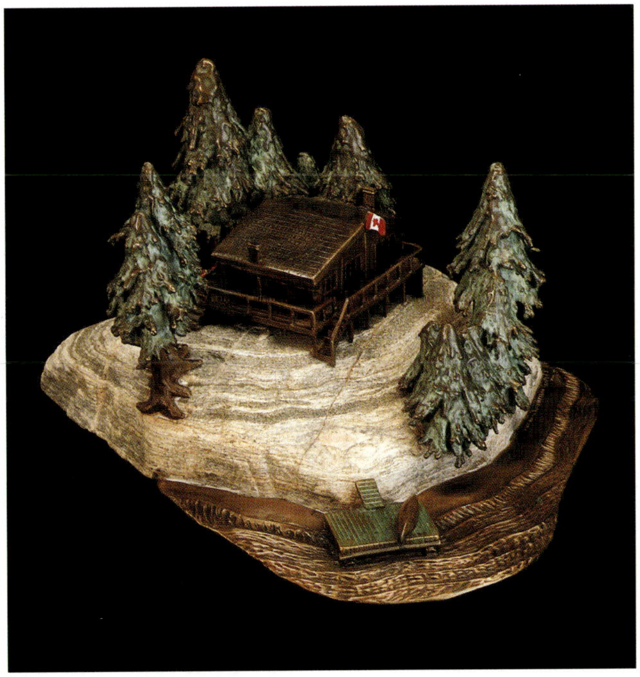

Brenda completed *Spirit* in the late 1970s, toward the end of her studies at the Ontario College of Art[1] (now the Ontario College of Art and Design) in Toronto. Soon after graduation, Brenda won her first major sculpture commission. She learned later that the judges had selected her over Disney Studios. "Had I known in advance that I was competing against Disney," she says over lunch in her kitchen, "I would probably have thrown up my hands and walked away."

Despite this auspicious beginning, Brenda did not work full time as an artist until years later, when she moved back to Muskoka. Four years after that, in 1991, Brenda joined the Muskoka Autumn Studio Tour.

Winter 1959. Two silent figures are out walking. The man labours under the weight of water hauled from a nearby ice hole. A little girl, bundled up in a snow suit, keeps pace with tiny, fitted snowshoes. A chore for him, an imaginary expedition for her.

Brenda is a Muskoka baby, born in Algonquin Park to David and Joyce Wainman. David was the park's deputy chief ranger; Joyce, the postmistress of a community of 25. They first lived on Cache Lake, with no running water, no television or radio, and limited access in and out of the community from early December to late March. It was a magical time in a place of beauty and inspiration. Brenda learned quickly to draw on her own creativity for entertainment. "I guess I learned how to make my own fun."

Later they moved to Huntsville and, when Brenda was 9, to Toronto. The further from Muskoka, the more at odds Brenda felt with her environment. However, every summer Brenda came back, helping out at her father's new business, Algonquin Outfitters, on the shores of Oxtongue Lake. In her teens, she worked as a cabin girl at the Blue Spruce Inn, and waitressed at Deerhurst Inn.

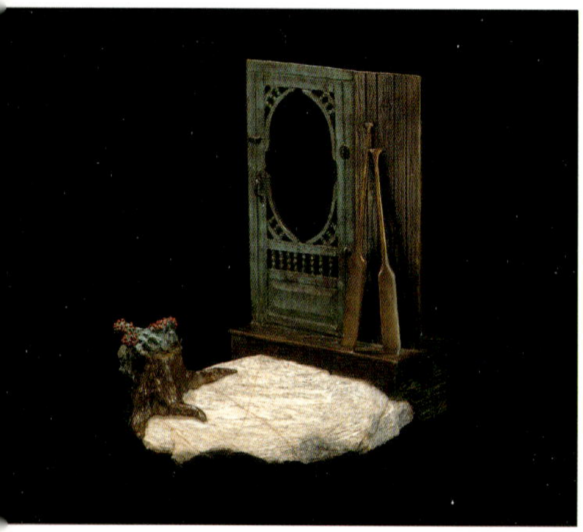

Even as a teenager Brenda knew she wanted a career in art. "I decided that if I was going to do something for 40 hours a week for the rest of my life, it had better be something I really enjoy – and the only thing that made sense to me was my art." After high school, Brenda spent a year preparing a portfolio for OCA. She painted by day and waitressed at night.

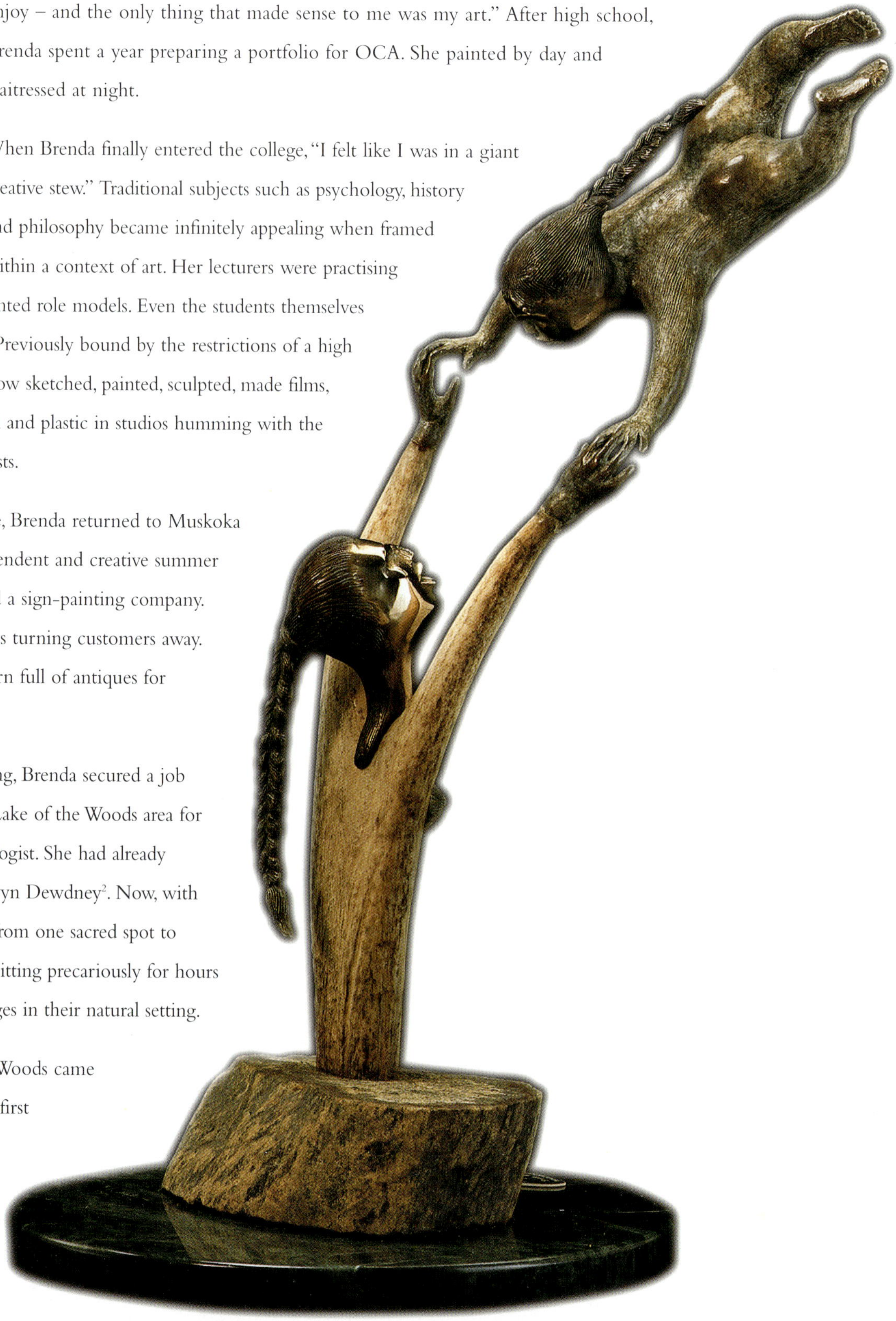

When Brenda finally entered the college, "I felt like I was in a giant creative stew." Traditional subjects such as psychology, history and philosophy became infinitely appealing when framed within a context of art. Her lecturers were practising artists: interesting, informed and talented role models. Even the students themselves were rich sources of creative input. Previously bound by the restrictions of a high school course curriculum, Brenda now sketched, painted, sculpted, made films, took photos, and worked with metal and plastic in studios humming with the inspiration and energy of young artists.

During summer breaks from college, Brenda returned to Muskoka but experimented with more independent and creative summer jobs. The first summer she launched a sign-painting company. By the end of the season Brenda was turning customers away. The next summer, she restored a barn full of antiques for Deerhurst Inn.

In her final summer before graduating, Brenda secured a job tracing native rock paintings in the Lake of the Woods area for Brian Leigh Molyneaux, an archaeologist. She had already studied native art at OCA with Selwyn Dewdney[2]. Now, with Brian and his team, Brenda canoed from one sacred spot to another, camping in the wilderness, sitting precariously for hours to capture details of the ancient images in their natural setting.

Out of her summer on Lake of the Woods came interests in spirituality and memory, first expressed literally in rock drawings and sculptures like *Spirit,*

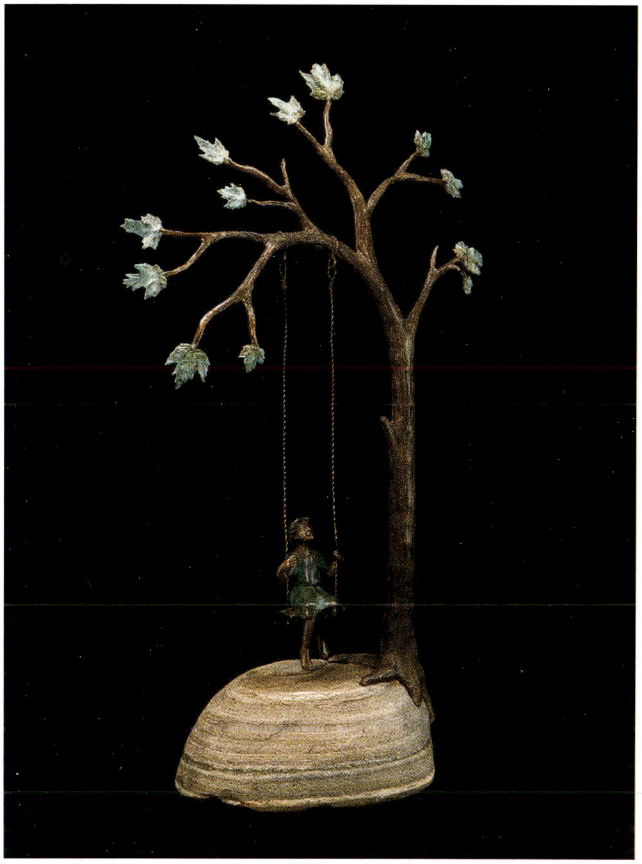

and later, more figuratively, in bronze sculptures of scenes and settings from childhood. Finding a means of expressing these interests came slowly.

While at OCA Brenda met Paul Goulet. Having grown up just outside Rondo Provincial Park near Chatham, Paul shares Brenda's love of outdoors. They married in 1981, lived in Toronto, then moved to Huttonville, a small town in the Caledon hills close to the city. Brenda promptly converted the garage into a studio. To supplement their income and finance her artwork, Brenda got a job at Artcast Inc., an art foundry in nearby Georgetown. There she learned the intricacies of the lost wax process for casting bronze sculptures.

Brenda had already worked with bronze, but as Artcast's chief mould maker and patina finisher, she became more intimate with and intrigued by its powers of expression. However, working full-time and looking after Halley, the first of their three children, left little time or energy to indulge her growing passion.

Summer 1965. Brenda and her brother Mike decide there aren't enough frogs at their end of the lake. They paddle over to the other side. On the return trip the bottom of the canoe is alive with frogs. The next day they're gone. Brenda and Mike try again, but the frogs keep migrating home.

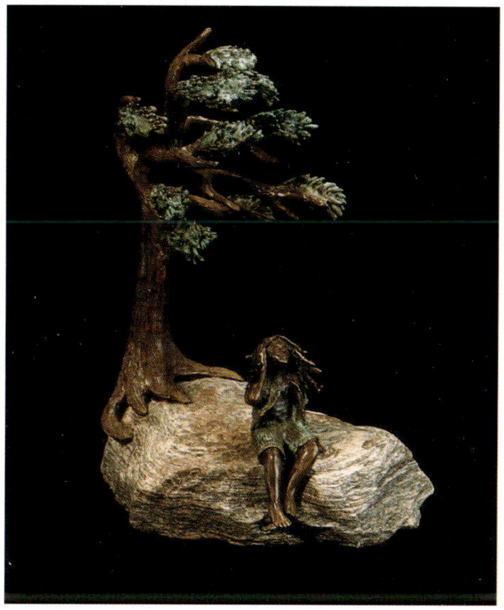

In 1987, Brenda migrated back to Muskoka, this time permanently. She and Paul moved north to Walker Lake, where they both felt safe and at home. Politely ignoring her fears, Brenda resolved to sculpt in bronze full time.

It wasn't easy. Despite good reviews from art shows and strong summer sales, Brenda faced financial and creative challenges. One was sustaining revenue in winter, when the seasonal residents and tourists had gone. Another was finding a base that would complement her subject matter – increasingly Muskoka memories and settings – yet support the sculpture's immense weight. Traditionally sculptors have preferred figurative or abstract subjects, rarely landscape. It's hard to find a pedestal that thematically supports a landscape. Brenda found her solution under her feet.

The Muskoka landscape is famous for its lakes, trees and rock – massive slabs of precambrian shield thrusting out of the ground at impossible angles, veined, weathered and, to Brenda, eloquent. The colours, shapes and textures of individual rocks coax memories from Brenda's past that enable her to express unique life experiences: a kayak enthusiast hurtling down white water on a backdrop of sodalite; a little girl swinging, braids trailing, from a maple tree rooted in granite; ice skaters practising pirouettes on a thin wedge of cheverie spar.

Casting Bronze

Asked to describe how Brenda Wainman Goulet creates her bronze sculptures, she stalls for time. "You mean, describe it in words? Oh, I don't know. When you're here in my studio, I can show it. But words?

"What I really enjoy about it is that it's a series of steps. You're not doing the same thing all the time. First you create a sculpture in wax, then you take it to a foundry where they attach a series of funnels, called a sprueing system. Then the foundry applies a ceramic coating. This coating's actually silica liquid and sand, into which the wax sculpture is dipped.

"Then you fire the dipped sculpture in a kiln. The heat from the kiln hardens the shell and melts the wax, which drains out through the funnels. That's why the process is called 'lost wax.'

"After the wax is gone, you're left with a ceramic shell, which is what you pour the molten bronze into. It's tricky. You have to let the bronze in quickly, before it cools, and let air out through the sprueing system.

"Once it's cooled, you chip off the ceramic shell. After it is gone, you have to grind down and retexture the places where the sprueing system had been attached to the wax sculpture. This is called fettling.

"Then you sandblast the sculpture to create microscopic pits in the surface. The patina you apply fills in these pits and reacts with the surface of the bronze, which creates the final look. Bronze is 94 per cent copper, so if you don't apply a patina the sculpture will turn green like a copper roof. Then to preserve the patina, you seal the sculpture with a thin coat of wax." And the job is done.

Winter 1988. Inspired by her preliminary success with rocks, Brenda assigns herself a goal: landing a sculpture commission. She waddles, eight months pregnant with her second child, into the Huntsville Professional Building. Sitting before a panel appointed to select artworks for the building, Brenda launches into loving detail about her rocks. She hears the room fill with silence after she declares that rocks speak to her. Nonetheless, she wins the commission.

Today Brenda balances her sculpting with varied responsibilities: homemaker and mother of three daughters, Halley, Mallory and Danielle; community volunteer; Muskoka Autumn Studio Tour executive; and member of Pentad, a group of five Muskoka women artists. She also pursues other interests depending on the season, the day, the hour. Her energy and resourcefulness spring from simple concepts on how to live. Life is what you make of it. Attitude is more important than skill. Negative breeds negative, positive breeds positive. Go for your dreams, even if it means going in a direction that's different from those around you.

"I've never felt I was one of those gifted children who was a natural at drawing or combining colour or composing a picture," says Brenda, "but I discovered you could learn to do these things and it gave me satisfaction when I did. Then it's like anything you work hard at. Your creativity becomes a muscle. Once you work it a lot, it becomes fit. Your art may appear to others like a natural talent, but it's something you've built and grown until you become strong in it."

Brenda's philosophy is simple. Follow your heart, have faith, work hard, and eventually you'll find the rock beneath.

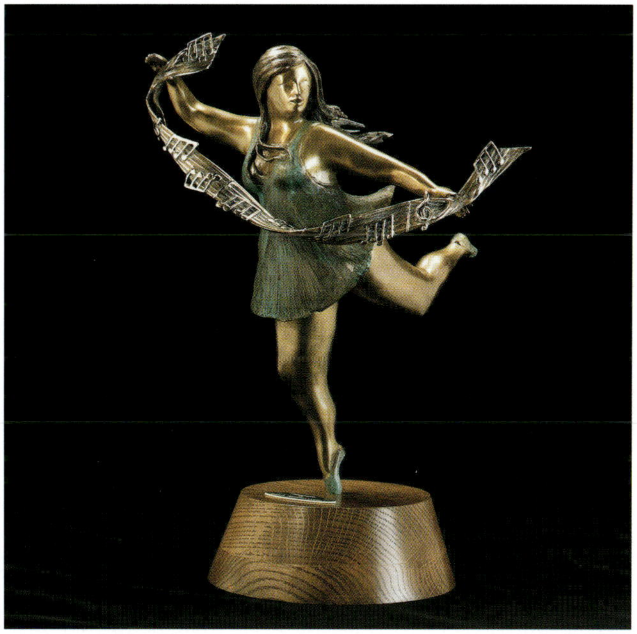

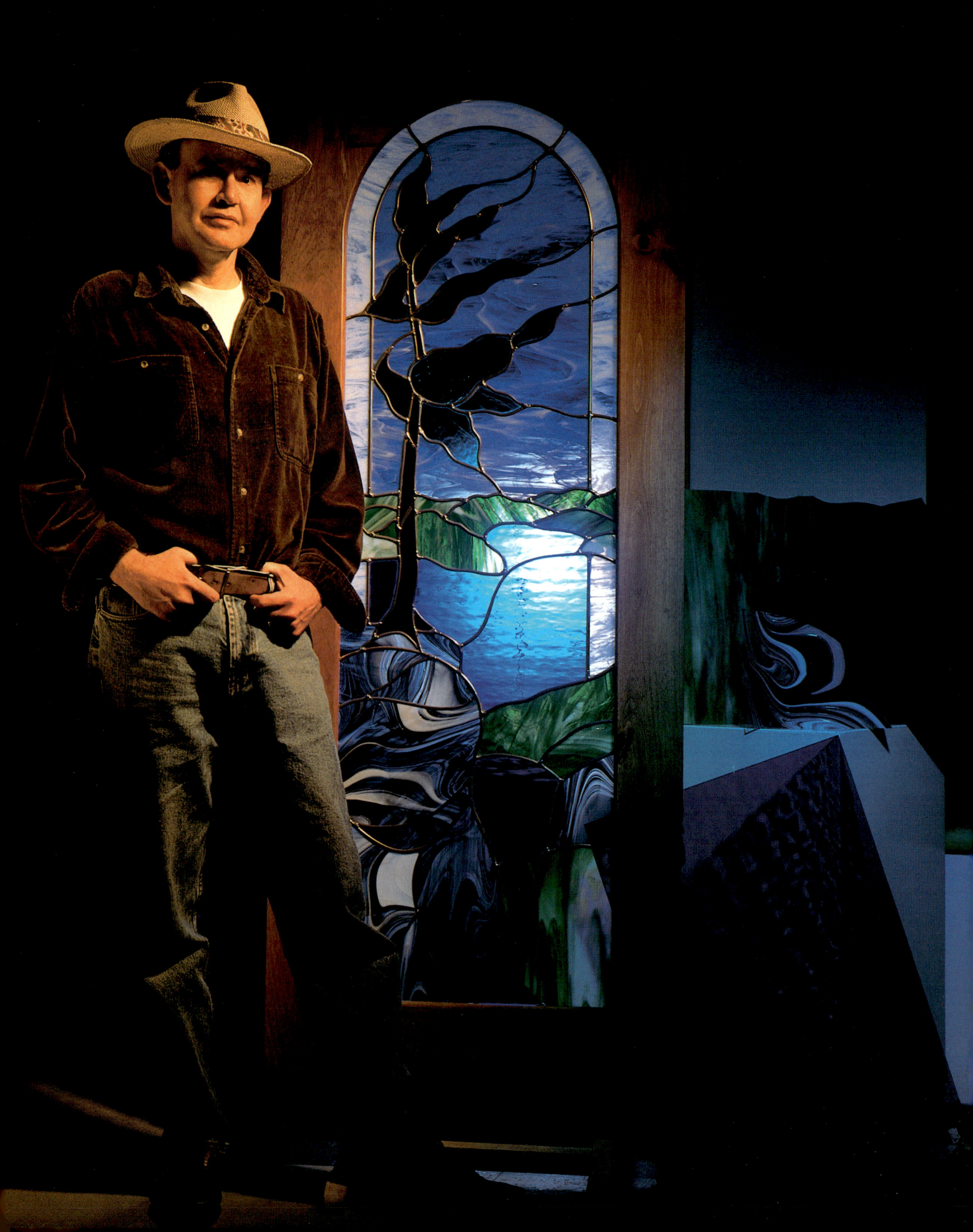

C H A R L E S   K N A P P

The harder I work, the luckier I get. – Mark Twain

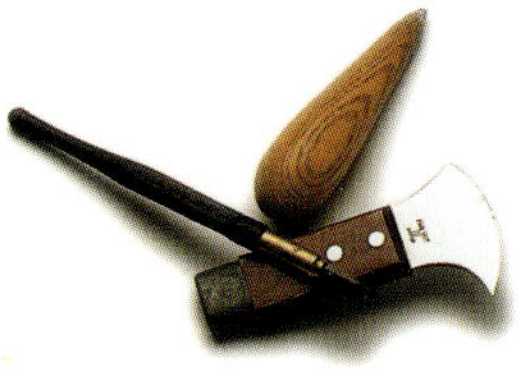

Wheel of Fortune

In the mid 1980s, Charles Knapp stepped back from his workbench and put down his glass-making tools. "If I'm going to continue working so hard," he told himself, "then it has to be at something that will earn a better living."

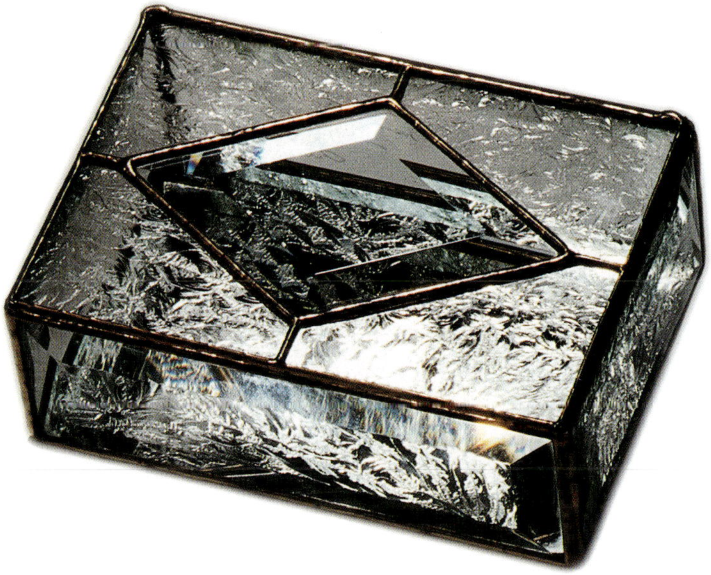

This wasn't the only time Charles had struggled with his choice of career. "I didn't have to climb the corporate ladder, but I've had my own pressures, including that gut wrenching fear of not being able to pay the bills." The only constant in his work was a love of glass.

"It's an unforgiving medium," says Charles. The words are respectful, but the tone is enthusiastic. "And it's physically demanding, but I like physical work. It keeps me focused. If I don't pay attention, the glass cut goes where it wants, usually following the path of least resistance.

"What sustains my interest, after 24 years, is the constant process of creation. The colour and design possibilities are infinite. In the beginning, the major challenge was to gain control of the glass, solder and lead. As you progress, the challenge becomes what to create. The colours and textures available in glass provide abundant inspiration."

As a child squirming on a hard pew, Charles would inevitably drift away from his father's sermons and up toward rainbows of colour framed in high, slender windows. Charles' father was a Baptist minister, and his mother, a nurse. Charles was the youngest of three children. In 1950, when he was a year old, the family moved from Toronto to Louisburgh, Pennsylvania. In 1953, they moved to Evanston, Illinois, where Charles lived until he completed high school.

After graduating, Charles studied biology, intending to become a doctor. However, he began to wonder whether pursuing a career in medicine was what he really wanted. In 1971, BSc degree in hand, he decided to take time out. He spent the summer working on his uncle's farm outside Whitby, Ontario. Still undecided, he enrolled at the University of British Columbia in Vancouver, intending to earn Canadian equivalency credits.

Why UBC? "Go west, young man," he says. It was that simple? "Pretty much."

Charles' commitment to medicine faltered. He left school after five years of post-secondary education. One day while watching a friend make a leaded glass terrarium, Charles became intrigued. As a child he had always enjoyed working with his hands, engineering mechano bridges, assembling gas-powered model airplanes, or tying flies for trout fishing expeditions.

Charles promptly set up shop in the only space available, the balcony of his Kitsilano apartment. As a hobby, glass work was ideal, but he wasn't thinking of it as a career.

His first attempt with glass was a terrarium. "It was the ugliest thing I'd ever seen." The lead was crooked; the soldering, peaked and rough; the form, misshapen. He took it apart and

The Power of Fear

"Fear is a great motivator. It causes you to find a way through the difficult times, and in turn you grow and gain confidence. On the other hand, focusing on the fear can paralyse you.

"I'm busy all the time and grateful for that, but success can be temporary. I may experience it today, but if the stock market crashes tomorrow, my customer base could go with it. Security has to come from your own life. It can't come from outside.

"Our minds create our lives. Ultimately, it's up to us."

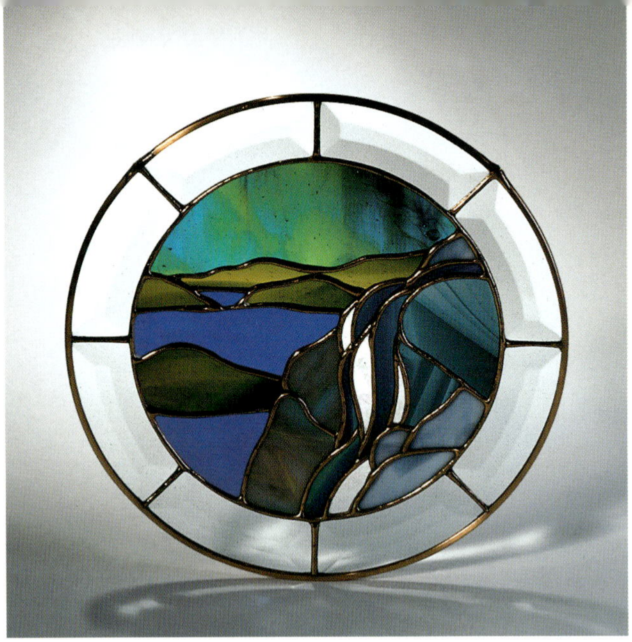

made a second, which turned out much better. The first store he approached liked the terrarium enough to order more.

Shortly after Charles' initial success, the owner of Creators' Corner, a Kitsilano landmark, offered him space. Creators' Corner stocked arts and crafts supplies, and rented work and display space to artisans. Accepting the offer would mean pursuing glass as a career.

While standing on his balcony debating his future direction, he heard a voice from on high: "What are you doing?" A hydro worker dressed in orange and yellow shimmied down from his perch on a utility pole and asked Charles how much he wanted for the glass box he had just finished making. For Charles, this was the closest he would come to a sign from above. His mind was made up.

The apprenticeship of Charles Knapp consisted of informal lessons over scotch with a friend who had a stained glass studio and ran a glass supply store. As for the rest – both art and business studies – he was on his own. Charles quickly grasped that, to work on commissions, he had to learn to draw. "In my Creators' Corner space, people would ask, 'Can you do this or that.' I'd say, 'Sure.' Imagine trying to draw a bull terrier sniffing a tiger lily. My favourite tool in those days was an eraser.

"If I had known how much there was to learn, I would have gone to art and business school. But one attribute I did bring to

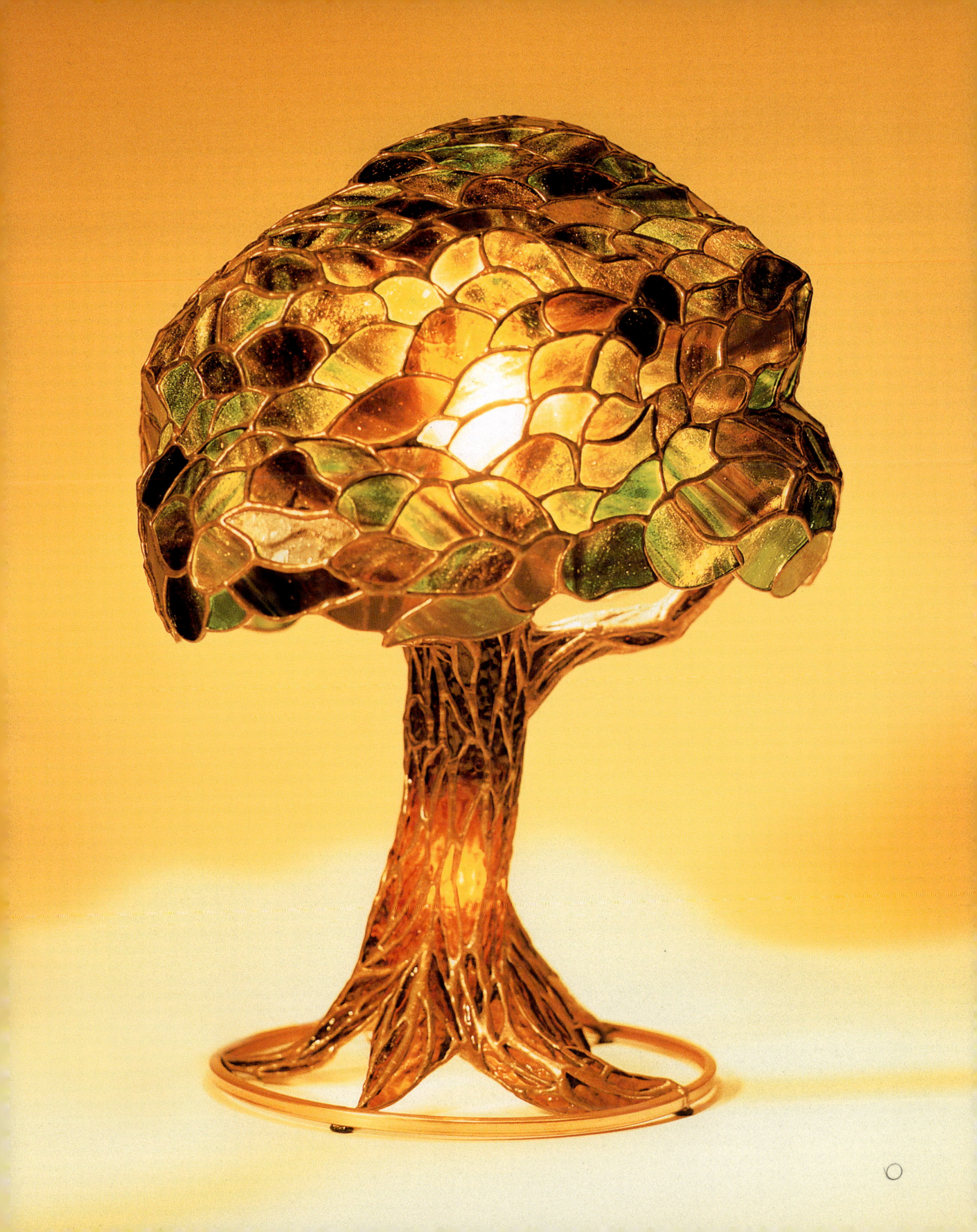

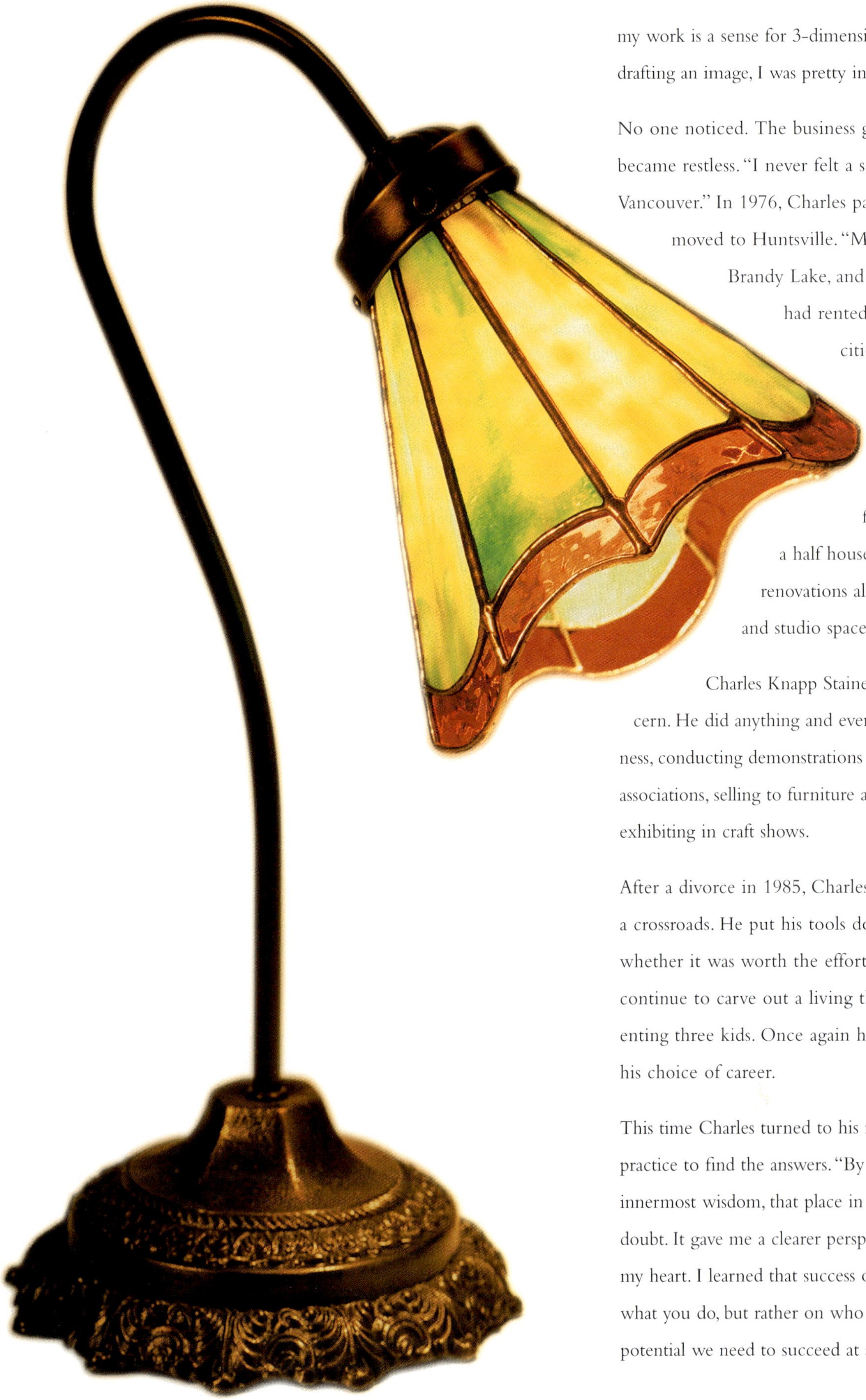

my work is a sense for 3-dimensional form. As for drawing or drafting an image, I was pretty inexperienced."

No one noticed. The business grew steadily, but Charles became restless. "I never felt a sense of belonging in Vancouver." In 1976, Charles packed up his family and moved to Huntsville. "My aunts had a cottage on Brandy Lake, and for a few summers my family had rented on Lake Joseph. I'd lived in cities all my life. It was time for a change."

Charles set up a stained glass studio and shop at the front of their quaint storey and a half house on Main Street. Gradually renovations allowed him to expand his work and studio space.

Charles Knapp Stained Glass became a going concern. He did anything and everything to promote his business, conducting demonstrations for church groups and business associations, selling to furniture and home furnishing stores, and exhibiting in craft shows.

After a divorce in 1985, Charles once again found himself at a crossroads. He put his tools down and asked himself whether it was worth the effort. He didn't know if he could continue to carve out a living through glass while single parenting three kids. Once again he was debating his future and his choice of career.

This time Charles turned to his recently acquired Buddhist practice to find the answers. "By chanting, I tapped into my innermost wisdom, that place in all of us that's free of fear and doubt. It gave me a clearer perspective so that I could follow my heart. I learned that success or failure isn't dependent on what you do, but rather on who you are. We all have the potential we need to succeed at anything we set our minds to."

Charles decided to take up his tools again. "Why throw away years of experience with glass when that's what I wanted to do? When I realized that success was up to me, things started to happen. Things fell into place."

In short order Charles took on an apprentice and focused on strengthening the business until it was where he wanted it to be. "I also opened myself to new directions. I found the courage to take my designs to a publisher, and my first book came out 10 years ago. It's sold 60,000 copies. Now I'm on my fourth book." He also began winning contracts, including one with a Muskoka company to supply stained glass windows for theme parks in Las Vegas and Orlando, and casinos in Atlantic City and Kansas City.

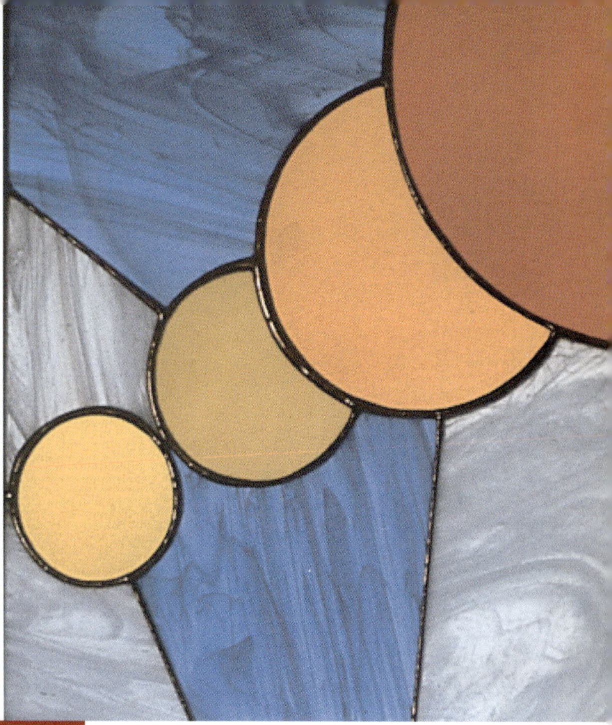

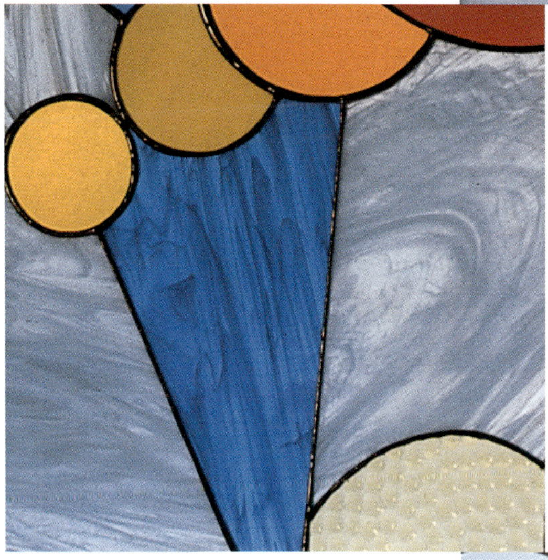

In 1987, Charles met Theresa O'Keefe and they married in 1993, sharing a blended family of five teenagers. They moved to a beautiful, serene location outside Huntsville that Charles finds inspirational for his work, and ideal for hosting the Muskoka Autumn Studio Tour.

A founding member of the studio tour, Charles remains enthusiastic about the event. He enjoys readying his home, the challenge of creating for display some of his finest work, and the chance to demonstrate his craft to the public. He is grateful for the visitors who flock to his studio, and appreciates the support of the local community, which accounts for many of his commissions.

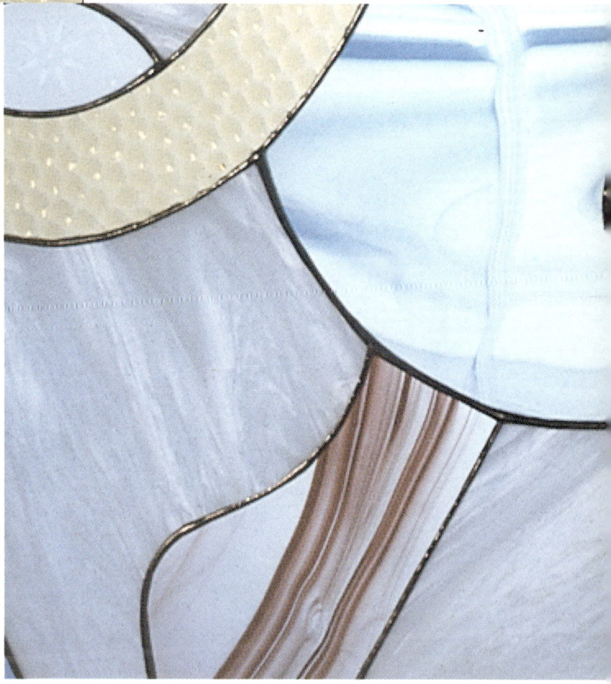

Charles doesn't romanticize his life as an artist, but he wouldn't have it any other way. "It's not always easy going after what you want, but the rewards of hard work and discipline and the spontaneous joy of creation make it all worthwhile."

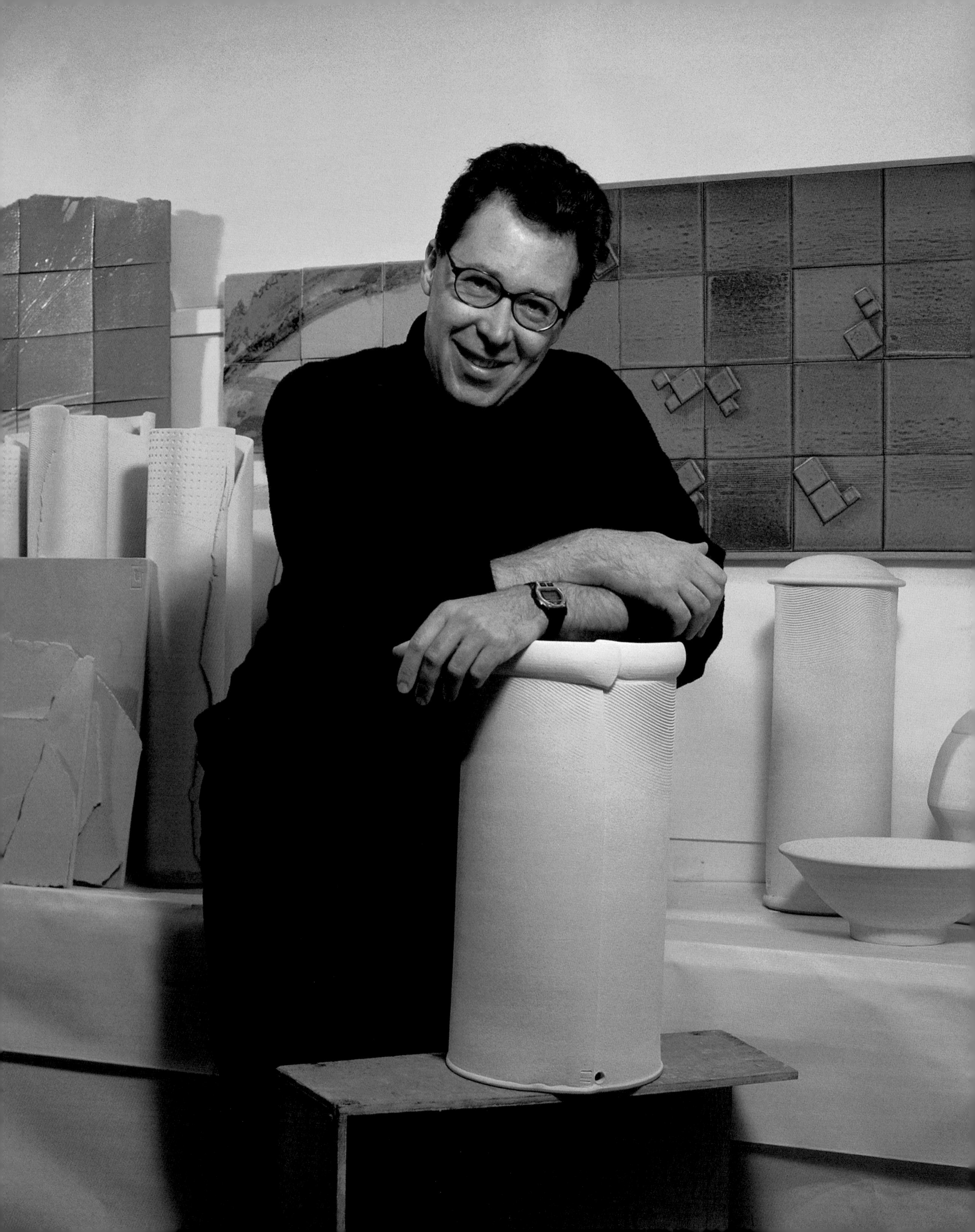

Though we travel the world over to find the beautiful, we must carry it with us or we find it not. – Ralph Waldo Emerson

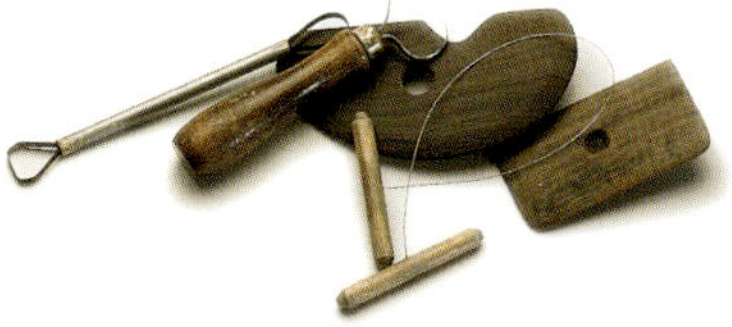

The Drive to Lindgren Road

After you exit Highway 11 onto Lindgren Road, the buzz of traffic quickly subsides. The resulting stillness provides a soothing backdrop for the occasional swish of reeds against the side of your vehicle or the rattle of pebbles on the road.

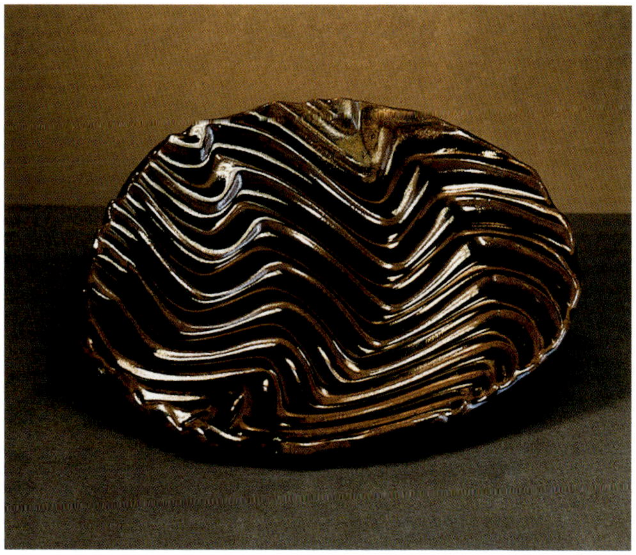

Because the gravel road twists and turns as it cuts its way through thick brush, tall pines and sweeping maples, the two kilometre stretch that takes you to your destination seems longer. You're relieved to see the sign for Lindgren Pottery. When Eric and Cathy Lindgren step out from their 100-year-old farmhouse, you can't refrain from asking the obvious: "How did you manage to get the road named after you?"

It was 1905 when Eric's great-grandfather, Fredrik Wilhelm Lindgren, arrived in Huntsville. He had endured a long trip from his native Sweden, first crossing the ocean by boat, then by rail from Halifax to Toronto. His final leg of the journey took him to Huntsville, a community promoted in 1900 from village to town, when its population surpassed 2,000.

He knew immediately Huntsville was a place he could call home. Its lakes, trees and rock reminded him of Eriksdal, the Swedish village he'd left behind. The following year, his wife Karin joined him with their five children, including Eric's 7-year-old grandfather, Tycko. By 1911, they had saved enough to purchase their farm just outside Huntsville. They moved into the existing farmhouse that, seven decades later, became home to Lindgren Pottery.

By the time Eric visited the area as a boy in the 1950s, Lindgren Road had become the official name of the winding road to the farmhouse. The family had stopped working the land in the 1940s and the house had become a summer retreat.

Like his great-grandfather before him, Eric would, in his own way, travel a great distance before finally settling on Lindgren Road. Born in Toronto in 1953, Eric Lindgren has lived in many places in Canada, including Vancouver, Winnipeg and Halifax. Influenced by his father, an architect, and his mother, an artist, you could say he was genetically and environmentally programmed for a career in visual arts.

From a young age, Eric painted and sketched. In high school, his talent earned him a scholarship to the Nova Scotia College of Art and Design. Like most youth, Eric's academic interests ranged widely, from art to languages to astronomy and science.

Eric also discovered computer programming while participating as an experimental subject of a study to see if a child could run a computer. A high school summer job in programming further sparked his interest. Two years in computer sciences at the University of Waterloo led to summer and part-time jobs in computer programming and operations, then a full time position in the computer operations department at Dominion Life Insurance. "I enjoyed programming for the summer but, full time, it was too confining."

Searching for a new career, Eric discovered the Three Schools of Art, a small school in Toronto funded and managed by artists. "I chose it because all the teachers were practising artists. There were no marks, no diplomas. You were there studying intensely only because you wanted to." He followed a program including anatomy, painting and life drawing.

Into a free time slot on his schedule, Eric inserted pottery. Just for fun, he thought. He discovered instead a serious fascination. "Going from a weekend painter to a daily one, I had become disenchanted. Painting full time was less satisfying than I expected. But you had to tear me off the potter's wheel. My ears perked up when I heard that people do this full time. It got the wheel turning in my head."

In 1975, Eric settled in for a summer on Lindgren Road to test his desire to be a full time potter. "I enjoyed it, and had no trouble putting in long hours. To create something with clay, water, motion and my hands was so satisfying, and so immediate. When you're making pots, you're really only using your fingertips and the simplest tools."

After his summer experience, Eric enrolled in a 3-year ceramics program in the art department of Georgian College[3] in Barrie, studying with established Canadian potters Roger Kerslake, Ann Mortimer and Alek Sorotschynski. Through mutual friends, he met Cathy Reid, a student specializing in textiles who later became his wife and business partner.

Eric's resolve to work in pottery was tested only once, by glass-blowing. He studied it for a year after graduation. "Hot glass

Firing the Car Kiln

"My big propane-fired kiln is called a car kiln because it has a movable portion: a four-wheeled platform carrying the floor and the door, that rolls on tracks to the stationary part of the kiln, housed outside in the kiln shed. This arrangement enables me to load and unload shelves and pots on the car while inside my studio, but keeps the actual firing out in the kiln shed.

"I make high-fired pottery in stoneware for its durability and visual character. On one hand high-firing (2300°F, 1280°C) tends to be simpler than low-firing because the glazes have a wider firing range, and subtleties of the heating action may make beautiful, natural variations in the glazes. On the other hand, there is an increased likelihood of flaws and catastrophes.

"There is always an element of chance in the outcome of a firing. Sometimes the kiln's contribution to the final result is a disappointment, but occasionally there is a wonderful surprise. Firing for me is very nerve-wracking because it's only partially under my control, yet so much work precedes a kiln load. It is the final reckoning for the pieces loaded and for my effort."

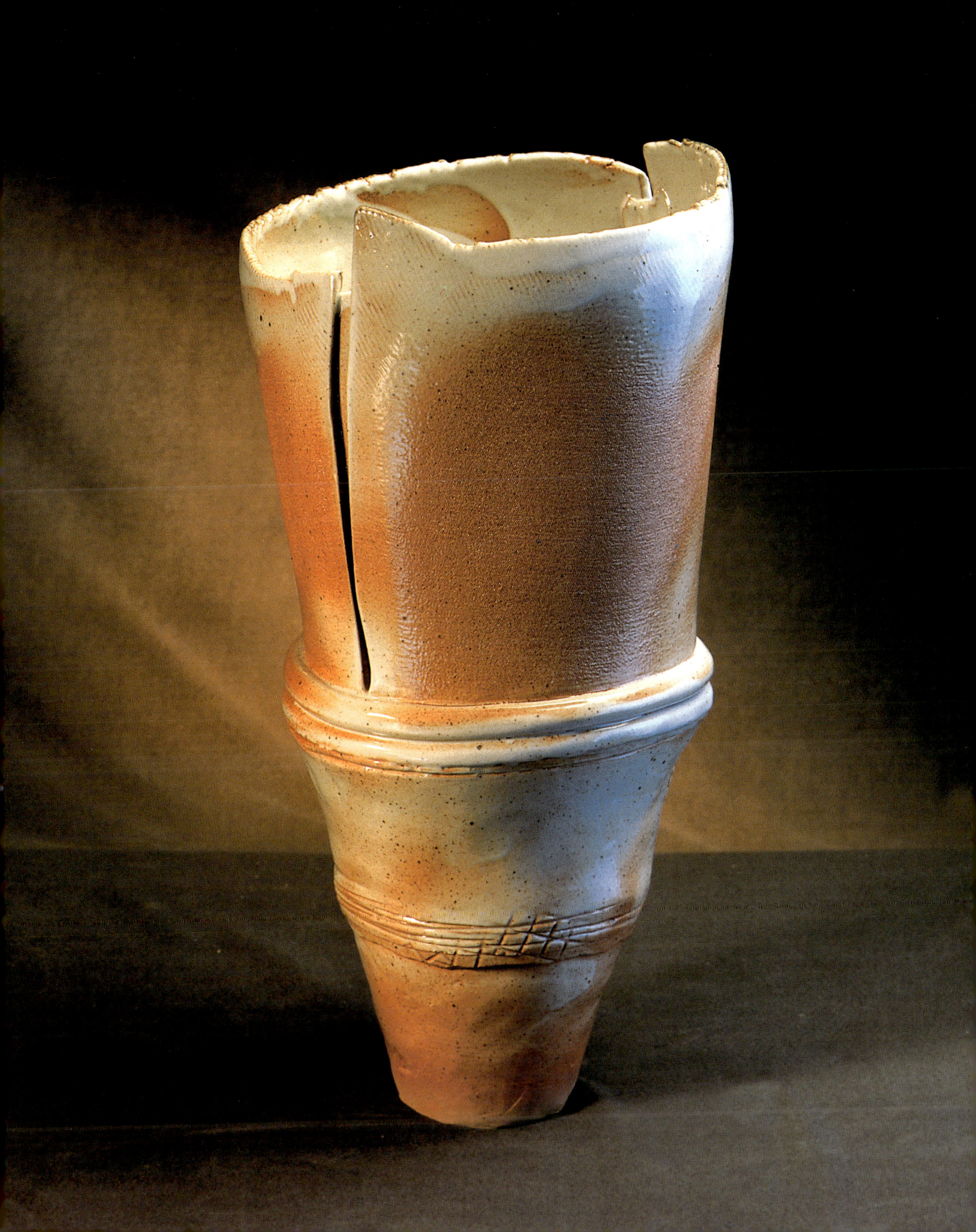

was a challenge. I tried to take advantage of the properties of glass that clay didn't have. Glass will stretch, it's instant and irretrievable. In clay, you have more time to react, it's a bit more forgiving. Also, I knew that earning a living as a glass blower would be even more difficult than as a potter."

Not that it's easy for potters. Establishing a studio presents serious financial challenges. Equipment alone requires a major capital investment. Eric taught workshops and a summer course in pottery at Lakehead University in Thunder Bay. At Georgian College he was the pottery studio technician, later teaching chemistry and history courses. These experiences gave him a solid foundation for managing the technical and business aspects of his own studio, and the means to purchase a kiln.

Eric started his first studio in a rented garage south of Barrie. He specialized in stoneware, preferring its water-tightness and strength over earthenware, which tends to be more porous and less durable. The One of a Kind Canadian Craft Show[4] in Toronto provided a wide audience for his dinnerware, vases, serving pieces and planters. His annual list of shows expanded with time to include more than two dozen across Ontario.

"The craft shows were an education. It was good to see other peoples' techniques in marketing and in clay and to get more of a sense of the buying public."

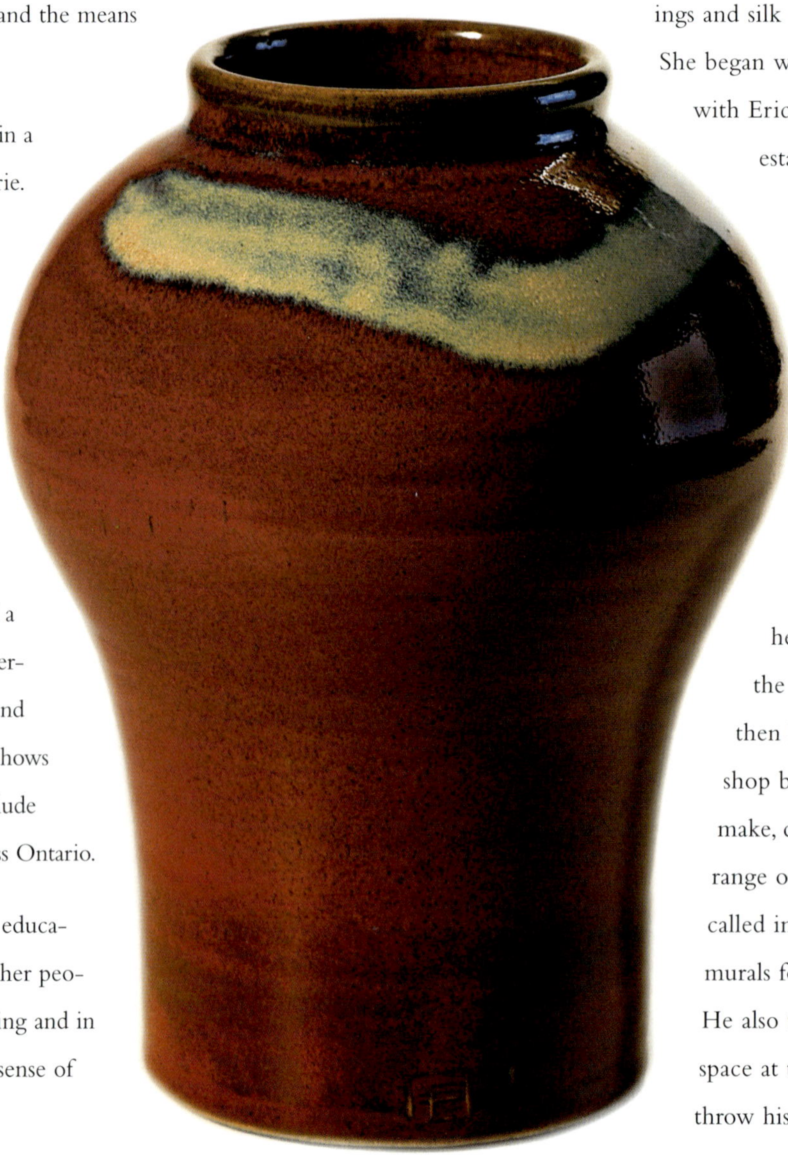

In 1981, this time accompanied by his wife Cathy, Eric returned to Lindgren Road and settled into the family homestead. That same year, they joined the Muskoka Autumn Studio Tour. Eric continued his work in stoneware and began experimenting with new lines and processes. Experiments in raku – a Japanese firing technique for tea ceremony vessels using a special kiln and glazes – led to a line of containers popular for Japanese style flower arranging. Other lines, such as his signature square plates, presented a dramatic counterpoint to the familiar roundness of wheel-thrown articles.

The 1990s ushered in a new direction for Cathy, who had until then had shown her handpainted silk wall hangings and silk scarves during the tour. She began working more closely with Eric. In 1991, the couple established The Huntsville Tile Company. Just four minutes from their home, the 2,000 square-foot plant they operate is a prime example of their entrepreneurial spirit. Cathy manages the operation, helping clients through the custom design process, then heads to the airy workshop behind the showroom to make, decorate and fire a wide range of tiles. Eric is often called in to decorate stoneware murals for various installations. He also takes advantage of the space at the tile company to throw his sinks.

For Eric and Cathy, their craft is a way of life. From morning coffee to day's end, pottery and tile design is never far from the centre of their conversation. Working with three-dimensional space, Eric is fascinated by form. Cathy is intrigued more by colour and pattern.

Eric and Cathy's enterprising ways go further than the tile company. Since 1994, they've headed for the Caribbean twice a year, a month at a time. In partnership with a Canadian hotel operator, they started a pottery studio that trained, and now employs, three islanders. Products include small handbuilt and wheelthrown candle holders, soap dishes, cups and bowls, sometimes illustrated with the native 5-petalled hibiscus or a whimsical fish. After a hard day's work, they don masks, fins and air tanks, then fishtail out to some of the best scuba diving sites this side of the equator.

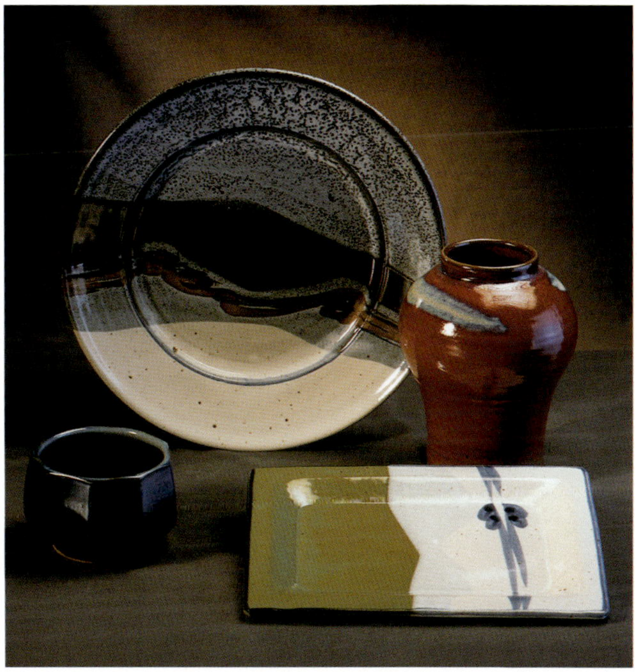

About this venture Eric is cautiously enthusiastic. "We were motivated more by lifestyle than artistic challenge or financial gain. It was a chance for us to be in a tropical place and perhaps earn a little money to defray travel costs," says Eric.

As a 23-year veteran potter, Eric has achieved a balance among his artistic, business and technical priorities. "My goal as an artist is to make strong pots. Strong in form, strong in use. The best pots have an elusive liveliness, a subtlety that can't be forced. As for business, I think it's a function of design. Design requires you to look at all aspects of an object and how it's going to be used. You must make compromises as part of any decision-making process. You have everything from the choice of materials through to how it works, for example making a spout that is dripless. And as for technology, there are inevitable variations in how pots accept glaze, and how they are transformed and enriched by firing, so that the kiln is like a magic box."

Belonging to a ceramic tradition that began in the Stone Age, Eric benefits from a rich storehouse of ideas, tools and techniques. In his travels, he can visit pottery studios anywhere and feel connected. An active Internet user, he exchanges tips with potters around the globe, sharing his experience in constructing a car kiln or discovering a recipe for a new glaze. Most important is the connection to the people who use and enjoy his pots. "A lot of pottery relates to food – the centre of a constant human activity. People will have their morning coffee or cereal using my pottery. It's part of their day. It's ritual. It's also human connection. We can't perform the same activity with as much richness if we're using something made by machine. More and more in this automated world, we need to have things that are handmade."

A self-employed craftsman, Eric also enjoys freedom and independence. "As an employee, I was a bus driver for someone else. Today, I drive myself. As a craftsman, I decide where I will go."

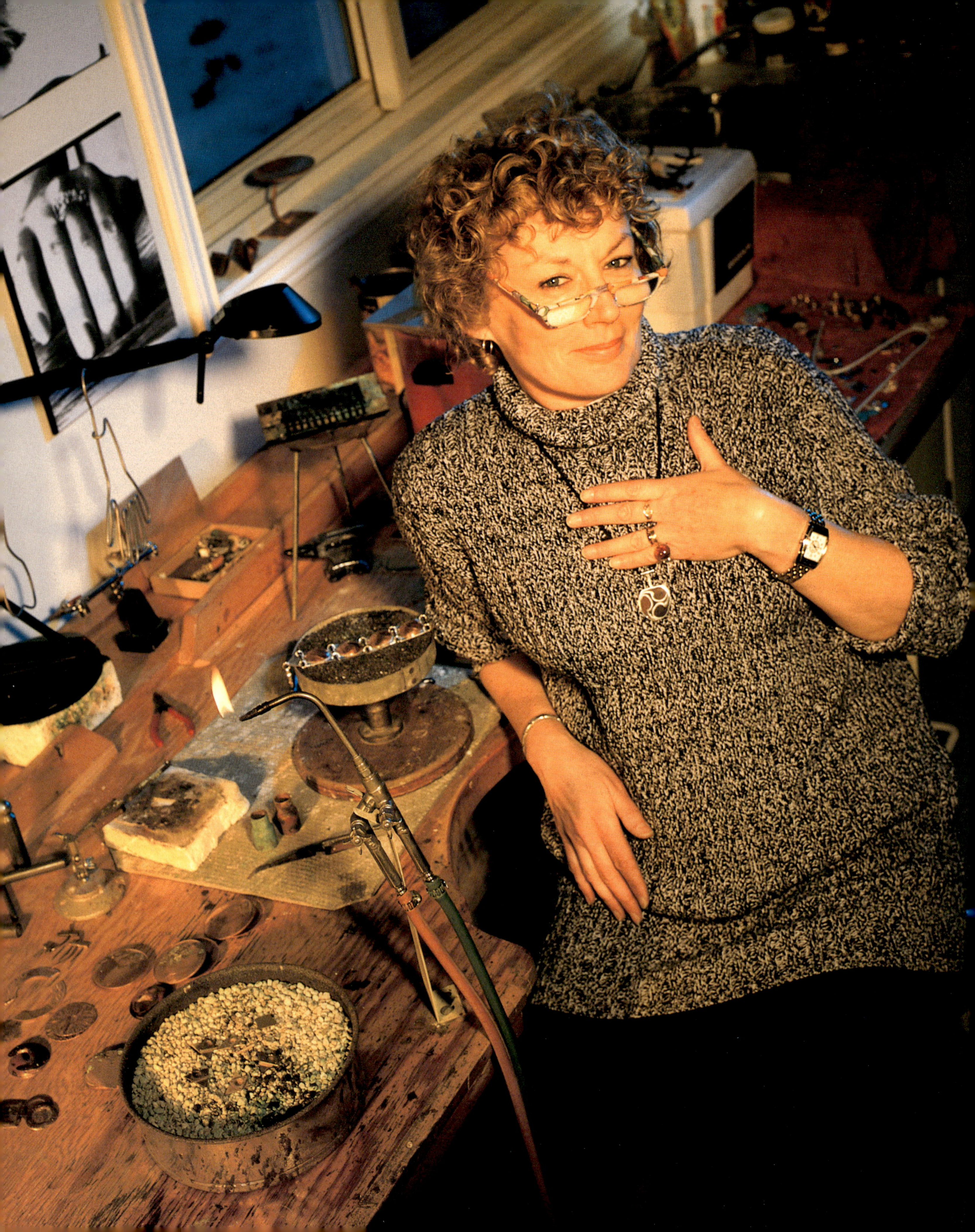

There is nothing in a caterpillar that tells you it's going to be a butterfly. – Buckminster Fuller

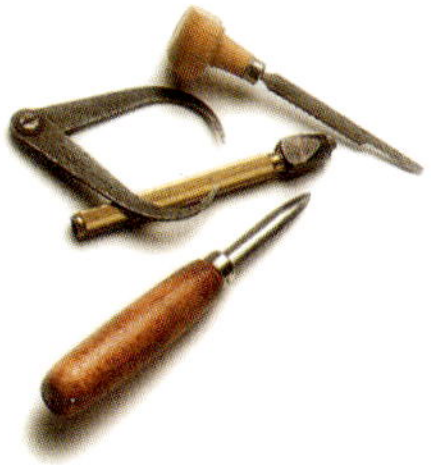

Journey of Discovery

The 1967 graduates of Toronto General Hospital Nursing School pose proudly for their class photograph, certificates in hand, ready to serve. The black and white photo hangs on the wall of Penny Varney's studio, next to a diploma in jewellery design from Georgian College. Four framed awards for excellence in jewellery design are further evidence of mid-life metamorphosis.

Penny Varney arrived at her first career crossroad when respectable choices for women included teaching or nursing. By the time she was a wife and mother, her spirit longed for something she couldn't name. She looked to learning for answers. At 40 years old, she went back to school, studying drawing, ceramics, design and art history. Eventually introduced to the craft of jewellery, Penny discovered a release valve for pent-up creativity. Possibilities came spilling out, first as lines on paper, then, with time, energy and understanding, as objects of grace and beauty.

Also a pragmatist, Penny first realized the commercial potential for her work during a college co-op term in 1989. Given a shortage of placements in the Gravenhurst area, she and another student created their own opportunity. Together, they developed a line of jewellery from anodized aluminium. Sales trickled in at first. Then the two friends offered their line to a shop on the campus of Georgian College, as an example of student enterprise.

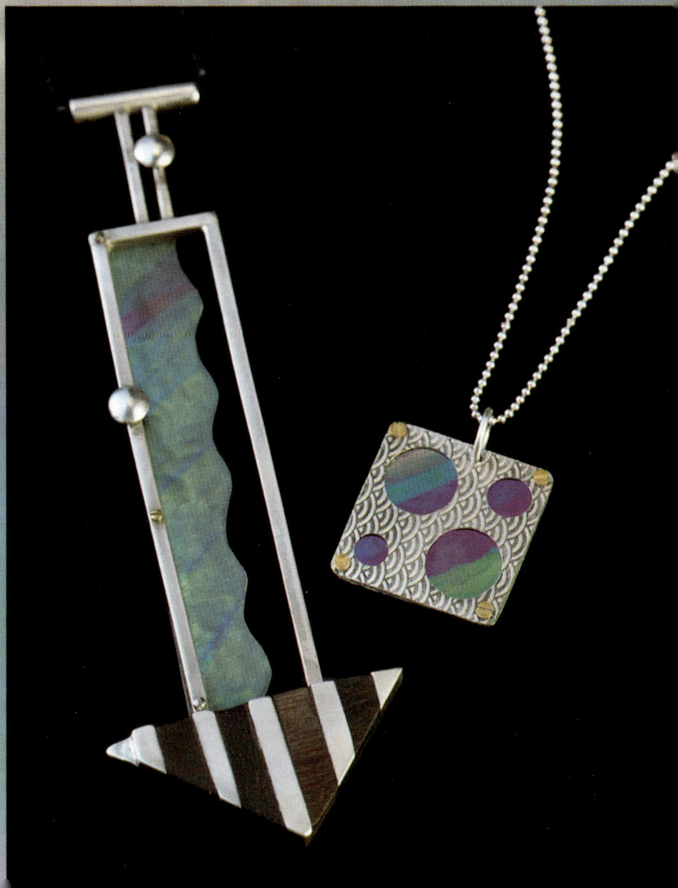

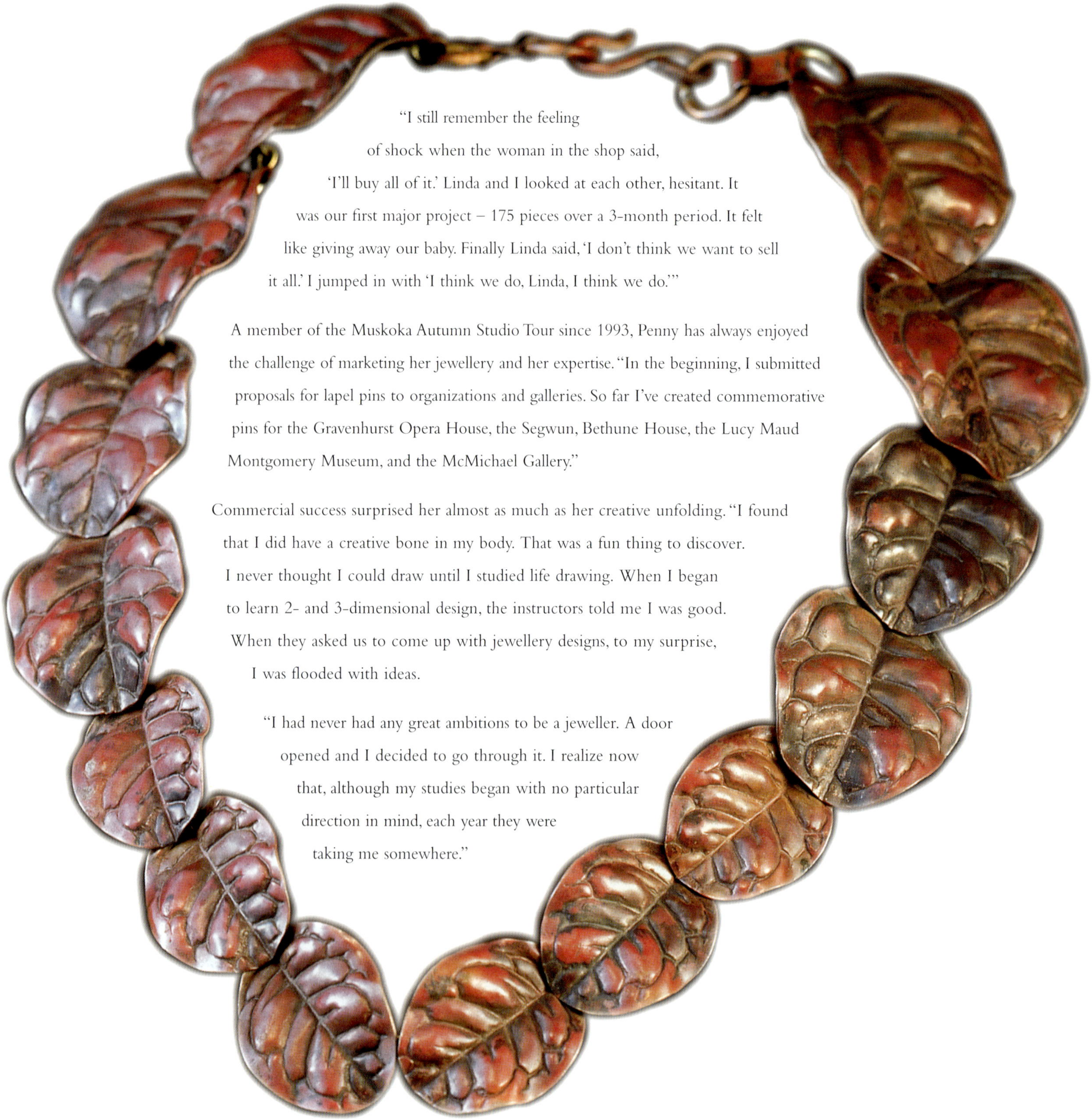

"I still remember the feeling of shock when the woman in the shop said, 'I'll buy all of it.' Linda and I looked at each other, hesitant. It was our first major project – 175 pieces over a 3-month period. It felt like giving away our baby. Finally Linda said, 'I don't think we want to sell it all.' I jumped in with 'I think we do, Linda, I think we do.'"

A member of the Muskoka Autumn Studio Tour since 1993, Penny has always enjoyed the challenge of marketing her jewellery and her expertise. "In the beginning, I submitted proposals for lapel pins to organizations and galleries. So far I've created commemorative pins for the Gravenhurst Opera House, the Segwun, Bethune House, the Lucy Maud Montgomery Museum, and the McMichael Gallery."

Commercial success surprised her almost as much as her creative unfolding. "I found that I did have a creative bone in my body. That was a fun thing to discover. I never thought I could draw until I studied life drawing. When I began to learn 2- and 3-dimensional design, the instructors told me I was good. When they asked us to come up with jewellery designs, to my surprise, I was flooded with ideas.

"I had never had any great ambitions to be a jeweller. A door opened and I decided to go through it. I realize now that, although my studies began with no particular direction in mind, each year they were taking me somewhere."

Penny's willingness to go places unknown began much earlier. After high school, she trained in nursing at Toronto General Hospital, specializing in psychiatric nursing. "In this type of nursing, it is important to talk with patients. Often we would do something with them, maybe introduce them to a craft and talk to them while they were doing it. Art is therapeutic. Perhaps because it's tactile and engages your senses, maybe because in doing something with your hands, your mind is free from thinking about things."

Though Penny loved the interaction with patients, she wasn't convinced that nursing was for her. After working for a year, she left Canada in search of adventure. In London, she began wondering about the possibility of working. "Is there anything a nurse can do who doesn't want to do traditional nursing," she asked an officer at Canada House. Her question landed her a position with Boots Chemists in Picadilly Circus. For the next few years, she shared a flat in trendy Chelsea with three other women and dated a young pharmacist, Tony Varney.

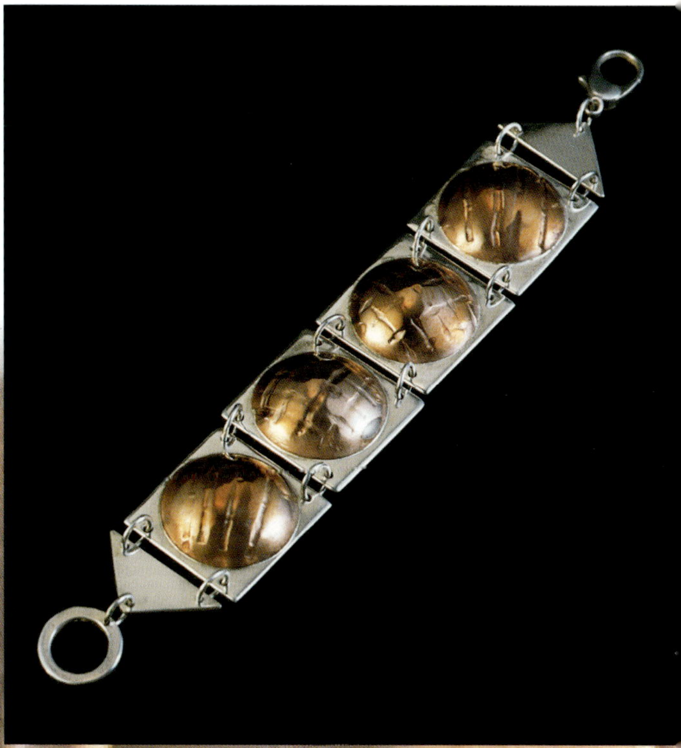

Following their marriage in 1970, the couple spent a year working in Canada, Tony taking a temporary position as an assistant pharmacist in Gravenhurst, Penny as a nurse with the South Muskoka Memorial Hospital in Bracebridge. When Tony's job came to an end, Penny resigned and the couple travelled through Europe and the Middle East. While abroad, Tony received a letter offering to sell him a partnership in the Gravenhurst Pharmacy. Six months later, they rolled into Gravenhurst with the sum total of their possessions: a van, a canoe, a black and white TV and a bank book showing a $500 balance.

The couple took out a loan to finance the partnership, fulfilling for Tony a long-held ambition to manage his own pharmacy. Besides taking on part-time nursing jobs, Penny helped out in any way she could, working behind the cosmetics counter, assisting in the pharmacy, hiring and managing staff. "We worked hard. I didn't know much about running a business. For that matter, I didn't know much about hair colour when I had to take over the cosmetics counter. But I learned."

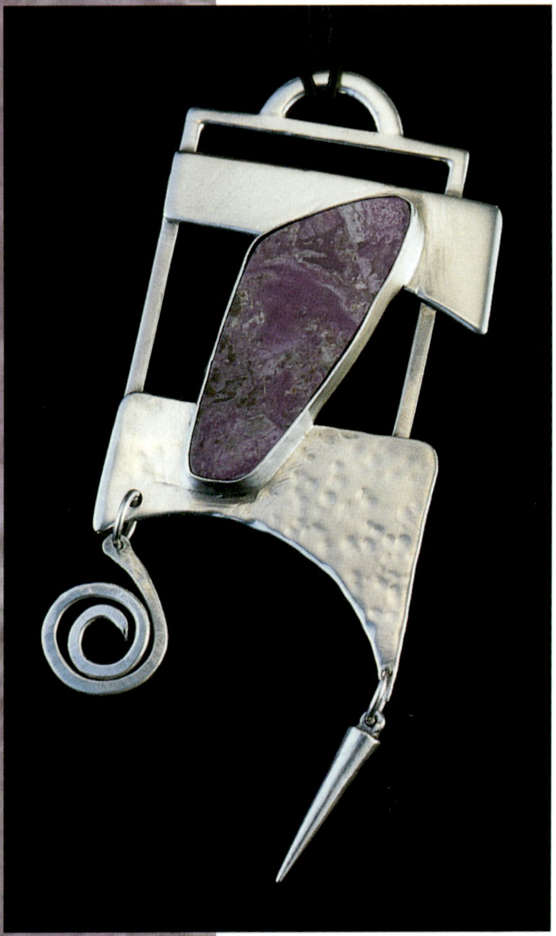

By the early 1980s, the couple had two young children, were sole proprietors of a thriving business, and had built a charming home with a country garden. It was picture perfect, but for Penny something was missing. "I thought, 'There has to be more to life than this.' Tony encouraged me to take courses, and he was incredibly supportive the whole time I went to school. I wasn't looking for a career, just an outlet or an interest I could call my own."

For four years, Penny studied art part-time at Georgian College. When the college introduced a specialized jewellery program, she studied full-time for another three years.

Though art may offer certain therapeutic benefits, Penny insists there is nothing therapeutic about studying it full-time with young children at home. "Life was frantic. If I wasn't on the road to Barrie, I was in class or working in the pharmacy. In the evenings, I would put the kids to bed, then do my homework until 2:00 a.m. The program went from January to August, so for three summers in a row, my time with the kids was limited. I always felt guilty. However, it did make me strong. Today I feel that I can cope with just about anything."

From her storybook studio – a scaled-down companion to their home – Penny tackles business opportunities and creative projects. In addition to crafting lapel pins, she repairs jewellery and produces production and one-of-a-kind pieces for her on-site showroom and for galleries in Bracebridge, Orillia, Gravenhurst and Parry Sound.

Already working at high speed, Penny shifts into overdrive before local shows and the studio tour, racing through 12-hour days for weeks at a time.

For something so small and often simple in execution, jewellery has a diverse and complex heritage. It's not uncommon for a jeweller to specialize in a single technique. Not Penny. Like a medieval alchemist, she is fascinated by a range of materials and processes. Her training at Georgian College introduced her to the familiar metals of silver and gold. However, she also became interested in niobium. A refractory metal, niobium can be tinted to bright shades of the colour spectrum by passing an electric current through a solution into which the metal is dipped. The patination of copper and brass and "marriage of metals" also hold fascination for Penny. Recently, she's begun to experiment with enamelling, a technique that fuses glass to metal at high temperatures.

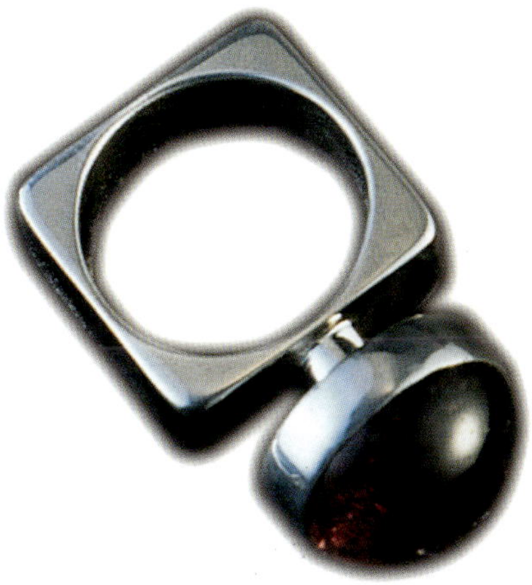

The new and different give Penny the enthusiasm and impetus to carry on in jewellery. "I don't enjoy doing production line jewellery as much as one-of-a-kind. I try to challenge myself to do five pieces of jewellery exactly the same way. By the sixth, it's transformed into something completely different.

"I love the learning. And I think that's really what life is all about, to keep an open mind." It's a lesson from her own mother, a woman who never stopped learning and encouraged Penny to do the same. Penny hopes to bequeath a similar message to her two children, Megan and Nicholas. "Tony and the kids put up with a lot while I was going to school, but I'd like to think it was good for them as well. They saw me go to school as an adult student. They came to my graduation. They help where they can, especially during the studio tour. They know how hard I've had to work to achieve something. It means more to me than anything else that I'm making a difference to my children, and that maybe my choices will help shape theirs in a healthy way."

Some Things Remain the Same

Growing up with three active older brothers, Penny was more into sport than art. Today, she keeps body and mind together with the help of a recently acquired past-time – rowing. You'll find her two evenings a week sculling with a four-person team on the Muskoka River in Bracebridge.

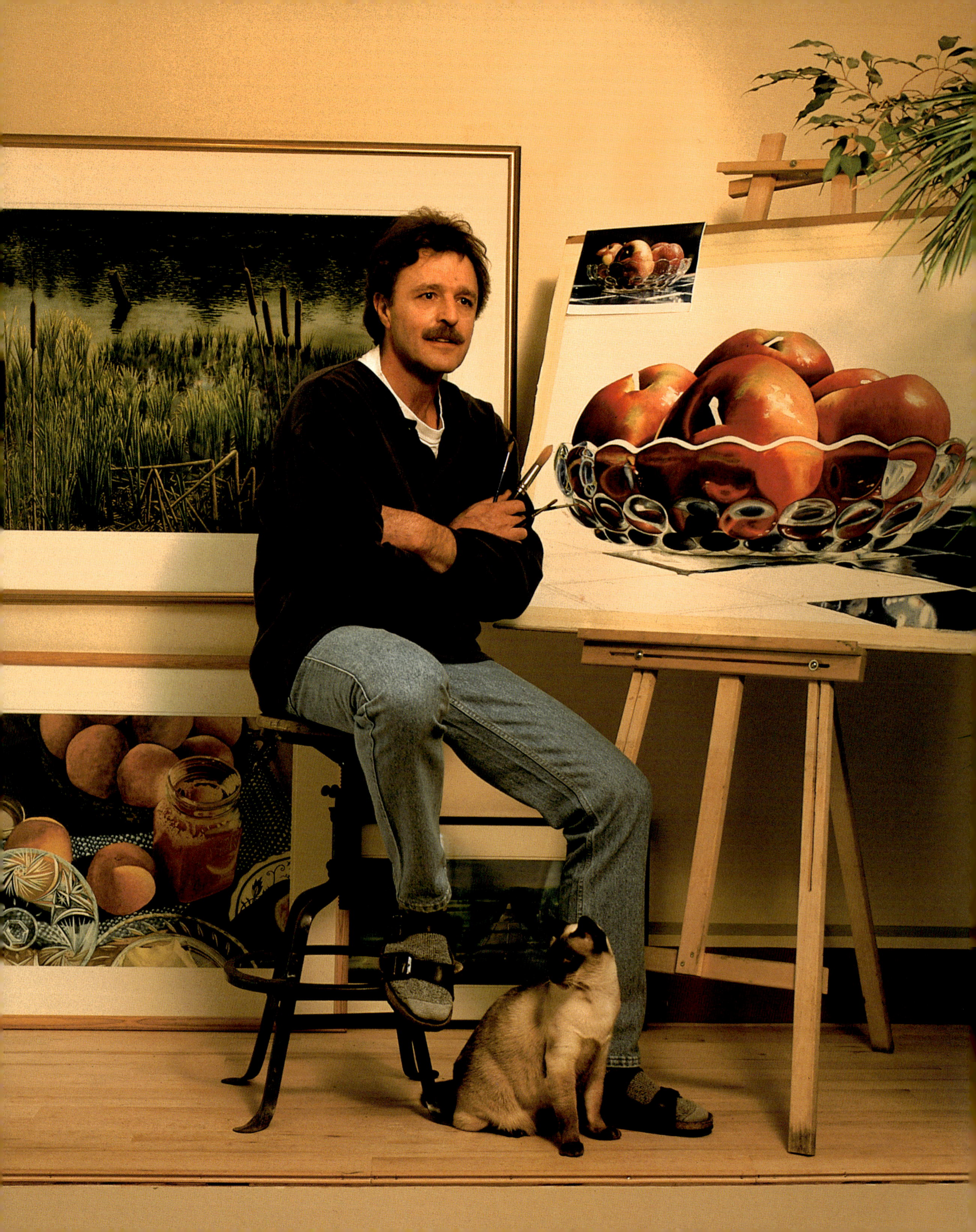

Blow up the TV / Throw away the paper / Move to the country / Build us a home. – John Pryne

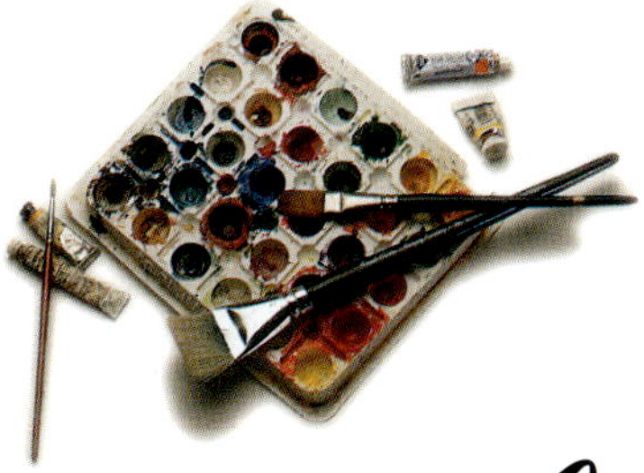

A Search for Light

The first five bricks just bounced off the picture tube. Number six shattered the screen and the TV leapt three feet in the air. Step one finished. No TV.

The next step was to kick a two newspaper per day habit, not that hard. Though Ed still craves for The Globe and Mail crossword.

Step three, Ed and Dawn's adventure began. "Pare down our lives to the basic essentials. From a big bungalow and the three cars that won't fit in the 2-car garage to something more streamlined – a VW camper van. Home and transportation all in one. Three cups, three plates, three spoons. A change of clothes, some bedding, and we were off."

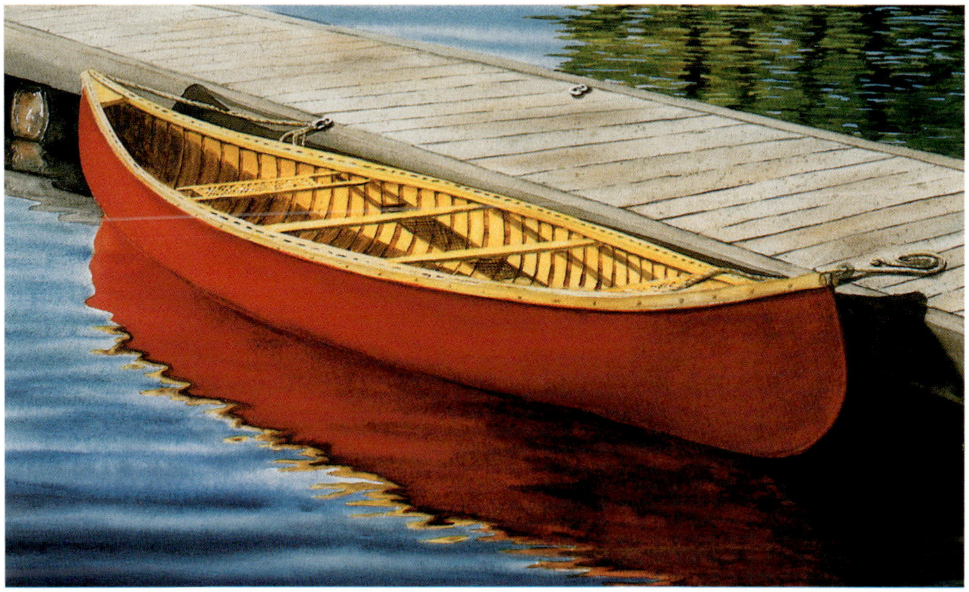

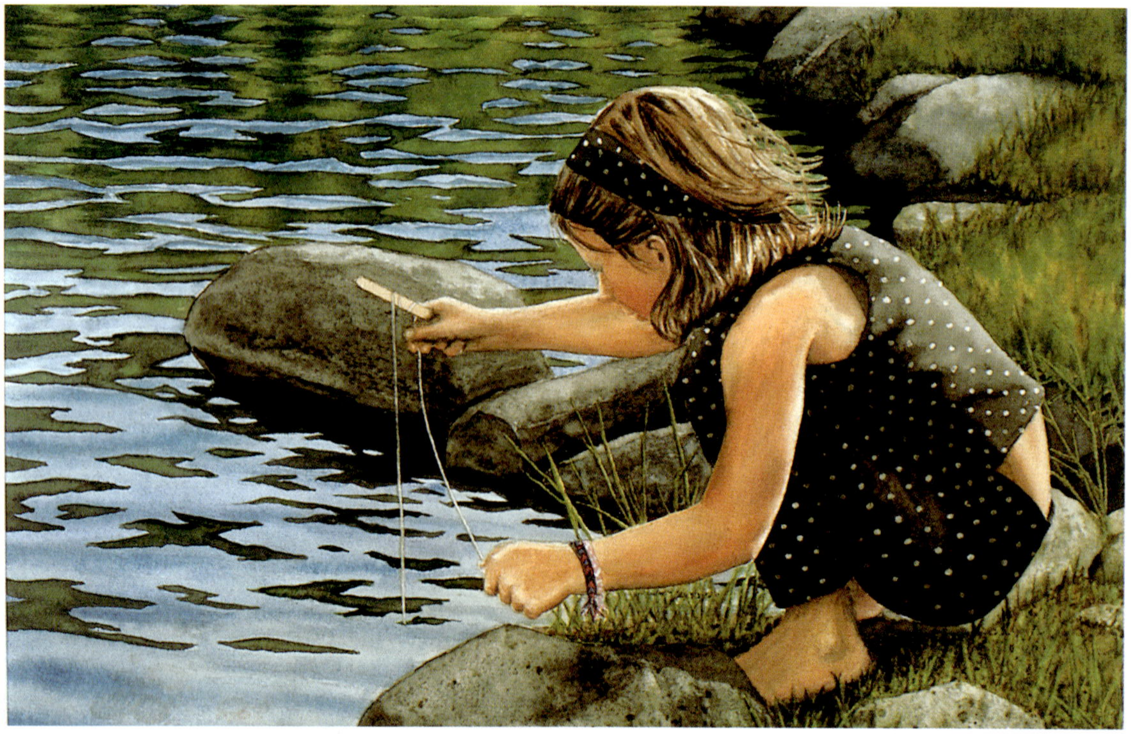

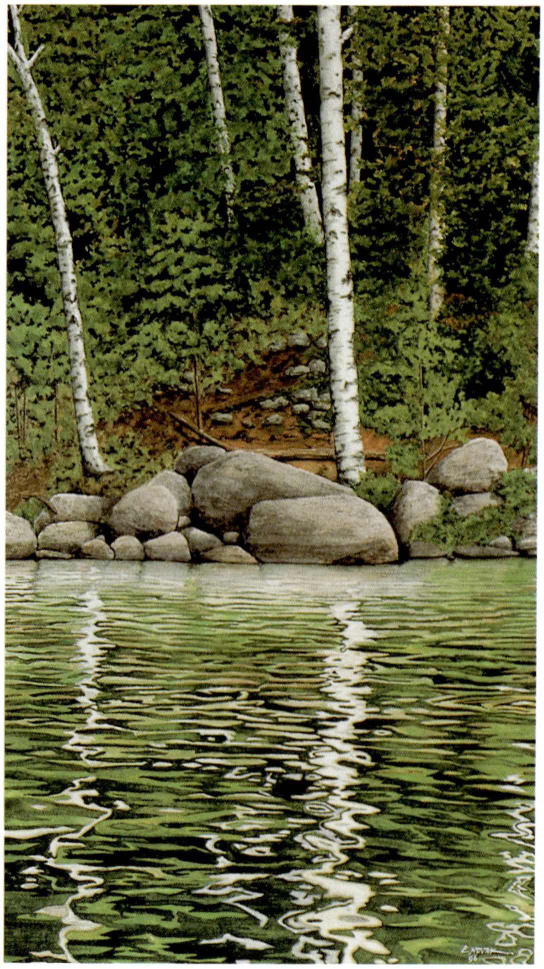

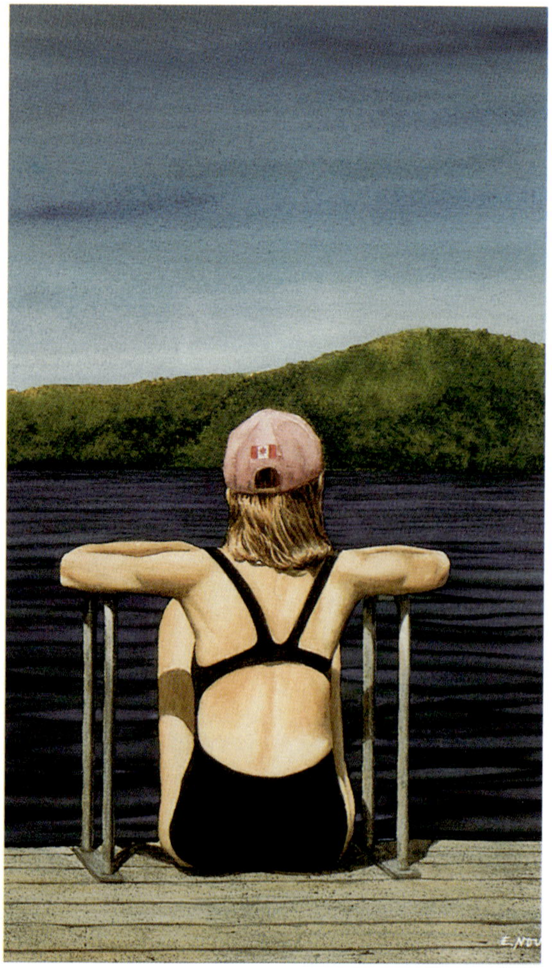

Off to a strange and beautiful place Ed and Dawn knew – Muskoka. "We had scouted out the area, finally deciding on a hilltop overlooking Three Mile Lake as the site for step four of the plan: build us a home."

Ed Novak was born in Hamilton, Ontario in 1951, the first of two children. His parents were immigrants from Poland who had the misadventure of being in Europe during the 1940s. Although their villages in Poland were only a few kilometres apart and they had shared an all-expense paid trip to Siberia courtesy of Stalin, they would not meet until years later in Hamilton.

"My dad was a machinist in a factory in Hamilton. He worked with his hands, was always building and fixing. 'Eddie' had to help. When my father wasn't working with his hands, he read. Two or three books most weeks. Reading and working with my hands – two great gifts from my father.

"During the misadventure of Europe in the 1940s, my mother and her two sisters became war refugees. They ended up living in Mexico for six years, acquiring a lasting Latino outlook on life. Christmas was a mix of piñatas and perogies. Spanish, Polish and broken English were spoken. This was not unusual in the East Hamilton neighbourhood where I grew up. English was my second language, Polish my first. It was a multi-ethnic neighbourhood filled with strange and exotic customs, foods and smells. My mother's greatest talent found expression in the kitchen. For this gift, I am grateful. So too are my wife and children who usually enjoy my daily forays into the culinary arts."

"My childhood was full of hockey and boy scouts, playing in the woods and drawing in my room. My first art was of hockey players. Not an unusual subject matter for Canadian male artists just starting out. I think I already knew at about 7 or 8 that I had some natural ability to draw, at least half-decent hockey players. My Grade 2 teacher would always hang my pictures up. Unlike my father who was not impressed by the tape on the walls that was wrecking the wallpaper in my room. Little did I know that this would help in step five of the plan: become an artist, paint a lot of pictures.

"So, I grew up in Hamilton during the '50s and '60s. It was in high school, just before my first pair of bell bottoms and just after colour TV, that I met Dawn. We were high school sweethearts. Madly in love. We both ended up at the University of Guelph. Dawn studied psychology. I studied fine art. Somewhere along the line, I switched from fine art to landscape architecture. I'd heard that this was a field in which you could develop your creative abilities and also get a pretty good paycheque. It seemed a natural choice at the time."

Ed and Dawn were married while at university. Though their marital status helped with student loans, they were still 'poor students.' That changed in 1976. Dawn became a teacher, Ed a landscape architect with the City of Hamilton. "To compensate for those poor years, we bought a lot of stuff."

Dawn eventually moved into special education and twenty years later still enjoys it. Ed spent the next five years as a civil servant in Hamilton's city hall. "I jumped in with both feet, often in my mouth. Building and running a city is a complex juggling act. Hence, miles of procedure. The procedure part was my weakest skill. Nonetheless, I happily immersed myself in building little green spaces where people could breathe, trying to figure out how to fit a whole town of people into a tight space and make it a more pleasant experience. In retrospect, I ended up leaving behind thousands of trees that have been giving shade for 20 years now. I hope they've provided pleasure to people.

"As luck or fate would have it, an art gallery opened across the street during my tenure at city hall. I had never been exposed to so much art before. One day I walked in and there was a painting of a bowl of fruits by an artist named Mary Pratt. The glass in the bowl was unbelievably detailed. She had also done an almost photographic painting of flames coming out of a garbage pail. I was awestruck. How did she paint something that's transparent and almost invisible and make it so real? It's still puzzling.

"My eyes were opened. I started to see in a whole different way. It's like a faucet that keeps dripping all night. No matter what you do, you can't get it out of your head. I began to see new light and shadows and colour where they never existed before. I was inspired by a new awareness. Nights and weekends I painted. And the more I did, the more I wanted to. I sold a few pieces. Gave away most. A familiar hankering was back. The force was pulling me back into art.

"In 1980, I attended the funeral of my father Nick; later that year, the birth of my son Nick. The ledger balanced. One Nick out, one Nick in. A new awareness, an awareness of time as a factor in my life, pressed hard. All of a sudden, I felt a sense of urgency. I quit my job. I stayed home, changed diapers, cooked and painted. We began to devise a plan. It was not long after that we blew up the TV."

Nick, Dawn and Ed moved into the VW camper van and headed three hours north. They parked themselves on a chunk of granite surrounded by a forest. Home at last, although it needed work. Winter came and all they'd done was clear the land.

"We hopped into the van and headed down to Mexico, planning to tour the country over the next six months. On the second day, we stopped in a little town in the mountains called San Miguel de Allende. It was just like the photos in my mother's album. Next day, we rented an apartment and stayed five months. I studied printmaking in a 500-year old former monastery, now art school. I worked with artists from Italy, France, Spain, Canada and Mexico, while nuns still walked the top floor and rang the big bell. It was magic. And the vital juices began to flow. Mexico was enlightening. After witnessing the day-to-day struggle that so many people there face, our personal task in Muskoka seemed easy in comparison.

"In Mexico, we made plans for the house, heavily influenced by an arrangement of space that Mexicans enjoy: a courtyard with breathing space in the middle of the house."

The next few years passed in a blur of cement mixers, 2x4s and drywall. Neither Ed nor Dawn had ever built a house. Every step had to be learned and tried. If they erred, they tried again. "The first summer, we made cement, morning 'til night. We were more tanned and fit than we'd ever been. Life was simple. Make cement, eat, sleep. What a welcome change to work with our bodies rather than our heads. In the middle of framing, our daughter Natalie was born. My cement-making partner was now occupied with child.

"The first winter we lived in our dining room. Our little family had everything we needed to survive: three beds, kitchen table, small stove and fridge, pots for cooking, tub for washing. It didn't seem that crowded to us because, after all, we had just finished living in a van.

"Slowly the house grew, the kids grew and we moved out of the dining room. Bit by bit, it got done. Kids played in the middle

The 9-Hour Egg

"During my first year in fine arts at Guelph University, one professor had a profound influence on me. I learned that art has much more to do with the eye than the hand.

"For one assignment, he gave us each a couple of eggs, and nine hours to draw them. Staring at something for so long gives you a whole new appreciation for texture and shadow and shape. Then we had to draw them again, this time in 30 seconds.

"We mounted all the drawings on the wall, and the professor asked which exercise produced better results. It was hard to say. The professor's advice to the class was, "Do what you do best."

Ed's best? "My 9-hour egg was pretty good. I had never been aware of the intensity of detail in something as simple as two eggs. Eggs were never the same again."

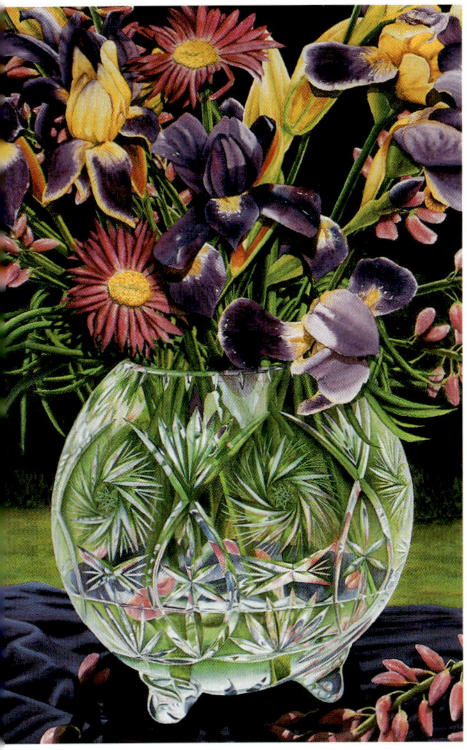

of construction. We spent a lot of time together, under circumstances that can only be called an adventure. That was the beauty of the experience. I still find it hard to believe that we did it."

Having built the house, it was now time for the last step in Ed's plan – paint. "Around 1987, I began painting all day, every day. I worked at a make-shift kitchen counter, standing up, a habit that has stuck with me. One of the advantages of building your own house is that you can pay as you play. Once the house was finished, we didn't have to worry about paying back a mortgage. This gave me time to paint rather than work for a bank.

"At first I painted everything, cows, trees, clouds, kids, water, boats, everything that's Muskoka. But my eye kept going back to a dance of light on the sugar bowl or a reflection on a vase or all that juicy colour in an apple. An endless fascination with nothing more complicated than a glint of light and a bit of shadow.

"My work has developed in the 10 years since I first stood at the kitchen counter. Most days I'm home where my inspiration is within a hundred yards of my studio. Since I'm the cook, the kitchen and dining room are places where I spend the most time. A great window lets in a flood of light across the table. Living on the 45th parallel affords an artist some of the best extremes of light around. Winter light shooting across a bowl of green apples with mile-long shadows can get me quite excited. As can green moss on the side of pink granite, or an arrangement of twigs and stones under my shoe.

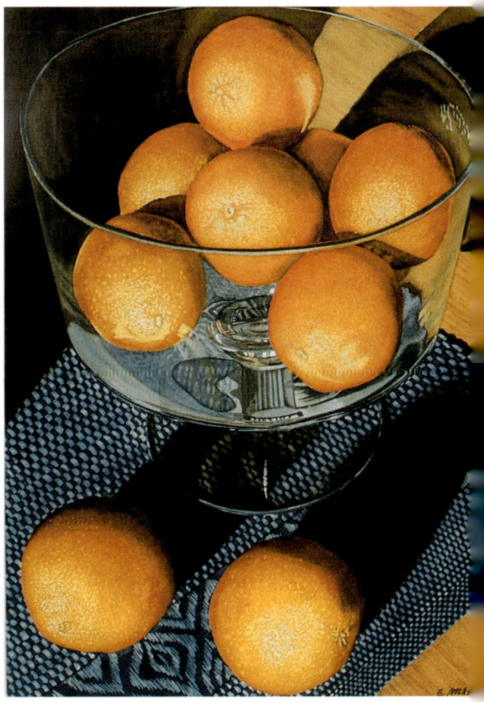

"My satisfaction as an artist comes in part from taking time to look at all the little things around me. The minutest of detail in the simplest of things. And then with only the power of a brush, some pigments and paper, I get to transform some object to a level that make others aware. To see in a new way the great beauty that surrounds us. And if I'm lucky, what I do might bring a bit of pleasure to someone else.

"That's the greatest power I have as an artist."

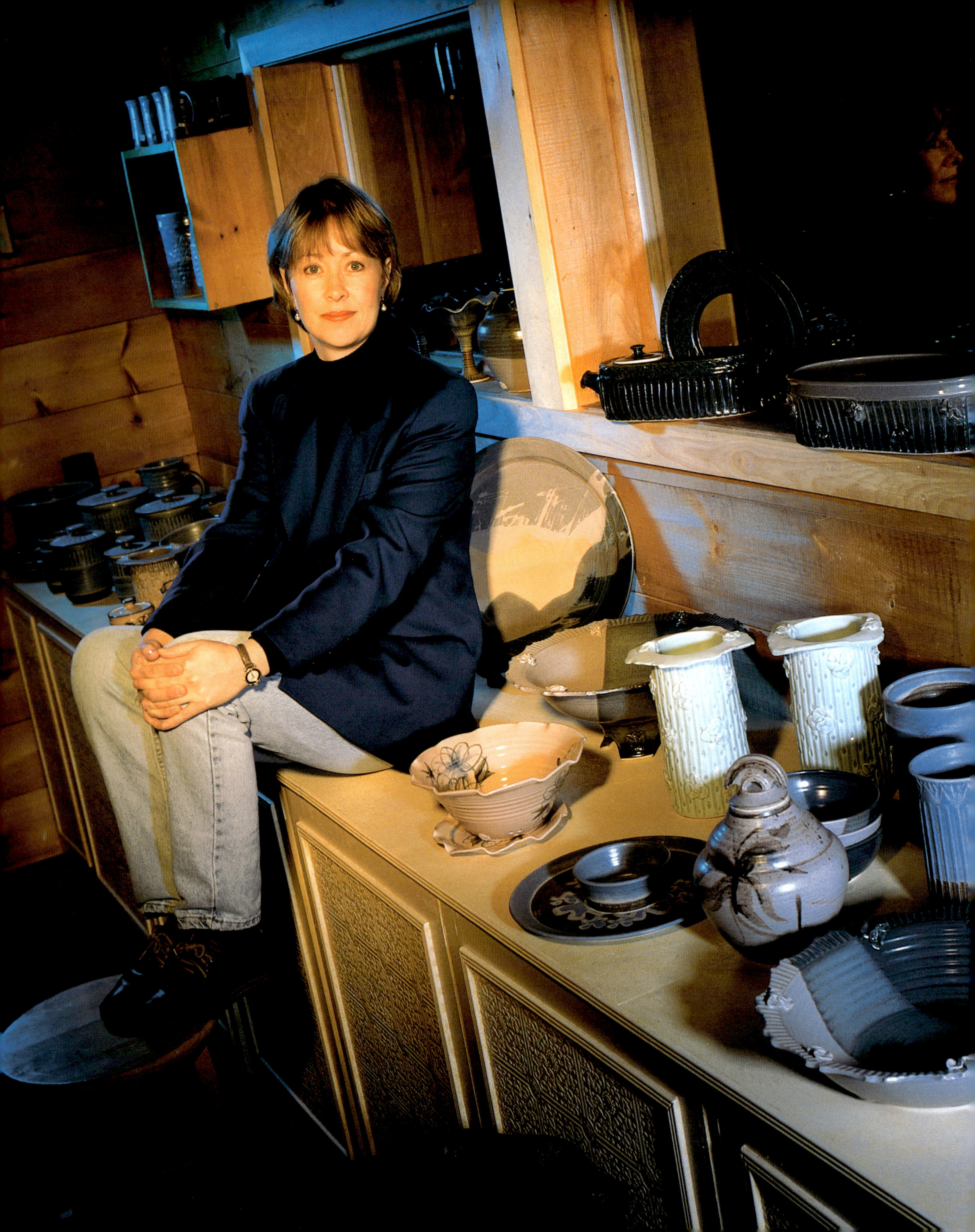

If I ever go looking for my heart's desire again I won't look any further than my own back yard. – Dorothy, The Wizard of Oz

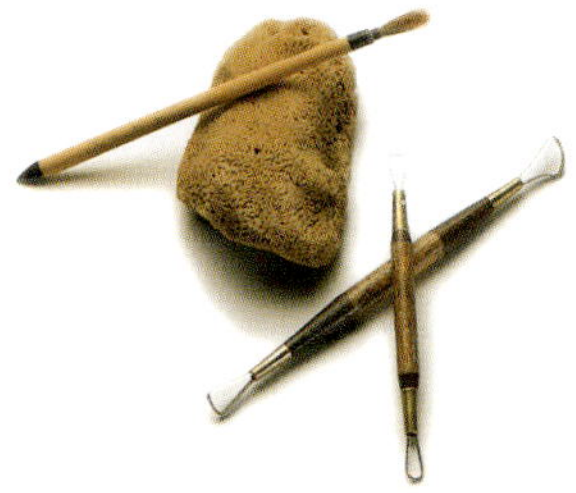

A Delicate Balance

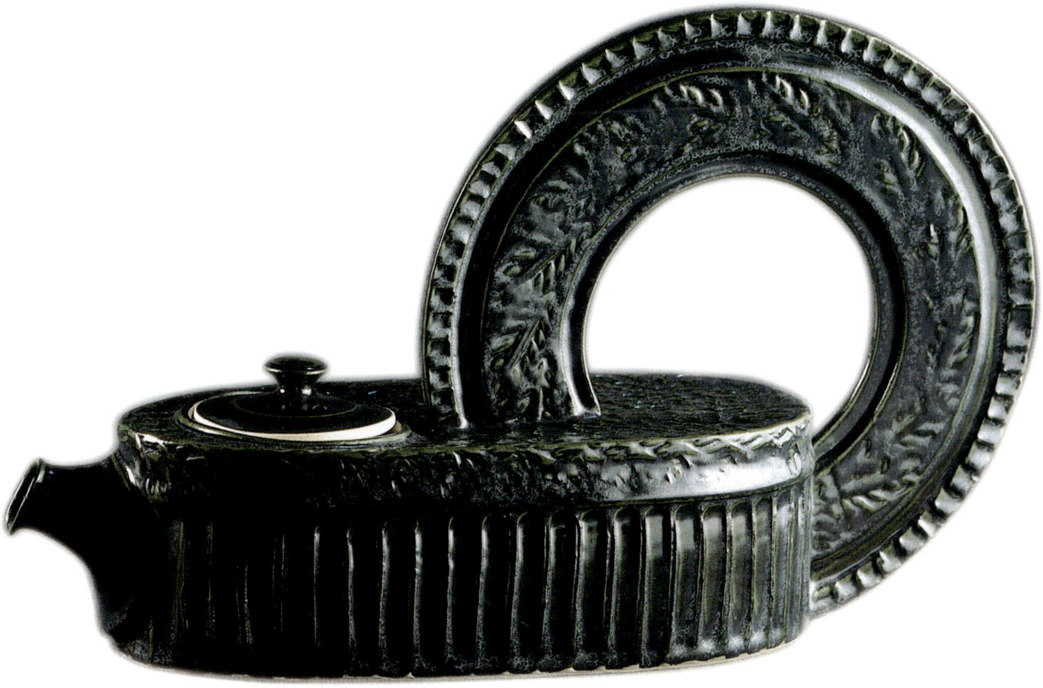

Linda Hrynyk's most recent resumé is dated April 2, 1991. The experience section for 1985 to 1991 reads, "running my own business for the past six years has been very challenging and rewarding. I've gained great experience in various aspects of business such as: finances, bookkeeping, organizational skills, inventory and public relations."

The job she accepted shortly after submitting her resumé gave her a regular paycheque for the next two months. She drew on all the skills listed above, but not the one she left out – creating exquisite pottery. Two months later, she went back to her studio. She hasn't updated her resumé since then. Chances are she won't until pots freeze over in her kiln.

Linda Hrynyk Pottery, west of Gravenhurst just off Highway 169, displays a diverse array of porcelain and stoneware articles for the home and garden. Says Linda of her pottery, "I like to make things that people will use." Attractively arranged throughout the showroom are place settings, teapots and mugs, casseroles and baking dishes that bring colour and function to the dinner

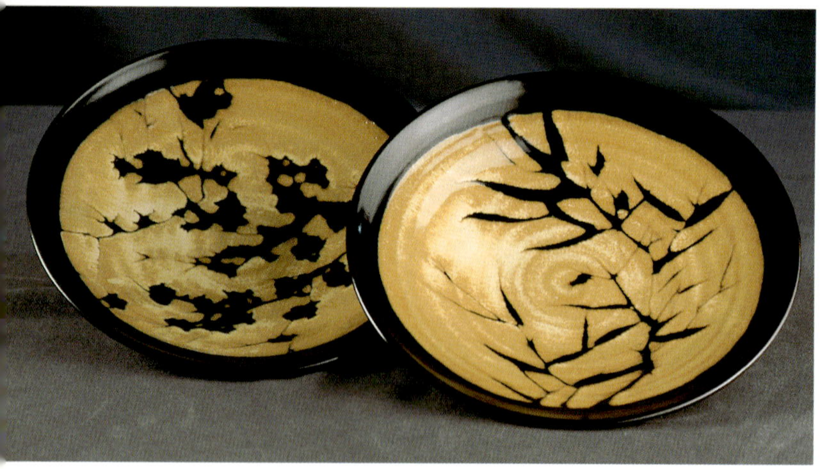

table. Her bird feeders and baths for the garden stand their ground against attack by enemy squirrels. Her large sculptural vases and window box planters provide a means of bringing nature indoors.

During the studio tour, a customer with a glimmer in her eye and a pastel blue platter in hand beckons to her boyfriend: "Look, I found something to buy."

"You already have several just like it."

"It's a gift," she explains, hesitating only slightly. Maybe yes, maybe no. Any pottery lover knows you can never have too many pieces. Each one is special.

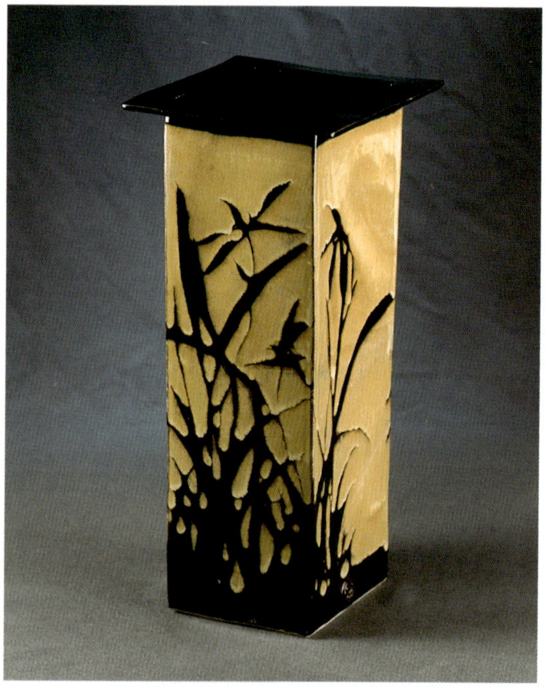

Linda, a long-time pottery collector before learning the craft, agrees. "There's a part of me in every piece. I think about each one that I make. There are so many details I care about. I put the handles on in a certain way. The rims have a certain look. I'm even finicky about the way I do glazes. If I had someone else helping me, it wouldn't be the same.

"Maybe no one else would know the difference, but I would. I would rather work harder than hire someone to help me. It feels good when someone asks if I do it all and I can answer, 'Yes, I do.'"

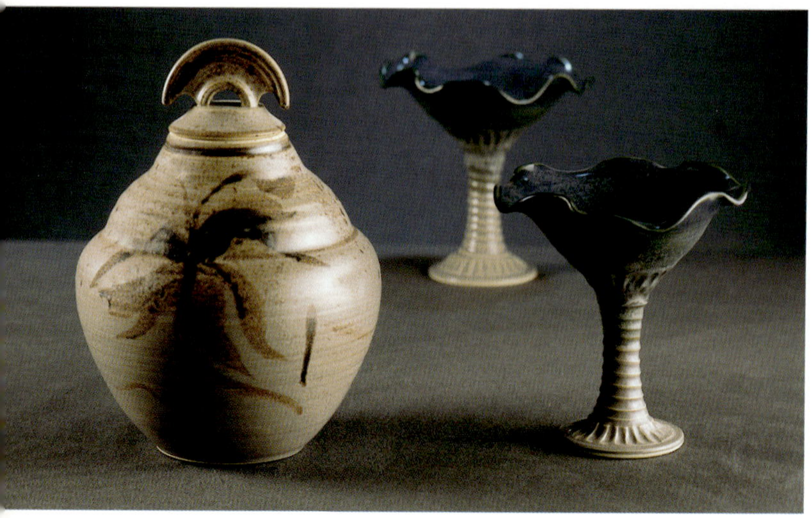

Trained in colour and composition by years in the field of professional photography, Linda draws much inspiration from the world around her. After squirrels destroyed a wooden bird feeder, she crafted her own clay version, and went on to make clay birdbaths. When mice ate a gingerbread house she and her son Kyle had made, she re-created it in stoneware.

At other times, inspiration comes from deep within. "I meditate a lot. It's amazing what will flow in if you just open up your mind. Some of my ideas come to me in the midst of meditating – a concept for a new sculpture or a new line.

"People are in such a hurry. Me too. But once a day, I just relax. A lot of good comes from that."

A studio potter since graduating from Georgian College in 1985, Linda grapples with the entrepreneur's challenge of producing and selling a high quality product, the artist's need for time to explore and play, and a parent's desire to nurture – and just be with – her child.

Kyle was only 5 when he produced his first clay dragon. After he made several more in various shapes, sizes and colours, mother and son sat down together to strategize. Challenge #1: pricing. In order to buy more Lego, how many would he need to sell and at what price? Challenge #2: promotion. On a piece of bristol board he advertised his dragons with a photo of the artist at work. When the doors opened for that year's Muskoka Autumn Studio Tour, a dragon was the first item rung up on the cash register.

"Growing up around the studio, he's learned a lot of values that took me a long time to learn, about how to use time well, how to manage money, what life is all about. It's also been good for me. When he was in daycare, I would work all day, maybe bring in a muffin and banana, and just keep going without a break. With him at home in the summer, I stop, cook something, and we have a nice visit over lunch. Then we go do our own thing. He's pretty independent and knows how to entertain himself, but I'm always here if he needs me."

Linda was born in 1958, the first of three children. She spent most of her childhood in the rolling hills outside of what was then the little town of Newmarket. "It's changed so much since I was a child. We didn't live on a farm, but it was like living in the country. We were on a rural route with farmers' fields on all sides."

Her father, an auto mechanic, sketched in his spare time. He encouraged Linda's interest in art, praising her work, enrolling her in classes, and sharing tips. A camera he had given her was always close at hand.

More interested in arts than sciences or math, Linda decided in high school to study photography. After graduating from Fanshawe College in London, she worked in a studio specializing in portrait photography, weddings and special events. She nurtured a love of landscape photography on her own time while camping and canoeing in Algonquin Park. Periodically, she sold her work at craft shows.

When a job as a transparency retoucher came up in a Toronto advertising agency, Linda moved to the big city. Ireland Graphics taught her the attention to detail that is characteristic of her pottery. "The agency managed production of catalogues, from photography to press. All of the articles – clothes or furniture or jewellery – were warehoused downstairs. My job was to go through one page at a time and compare the colour on the transparency to the actual article. If the colour was off, we would correct the page with dies. We'd retouch things as small as rings or buttons."

Her entrée into pottery came slowly. "I was 24 when I enrolled with my mother in a ceramics class. The pots were already made, we just painted them. I enjoyed it, but it wasn't enough. I wanted to make my own pieces. At the time I was commuting from Newmarket to downtown Toronto, Monday to Friday. I enrolled in a pottery course at George Brown College that had the additional benefit of keeping me busy until the traffic died down. I took evening courses for about a year and a half. My technique was shaky, but I just loved making pottery.

"People who come through my studio during the tour are amazed when I demonstrate. All of a sudden a pot or cup stands right up. You forget how amazing it is, that as a student you had the same reaction. When my instructor demonstrated, then said,

'Now we're all going to do the same thing,' I thought, 'Yeah right, there's no way I can do that.' Then you realize it's just a mental hurdle, that eventually, with practice, you'll master it."

Her desire to escape the bricks and mortar of the city grew more intense the longer she worked in Toronto. Whenever possible she escaped to Algonquin Park. "At one point I decided I wanted to be closer to the park. A lot of it was a gut feeling. I knew I didn't want to be in the city even though I enjoyed my job. So I had to ask myself what would make me happy, then figure out a way to do it." She moved to Muskoka in 1983.

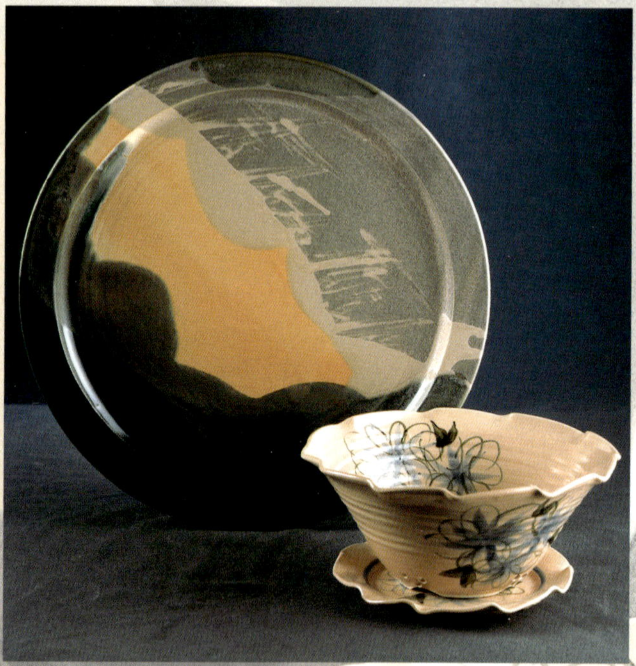

"I used to go on the studio tour every year prior to the move. From meeting the artists, I knew I wanted to be part of that kind of community. I was still into photography and initially thought I could sell my landscapes and nature pictures. Then I had second thoughts. I wasn't sure I could make a go of it financially. It was then I decided to return to school and study pottery professionally."

Circumstances forced another decision on Linda after she graduated from Georgian College in 1985. A new business loan had helped her buy a kiln and a second-hand wheel, but it wasn't enough to finance her start-up. To raise the rest of the money, she sold all her camera equipment except for one 35 millimetre camera. "That was tough. I had no idea whether the pottery would work out for me, but I had to try."

To supplement her income she worked part-time for an optometrist. "It was hard work to get the pottery business going while working part-time. When making pots, you need to be there at different stages of the process. For example, if you're making teapots, you have to be there when they dry in order to put on handles and spouts. If you're not there to trim items and put them together at just the right time, your work is ruined. I would work long hours, then go to the office, then come back and work some more. I'd have to switch my mind into a creative mode, which wasn't always easy. Then I'd find pieces didn't work because of poor timing – they had dried out too much or wouldn't fit together.

"Friends finally asked me, 'Why did you go to school in the first place? Take a year and work like crazy. At least you'll find out if it's possible to make a full-time living.' Eventually, that's what I did. In 1987 I jumped in and worked like mad. I advertised a lot, I did a lot of shows, and I was amazed at how well it all went."

Her year of concentrated effort helped establish a solid business foundation. The pressures didn't go away, they just changed complexion – from timing and production to finances and budgeting. "I no longer had that weekly paycheque. People didn't start coming up to Muskoka until May and I couldn't help but wonder, 'What if they don't come this year?' With a retail market of only eight months, you have to budget wisely or you're in trouble."

There's No Place Like Home

"I enjoyed my job in Toronto, but it doesn't compare to how I work today. Back then, I sat all day in a room with no windows.

"Today I look outside through picture windows. In spring and summer, I can see the birds. Autumn's my favorite time, when the leaves change. Then in winter, I look out on beautiful white snow. My studio is three steps from my home, no traffic to battle. On those occasions when I drive across town to run errands, I can see the lake.

"I enjoy living and working here. It's a great place to raise my son. It's also a peaceful place and, for a creative person, that's important."

Trouble came in the early 1990s when the recession hit, prompting Linda to dust off her resumé. "I was getting into a rut where I was working so hard, yet still worrying about money and bills. When the recession began, I just wanted a regular 9-to-5 job so I could at least budget from month to month. I thought life would be so much easier. I was wrong."

She accepted a day job producing advertising layouts, which ended after only two months. "I'd have to go back home to let the dog out for lunch. My boss would want me to stay late and work evenings, but I had to pick up Kyle at daycare. I was running everywhere."

She handed in her resignation, clicked her heels three times and was back in her pottery studio. Today, she wouldn't have it any other way, despite the long hours and periods of uncertainty.

"I'm doing exactly what I need to be doing. I love what I do. It's so satisfying to start with a lump of clay and create something that you like, and others like too. I love the feedback, when people tell me how much enjoyment they get from something I've made. When you work for someone else, you don't always get that feedback. And there's so much freedom. With pottery, if I get bored, I can branch into another avenue of work. For example, in the next couple of years I want to get more into one-of-a-kind pieces. It will give me the change I need, but I won't leave clay."

"It's true what they say – the grass always looks greener on the other side. It helps to have a reminder every now and then so you don't forget how good you have it."

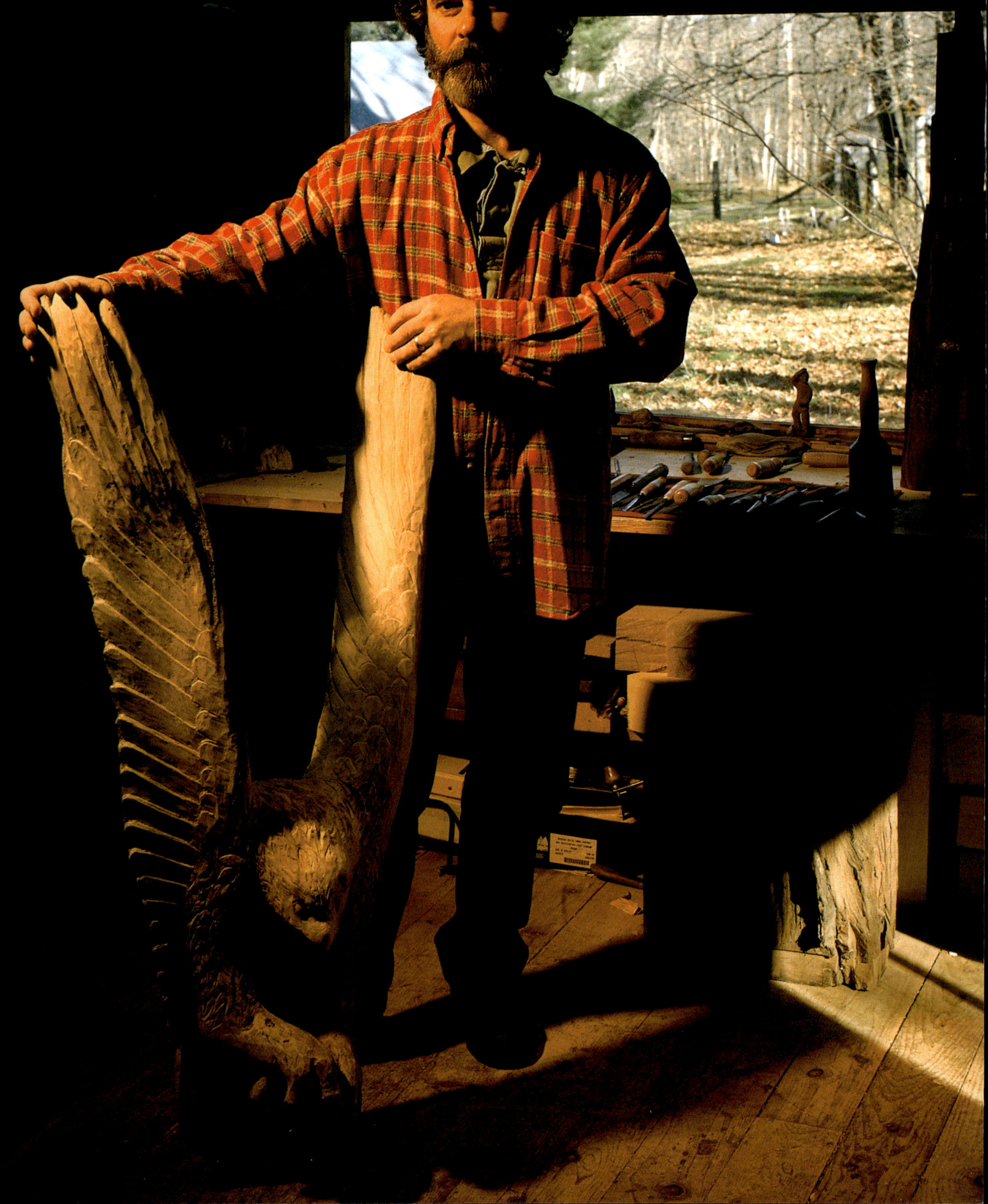

There is a season for everything, a time for every occupation under heaven. - Ecclesiastes 3:1

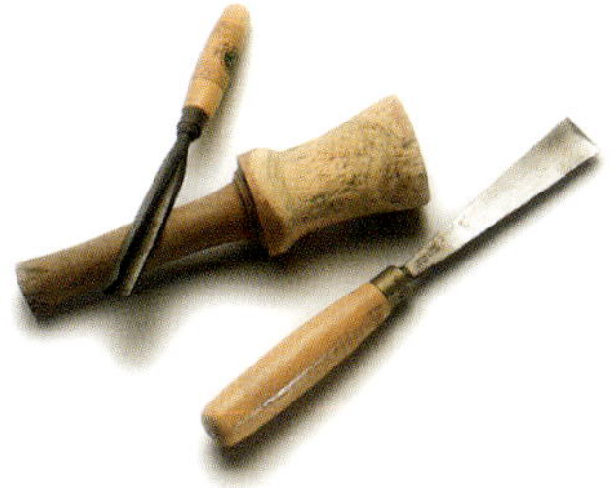

Seasons in a Woodcarver's Life

It's winter in Muskoka, a time for silence. Bill Hunnisett looks out his kitchen window at the fresh blanket of snow and sets down a half-finished cup of coffee. He dons a heavy winter coat and high boots, and clears a path to his workshop 100 yards from the house.

Crossing the threshold of the 70-year-old reconstructed barn, he smiles at a lifesize figure of John Lennon standing guard and nods politely toward a kneeling form of Jimi Hendrix at the other end of the studio. Five minutes later, the wood stove now radiating warmth, he heads back to the kitchen for breakfast with his wife Loie and their 7-year-old son Wesley.

By 8:30 a.m., Bill's re-entered his shop, and begun his daily time warp, wherein eight hours of carving, tool sharpening, designing and finishing rocket by in minutes. At the end of his day, he wishes for another four hours to work. He's busy with commissions and experiments. Too busy for town. It's been a week since he's left the farm or spoken with anyone other than Loie, Wes, John and Jimi. He never feels lonely.

Almost a hermit for several months of the year, Bill Hunnisett once worked as the social director for a Muskoka resort and led singles tours in the Caribbean. So how did this outgoing career man of the '70s become a modern-day Geppetto, carving life into forgotten limbs of driftwood found half submerged in the waters of Muskoka bays?

The second of three children, Bill was born in 1952 and raised in the Toronto suburb of York Mills.

The Woodcarver's Tools

HAND TOOLS

Type
knives and gouges

Number on hand – 50

Number used regularly – 15

Number Bill really needs to produce a carving – 10

Most valuable
a series of six purchased in 1978 under the eye of master carver Benoi Deschênes in St-Jean-Port-Joli

Most unusual
a set of six blades forged from the same steel found in samurai swords, sent from Japan by someone unknown to Bill, and who had received a carving as a gift

MOTORIZED TOOLS

Number on hand – 1

Purpose
grind and buff knife blades

Power source
washing machine motor

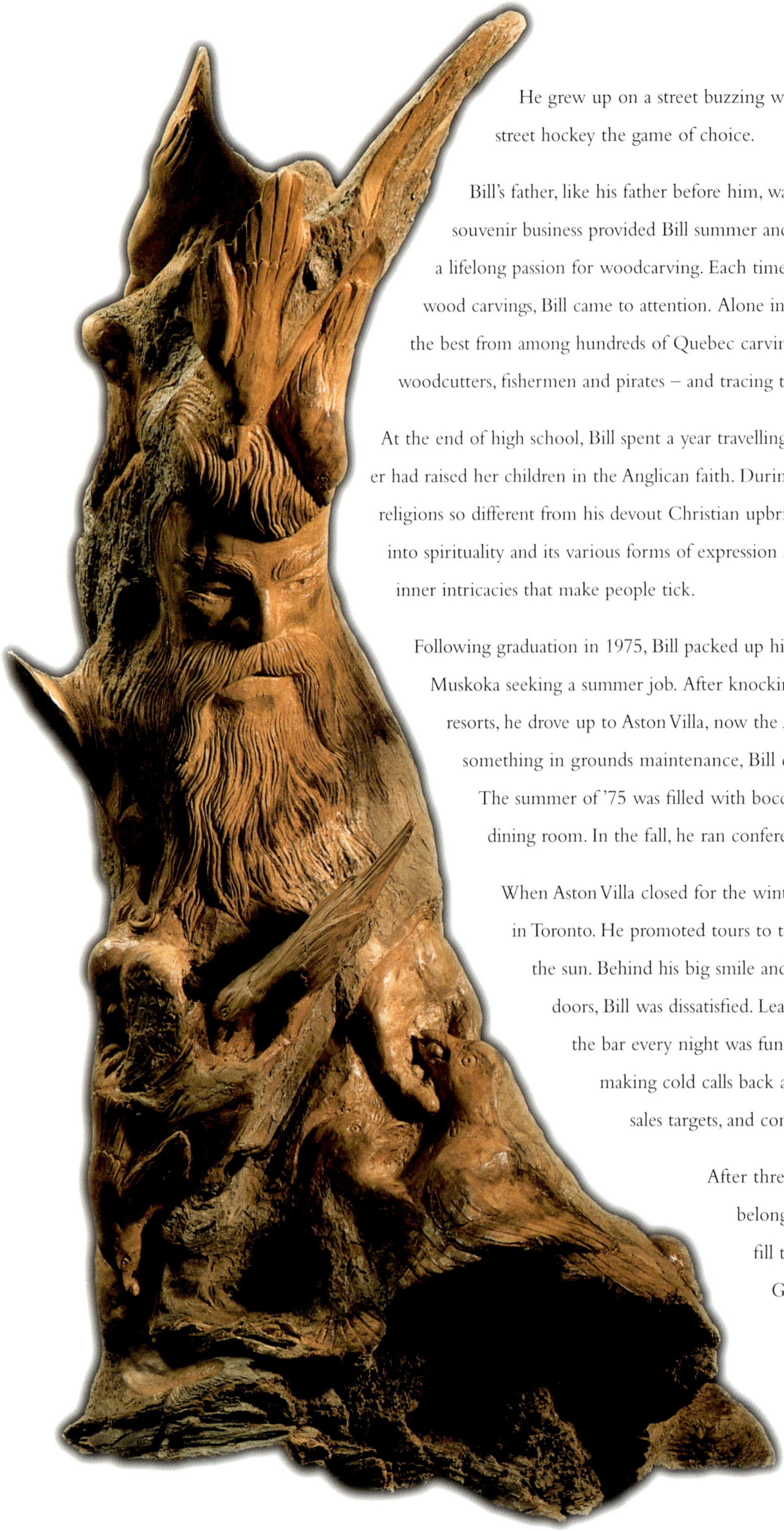

He grew up on a street buzzing with parents and children, a play haven with street hockey the game of choice.

Bill's father, like his father before him, was an entrepreneur. His wholesale gift and souvenir business provided Bill summer and Christmas employment. It also kindled a lifelong passion for woodcarving. Each time his father asked him to fill an order for wood carvings, Bill came to attention. Alone in the warehouse, he spun out time selecting the best from among hundreds of Quebec carvings, carefully choosing a variety of figures – woodcutters, fishermen and pirates – and tracing the intricacies with his fingertips.

At the end of high school, Bill spent a year travelling through Europe and Morocco. His mother had raised her children in the Anglican faith. During Bill's travels, the shock of cultures and religions so different from his devout Christian upbringing created a thirst for greater insight into spirituality and its various forms of expression around the world. He wanted to study the inner intricacies that make people tick.

Following graduation in 1975, Bill packed up his baby blue Volkswagen and drove to Muskoka seeking a summer job. After knocking unsuccessfully on the doors of three resorts, he drove up to Aston Villa, now the Aston Resort Hotel. Hoping at least for something in grounds maintenance, Bill drove away as the new social director. The summer of '75 was filled with bocci tournaments and announcements in the dining room. In the fall, he ran conferences.

When Aston Villa closed for the winter, Bill found a job with Skylark Holidays in Toronto. He promoted tours to travel agents and escorted groups south into the sun. Behind his big smile and a bronze glow from tropical hours outdoors, Bill was dissatisfied. Leading groups of singles intent on closing the bar every night was fun for a while, but exhausting. So too were making cold calls back at his desk, meeting aggressive monthly sales targets, and conforming to rigid management practices.

After three years Bill removed his tie, sold his belongings and bought a VW camper van. To fill the gap between this most recent and God-only-knew what next livelihood, he decided on woodcarving lessons with master carvers. He set out for St-Jean-Port-Joli, the heart of Quebec's wood carving community.

In Muskoka he had gone from resort to resort; now, in St-Jean-Port-Joli, from workshop to workshop, struggling with gestures and a limited French vocabulary to convey his desire for lessons. The current eventually carried him to the doorstep of Benoi Deschênes, today one of Canada's internationally respected wood sculptors. Deschênes offered two weeks; Bill wanted two months. At first reluctant, Benoi considered Bill's proposal and later that day offered him a trial period. If the first two weeks worked out, Bill could stay on.

Two months later, Bill shook hands with Benoi, packed up and headed off, uncertain about the destination but immensely satisfied with his experience. He had progressed from exacto knives

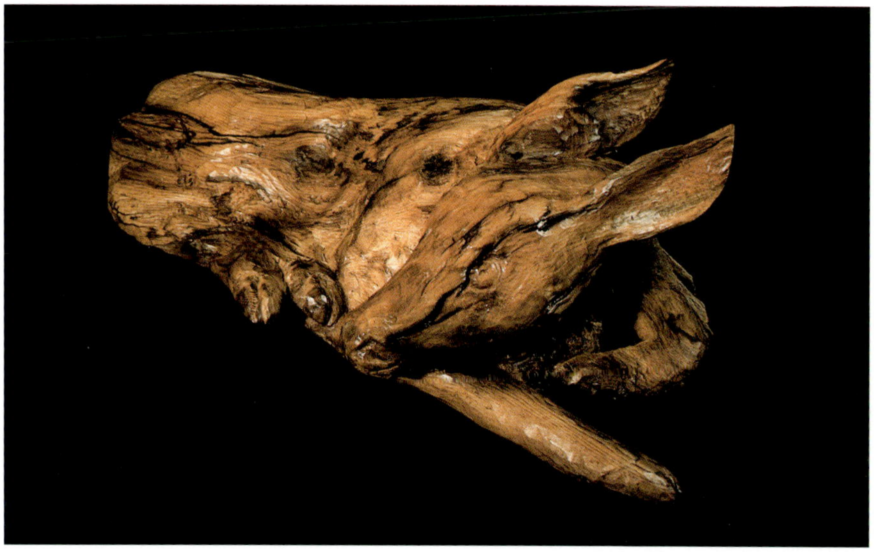

to v-tools, gouges, and straight knives, and drove off with a van full of carvings. In Quebec City, curious passers-by peeked in the van and asked if his work was for sale. Their questions gratified the artist and the entrepreneur. Within weeks of returning home, family and friends joined the circle of fans. He had left for Quebec in search of a retirement hobby. He would soon discover he had found a career.

It's spring in Muskoka, a time for creating. As the trees blossom, so too Bill's imagination. He inspects his inventory of driftwood from the previous year, now dried and ready for carving.

He lifts a few favourites from the pile. Over the next few months he'll start 15 or 20 carvings in readiness for summer and autumn shows.

Bill doesn't use a vice to work. It mars the wood. Instead, he holds the wood with his left hand and carves with his right. As curls peel off his blade, and the driftwood reveals its hidden image – a heron or fox, a ballerina or a pirate – he feels God helping him.

Over the years Bill has made gradual process toward full-time work as a woodcarver. After returning from Quebec in 1978, Bill worked at odd jobs in Toronto and Montreal to support himself and free up as much time as possible for carving.

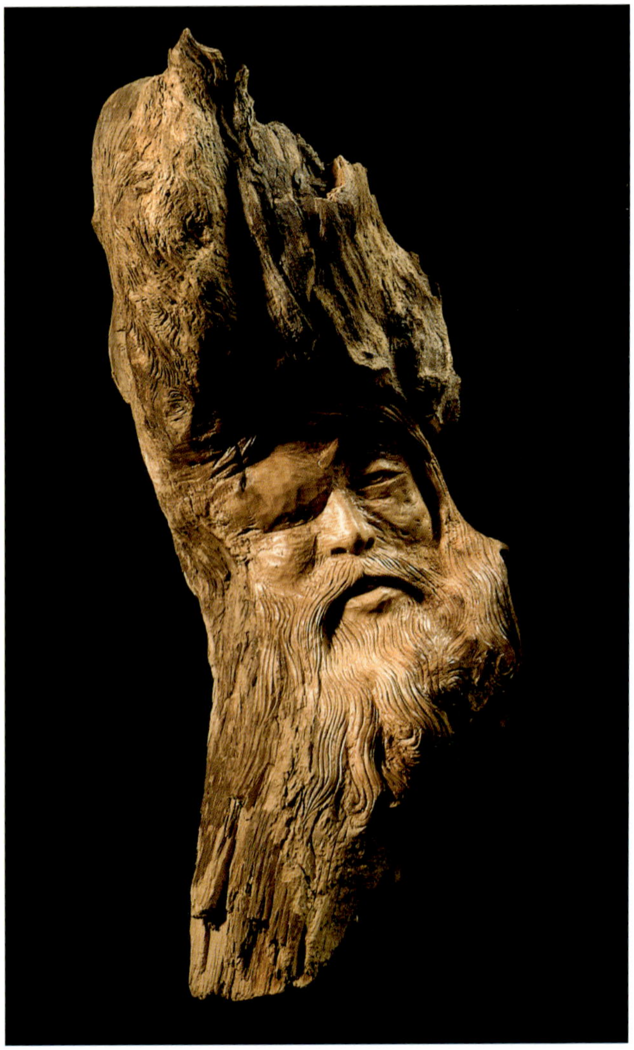

In 1979, his father learned of a retail gift business for sale in the Muskoka area and talked to Bill about buying it. Located on Gravenhurst's main street, "Hunnisett's Woodcarving and Crafts" became Bill's home, studio and gallery. He quickly became part of a growing community of artists, joining the Muskoka Autumn Studio Tour in 1980.

For five years, he combined retail management and carving, but eventually found that serving the public took too much time away from his creative work. His solution was to convert the store into Muskoka's first art co-op, The Courtyard Gallery. Teaming up with five other artists, he reduced his six-day tour of duty in retail management to one. Although an artistic success, the gallery foundered two years later due to low customer traffic outside the summer season.

Adrift again, Bill landed shared accommodation in Toronto's Kensington market, a multicultural community alive with shops, cafés and open-air stalls. Furnishing his bedroom with a work bench and a mattress, he whittled away the hours, preparing carvings for an upcoming show in Bracebridge.

It's summer in Muskoka, a time for gathering. Bill explores the nearby bays in search of buried treasure. Wading with running shoes in shallow waters, he combs the shoreline. He waits for the sun to come out and the water to calm. Driftwood is abundant, though not always in clear view. He spots an arm of maple wood breaking the surface. As Bill tugs at it, the whole piece emerges. He catches his breath, already envisioning a form waiting to find expression. He lugs the maple wood back to his canoe, a final addition to his catch for the day.

Summer is also a time for embracing. Setting up his booth at an outdoor arts show at the Muskoka Lakes Museum in 1985, Bill heard a voice offering him lemonade. Two hours later, he and the lemonade lady were still talking. Shortly after, Lois Anne Urquhart – officially responsible for maintaining the museum's gardens – left on a five-month trip to Australia. She wrote Bill daily. On her return, Bill set up his studio in downtown Guelph while she studied at university. They married in 1987 and a year later moved into their current home outside the town of Rosseau. Wesley was born three years later.

Bill had begun working with driftwood in the early 1980s. Each summer for two weeks, he gathers up driftwood, including maple, pine, cedar and oak. Bill selects only pieces that have remained immersed, because the water preserves what, in random cycles of wet and dry, would otherwise rot. Within a year, his rough cull dries out and is ready for carving.

"My goal with every carving is to put life and movement into it." Be it an osprey with a struggling fish in its talons or a merganser feeding its young, Bill's carvings leave part of the original wood untouched, creating a dynamic flow between natural wood and natural artistry. He loves carving driftwood because it allows him to work spontaneously. Each cut reveals characteristics of colour, texture or strength that require him to adapt as he goes along. A knot emerges as the eye of a fish; bad wood pared away, a new line or curve.

"I can't make a drawing because the piece changes as I shape it. I have to let the wood tell me how to work it." Sometimes the wood tells him what to do immediately. Other times, he must be patient. "There are days I don't even carve. I just stare at the wood. I used to feel impatient, but I've learned that seeing the image in the wood is the most important step." Once his hands start carving, one of Bill's greatest challenges is knowing when to let them stop. Otherwise, he risks overcarving, producing a piece that was better two hours earlier.

It's autumn in Muskoka, a time for reaping what has been sown. Three weeks before the Muskoka Autumn Studio Tour, Bill's shop contains 40 almost finished works. In the time remaining, while Loie prepares the grounds, Bill's adrenalin peaks. He finishes at least one carving a day, leaving five or six to work on as tour visitors watch.

Bill sees more people over the two days of the tour than he sees the rest of the year. And his visitors see a master carver, as well as a workshop full of finished works that, from culling to that last quick cut, have taken months of concentrated effort.

At tour's end, Bill is tired but satisfied. He moves on to a favourite chore, two weeks of chopping firewood for his home and workshop. The physical activity feels great. He's outdoors. The bugs are gone. Winter is just around the corner. Life is good.

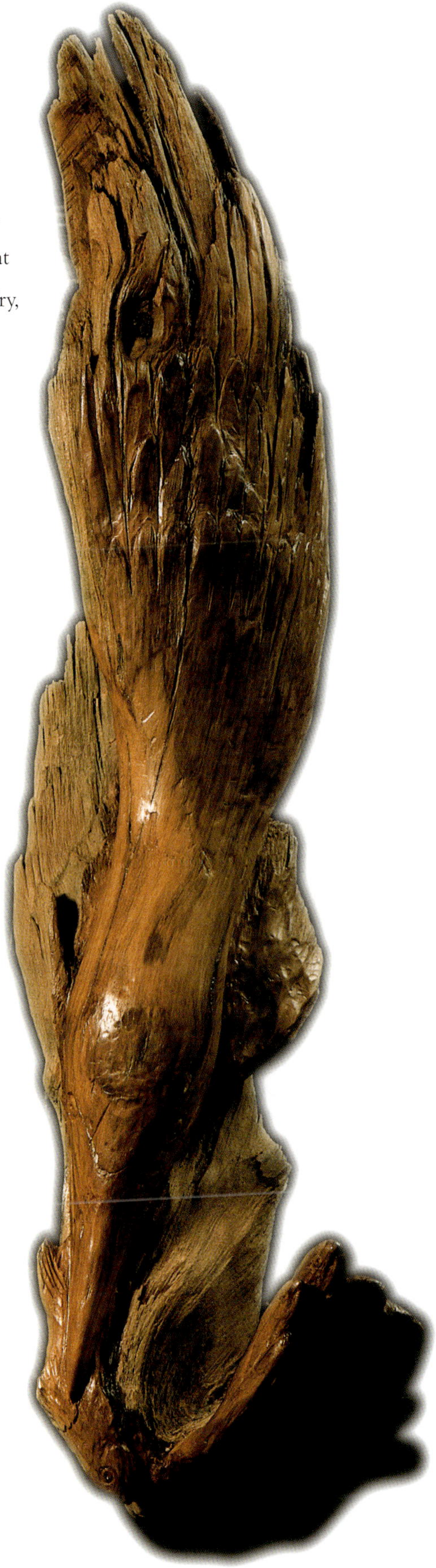

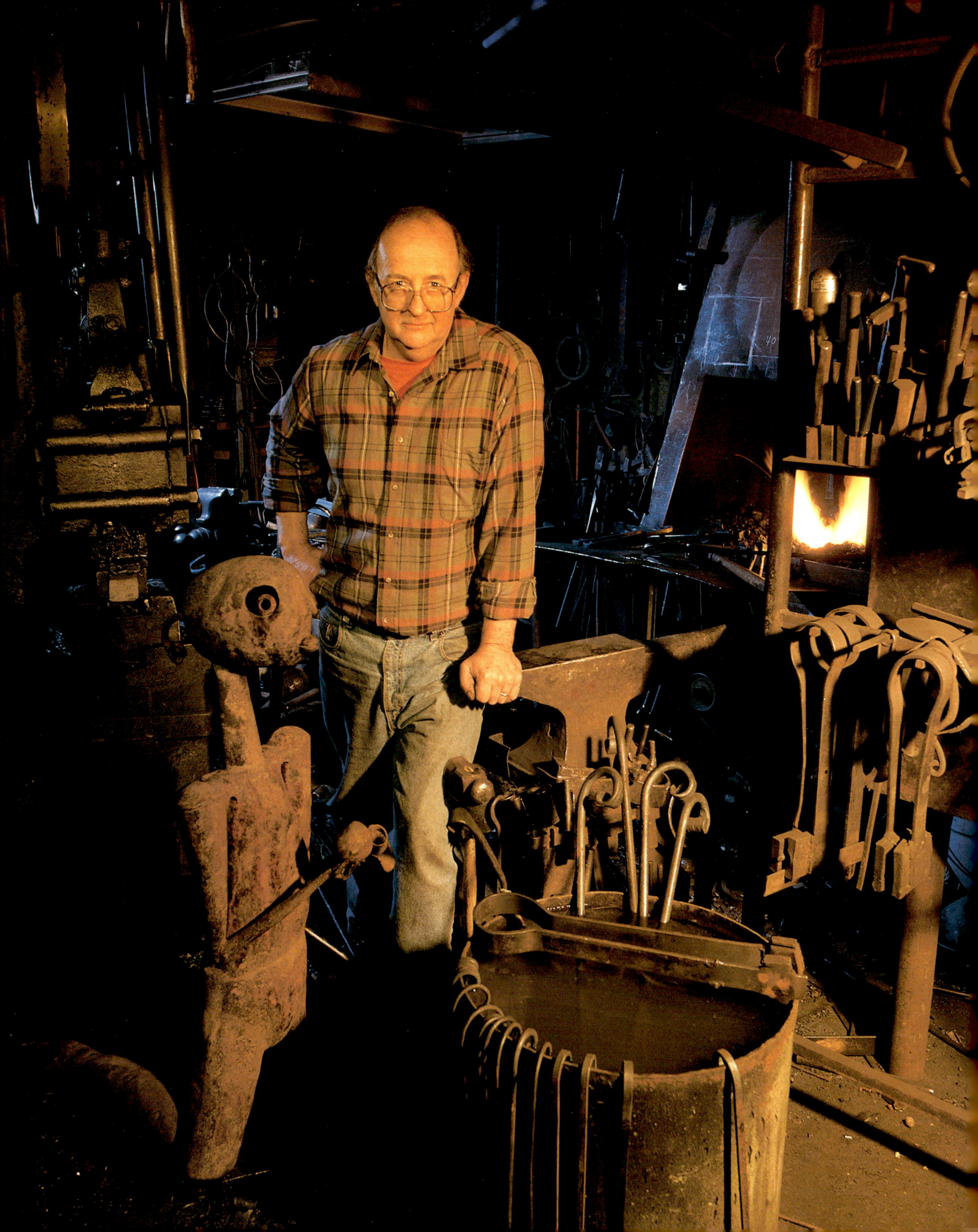

WAYNE CHURCH

They shall beat their swords into ploughshares and their spears into pruning hooks.
Nations shall not lift up swords against nations, nor shall they learn war anymore. – Isaiah 2:4

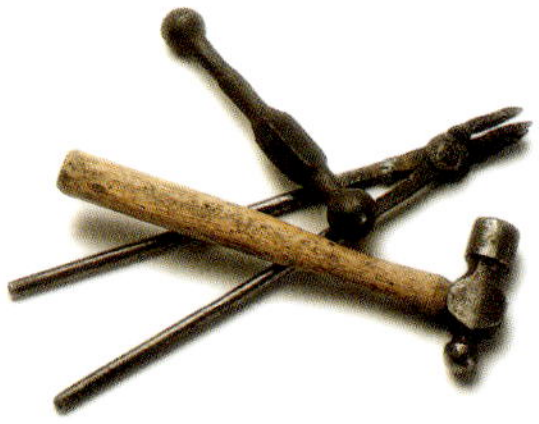

If I Had a Hammer

Heading south on Highway 11, just before crossing over the Severn River, you reach what has been for 20 years the last stop on the Muskoka Autumn Studio Tour. *Phoenix*, a 15-foot iron sculpture turned toffee from years of exposure to the elements, beckons you into the parking lot of The Artisan's Gallery. It's impossible to ignore the motley crew of steel figures that greets you – a permanent lawn party of unique and fascinating guests, frozen in time and space.

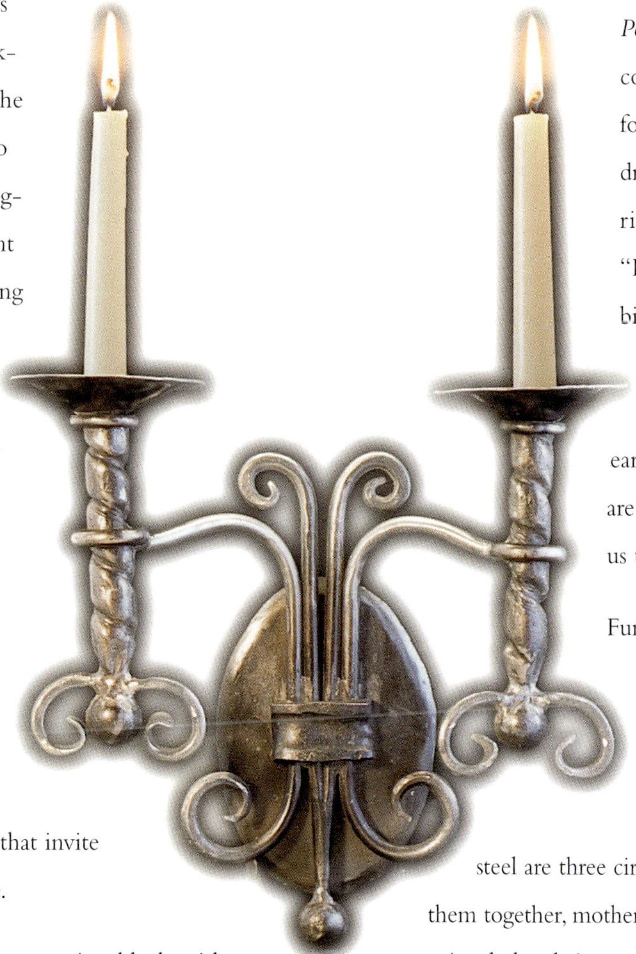

As you make your rounds, you might catch the gentle tinkling of wind chimes. Or spot a chrysalis preparing for its transformation into a butterfly. An emerald jewel no bigger than a jelly bean, its soft green body clings to a corten steel sculpture. Amid recognizable forms of Canadian geese poised in flight are abstract forms that invite the curious, ignite the imaginative.

Owner Wayne Church, a second generation blacksmith, created *Phoenix* in 1974 to symbolize a fresh start in his career. A graceful bird rising above a stylized flame, *Phoenix* represents the renaissance of a blacksmith from the embers of a dying trade.

Peace, also built in the 1970s, is a corten steel sculpture of cylindrical forms portraying the world's children, wrapped with a ribbon and riding on the back of a dove. "Initially, it wasn't meant to be a bird, but it became more birdlike as the concept evolved. I like the idea of utopian peace on earth, and the children of the earth are probably the ones who will get us there."

Further along is *Links*, one of 10 sculptures in a series originally called *Bondage*, but which evolved into *Bonding*. Bound together by a cord of painted steel are three circles. "This is a family. A link ties them together, mother to father to child. The link is generational, the chain continued by an empty link ready to start the next generation."

Wayne's father, Edward, was the family's first blacksmith. Wayne's son Matt continues the tradition. The youngest of Wayne and Pat Church's three sons, Matt will soon graduate from the Emily Carr School of Fine Art and partner with his father at The Artisan's Gallery.

Bird, Matt's sculpture, is made of found objects, begun with an old rake that conjured up for Matt a feathered tail. The tailpipe of a car became the bird's long neck. Its head, arms and legs are of fabricated metal. Matt comments: "Making something from found objects was for me a discovery. It was satisfying to have the freedom to create my own species, to take my imagination where it wanted to go, to be surprised by the end result. Surprising yourself is part of the pleasure of creation."

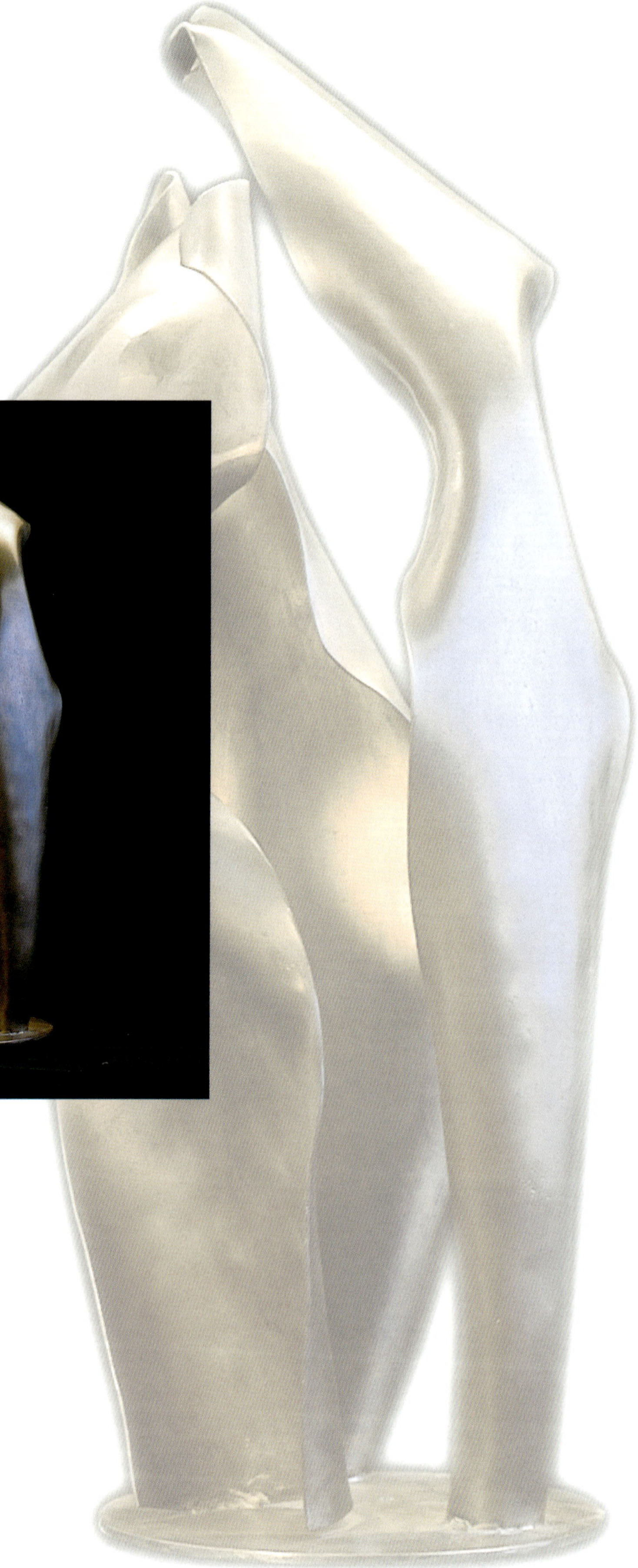

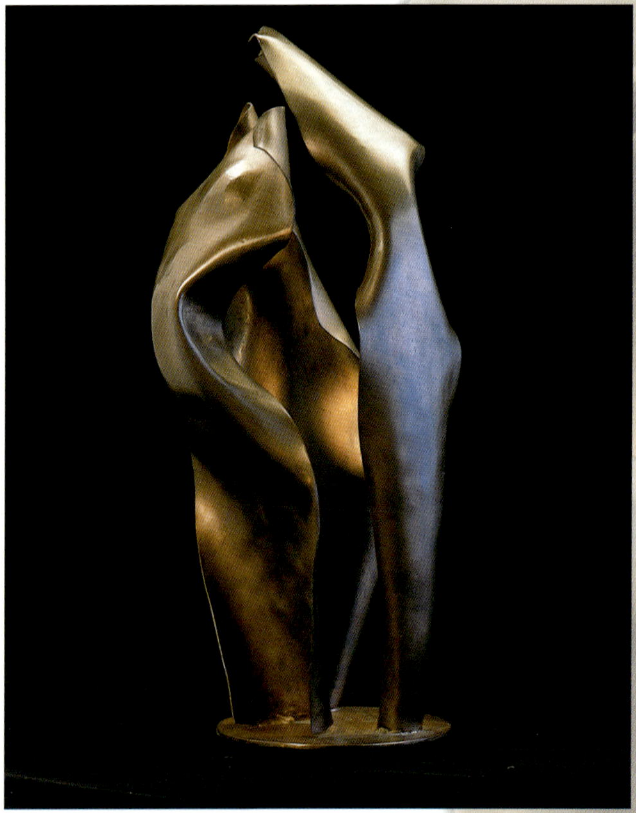

Wayne built *Ascending the Technocracy* in 1994. The base of the sculpture is three shapes, a triangle, rectangle and square which represents technology. In contrast to the linear forms is an organic form at the top, enveloping the heart and soul of humanity. Though Wayne is a master craftsman whose hand-wrought home and garden accessories are popular in Muskoka and beyond, he is passionate about his abstract expressionist sculptures. Reducing a complex topic to its simplest expression is a common process in his work. Asked to explain his triangle, square and circle, Wayne offers: "The base is the technical end of our society. Resting on it is the organic part of nature. It's like a human heart.

"I think we have problems today balancing the technical with the organic. We try to embrace technology, but all the technology in the world can't change our emotional attitudes. We're still very organic. We try to get rid of nature or rationalize it, but it's always there. The organic part, the heart, this is life. The technical, the mechanical, that should just be the support."

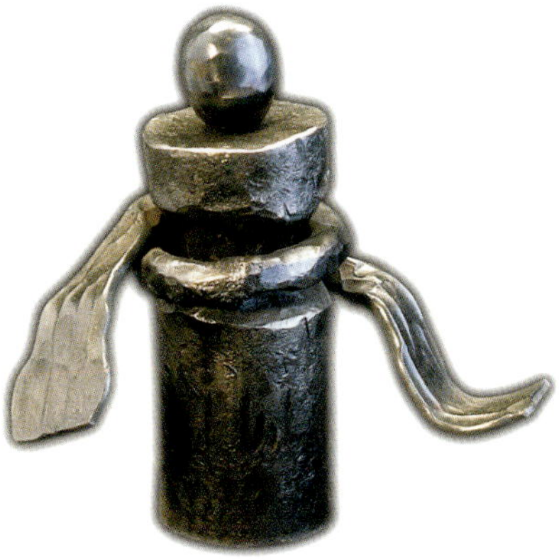

Wayne Church was born in Hamilton, Ontario in 1943, the third child of Muskoka blacksmith Edward Church, who had been relocated by the war effort to work in a Hamilton munitions factory. Edward himself was the son of a Muskoka pioneer who had cleared land and built roads.

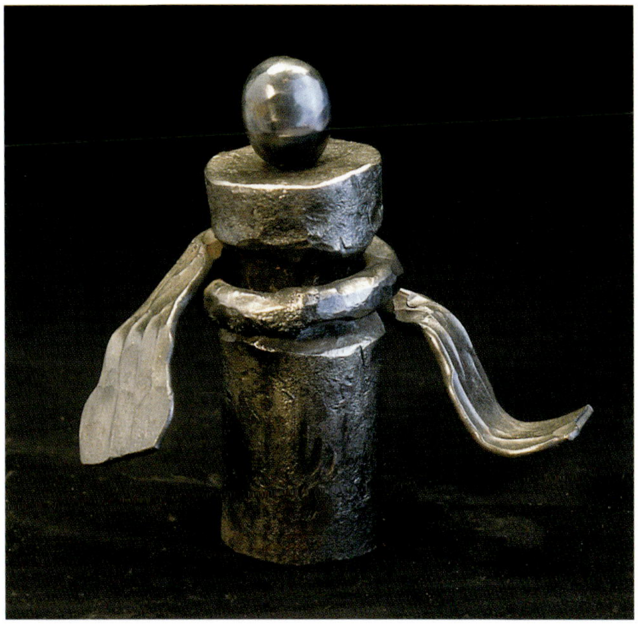

The Churches left Hamilton in 1945 because of Wayne's asthma, aggravated by the steel town's factory emissions. The family headed north. In the tiny lakeside community of Glen Orchard, Edward set up a fix-it shop, The Smithy. It provided repair services for equipment and fences, and made hand-crafted functional items like trailer hitches, building tools and fireplace accessories.

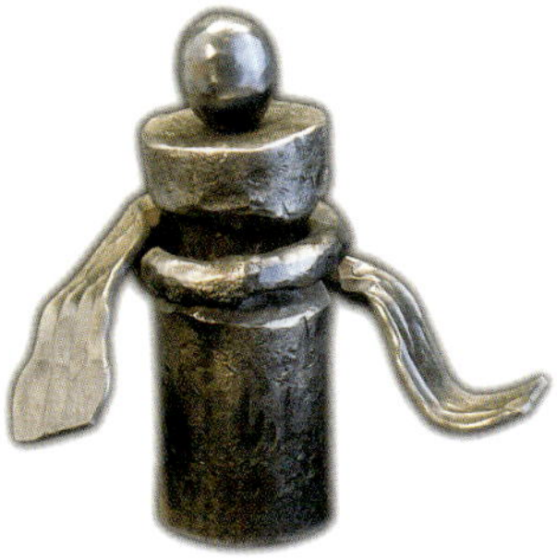

Of all the recreational pursuits a northern climate promotes, hockey ranks high for young boys. Wayne loved the sport, and it showed in his performance. Recruited into the Detroit Red Wings farm system at 15, Wayne moved back to Hamilton, juggling a gruelling training schedule with high school.

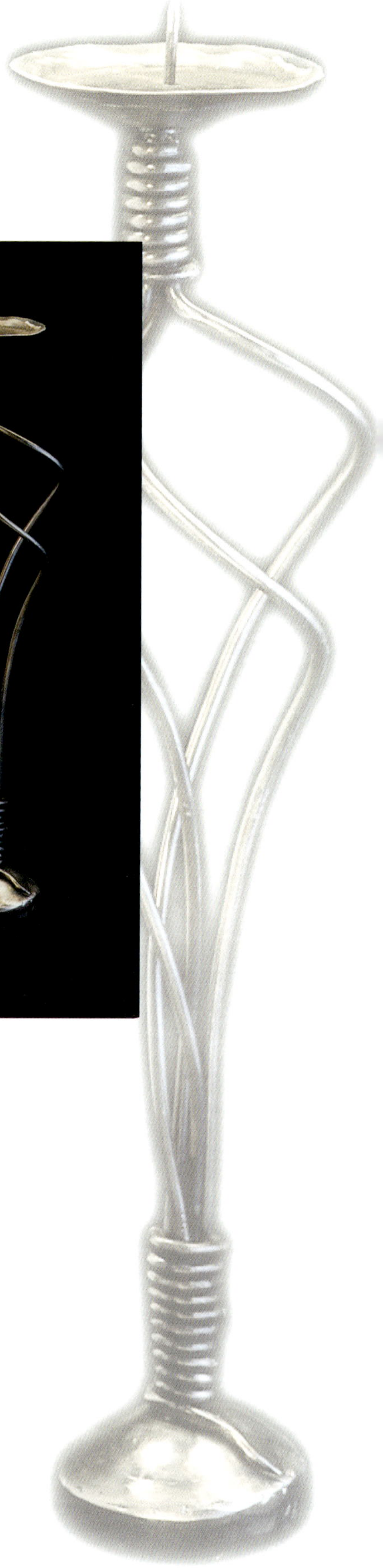

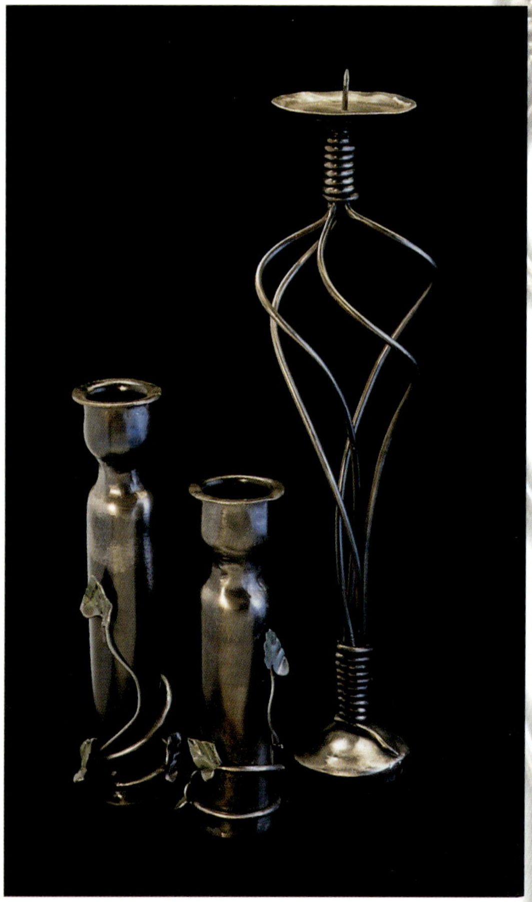

"I learned from hockey that you have to be dedicated to survive. I had to catch a streetcar before sunrise to make the 6:00 a.m. practice. I'd get home from a road trip at 3:00 in the morning and prepare for school the next day. It's the same for the arts. If you're not dedicated, you'll never make it."

Wayne decided to quit hockey after a full-body slam put him in the hospital. Introduced to paint and canvas by a high school teacher, he traded in his hockey stick for a paint brush and studied design arts at Central Technical School and Three Schools of Art in Toronto. After graduating, he apprenticed with commercial artist F.R. Halliday. He soon realized the feast or famine cycle of a painter's existence and reconsidered his future.

Returning to Glen Orchard for a visit, Wayne passed the time by hammering steel on his father's anvil. Leaning over the anvil sparked an idea that has kept Wayne going for over 30 years. "I'd always loved to watch my dad work. It just seemed like magic. Then it hit me that I could transfer that skill into sculptural forms, artistic forms. I got really excited. I was already enthralled with the plastic quality of metal when it's really hot, and I got to thinking that there's no limit to what we can do with metal, to where we can take it."

His marriage in 1963 to high school sweetheart Pat Vincent coincided with his move back to Glen Orchard and the start of a 10-year partnership with his father.

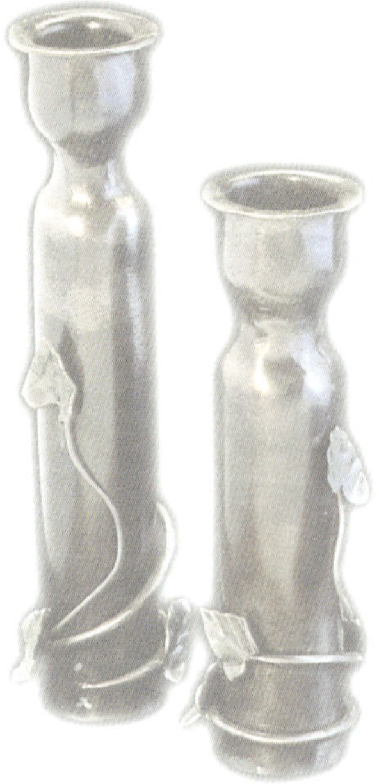

In 1964 a formidable influence entered The Smithy. Alexandra Luke was a member of Painters Eleven, a group of Canadian abstract expressionists. A fire had destroyed her family's boathouse, leaving metal remnants of boat motors and frames. She enlisted Wayne to help her weld the bent propellers and shafts into abstract sculptures. "Dad called them monstrosities, but Alexandra had a certain way of seeing things. She'd take a beat-up piece of cardboard and notice the beauty in the colours, or how interesting the spaces were around them."

For the next three summers, Wayne apprenticed under Alexandra, who taught him a new way of seeing. "Abstraction boils down to believing that beauty is everywhere."

In 1974, Wayne's two brothers joined the family business. Wanting more time and space to pursue his abstract sculptures, Wayne decided to go out on his own. Pat, a teacher, was firmly behind him and rounded up their three sons – 10-year-old Mark, 6-year-old Michael and 4-year-old Matthew – for an adventure in creative living. In the fall of 1974, they squeezed into a tiny 2-bedroom cabin close to a plot of land they had purchased on Highway 11, southern Ontario's thoroughfare to Muskoka. Wayne and crew first built their house, then the shop. The roof of The Artisan's Gallery went up during the first snowfall of the year.

An invisible hand helped them through what was in hindsight a traumatic experience. "We never thought twice at the time. It was just something we wanted to do. We wanted to be independent, and our plans seemed quite rational. But we survived."

Today The Artisan's Gallery enjoys a steady flow of private and corporate clients. Besides working on commissions, Wayne stocks his showroom with art pieces, as well as wrought iron tables, chairs, mirrors, and decorative articles. His work also appears in galleries in Toronto, Orillia and Haliburton, and in private collections on several continents.

Wayne starts his days in the shop at 7:30 a.m., but evenings he indulges a love of painting and designing. With watercolour and acrylic he explores the colour his day job lacks, and sketches ideas for sculptural projects. He tries to spend at least one day a week on his sculpture, often working on a series of pieces with a shared theme.

Empty nesters and recent grandparents, Wayne and Pat are proud of their links in the chain of evolution. Sons Mark and Michael are both immersed in computer technology – Mark an engineer in the manufacturing sector, Michael an independent multimedia expert in the music recording industry. Matt looks forward to joining his father in the family business. "By continuing in a trade that is so embedded in history, you can see yourself in a historical lineage. But it's hard to see the future. Mass production is putting a lot of smaller players out of business. On the other hand, there will always be a demand for custom work, for objects animated by the hand and heart of the maker."

Unto Ages of Ages

"The fact that our dad was creating large sculptures never separated us from other families. My parents always wanted to keep us grounded, and made a point of exposing us to a larger world. Travel was a priority. And just like other kids, we collected hockey cards and fastened the doubles to our bike spokes.

"More through example than by preaching, my father has passed on many lessons that go far beyond manipulating metal. We learned discipline by seeing him go to work each day like a well-tuned clock. We learned patience from his incredible ability to deal calmly with unsettling or stressful situations. We learned communication skills by seeing him interact comfortably with people from all walks of life.

"As for his sculptural work, I feel that abstraction so often has been either misrepresented or misunderstood in the art spectrum. Often the criticism is that it's impossible to understand without an art education. This has never been the abstractionist's intent. For through minimalism and abstraction, the artist calls viewers to read with their inner child, to respond free from adult thinking.

"My father is more of a minimalist, stripping the superfluous away in order to convey a complex message in simple terms. I'm more literal, preferring to start with a recognizable form, then take it in unpredictable directions. But we strive to communicate similar things. We're both concerned with what it means to be human, with connecting to others through our work, with breaking down barriers that keep people separate."

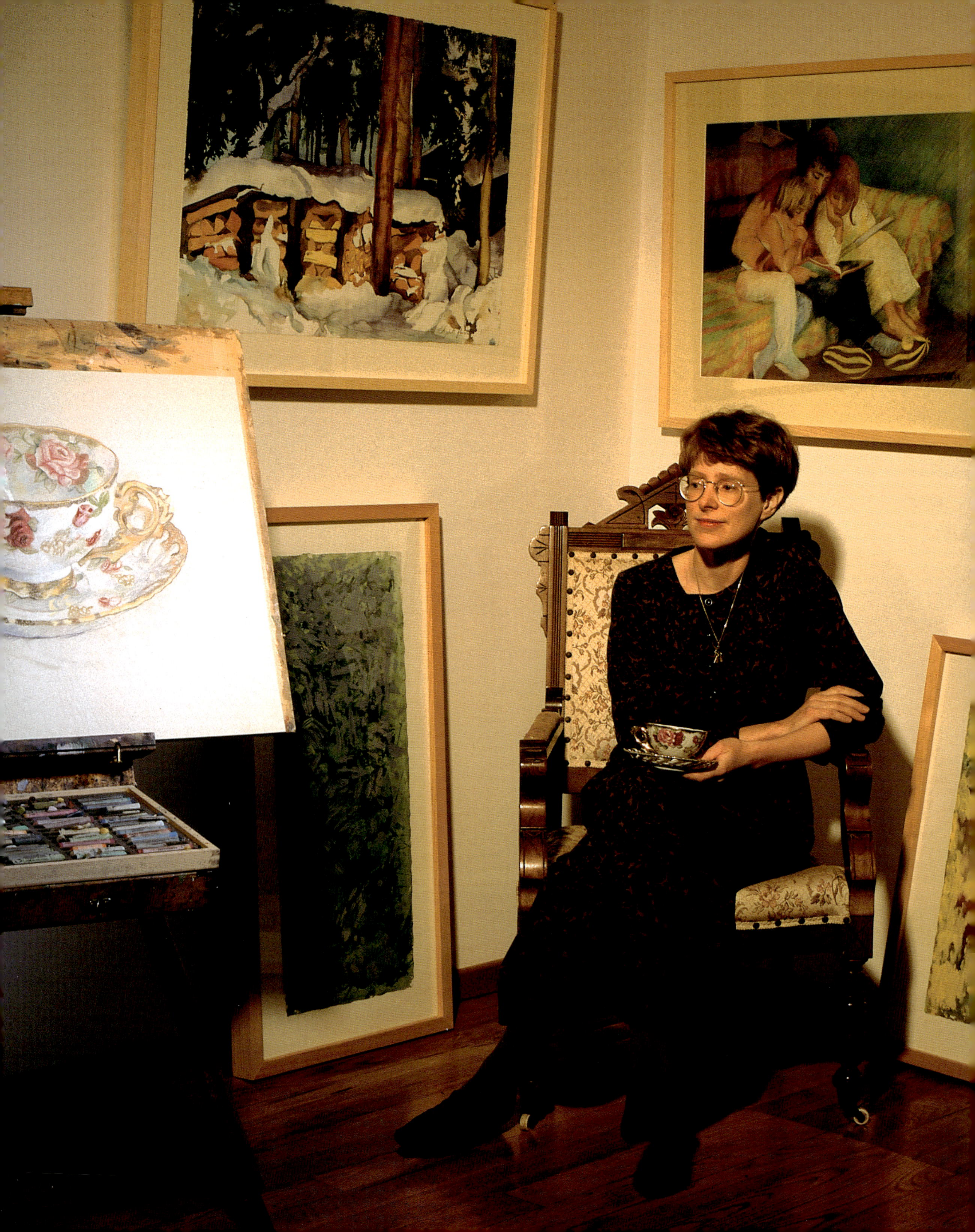

The purpose of art is not a rarefied intellectual distillate – it is life, intensified, brilliant life. – Alain Arias-Missom

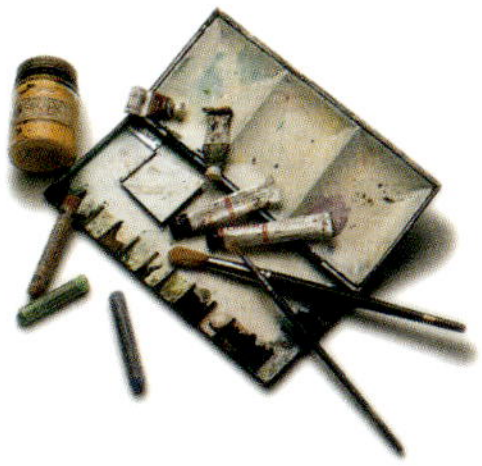

Life, Brilliant Life

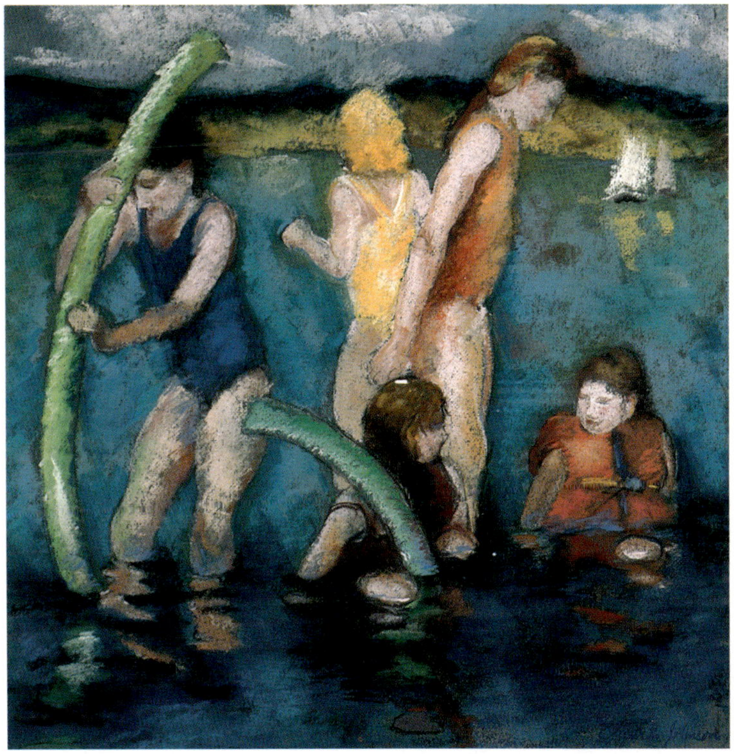

Elizabeth Nancy Nigh was 12 years old the day she rode a camel in the blistering sun of the Sinai desert. She remembers it clearly. So too a meal of flat bread, rice and lamb, shared under a star-lit sky with the men of a Bedouin tribe.

Elizabeth was nearing the end of a family adventure – a year of travelling through Europe and the Middle East with her parents and three older siblings in a VW camper van. Hard to imagine a more intimate journey or education. Twenty-five years later, the stars from that Middle Eastern sky still dance in Elizabeth's eyes: "It was a magnificent year." Family and learning continue as a motif in Elizabeth's life, often combined with a third motif, a passion for art and music.

Today Elizabeth Johnson lives on the shores of Shoe Lake just outside Dorset, Ontario with her husband Brad and their three children. Elizabeth captures landscapes, people and family life in watercolour, acrylic, collage and pastel.

Born in Fort Erie into a Mennonite family in 1959, the fourth and youngest child of Harold and Mildred Nigh, Elizabeth spent her first 12 years on the campus of Niagara Christian College. Her father, a Latin teacher, was the private school's principal. In 1971, Harold took a sabbatical leave from teaching. It was time to realize his dream of exploring antiquity overseas with his family.

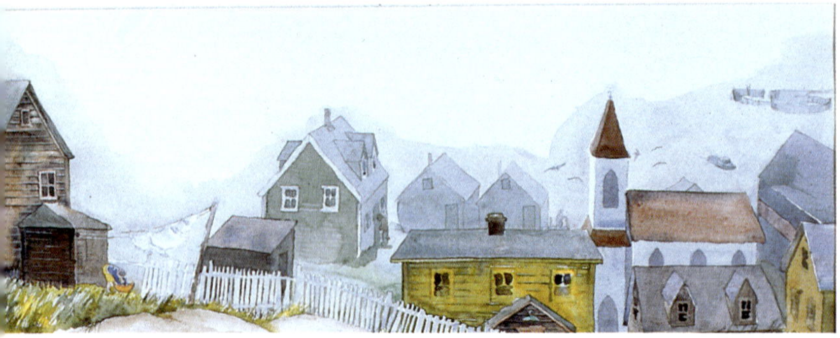

While not too keen on her correspondence courses, Elizabeth loved travelling. Imagine the daily itinerary. Practise French language skills in a clamorous Parisian café. Study mythology on

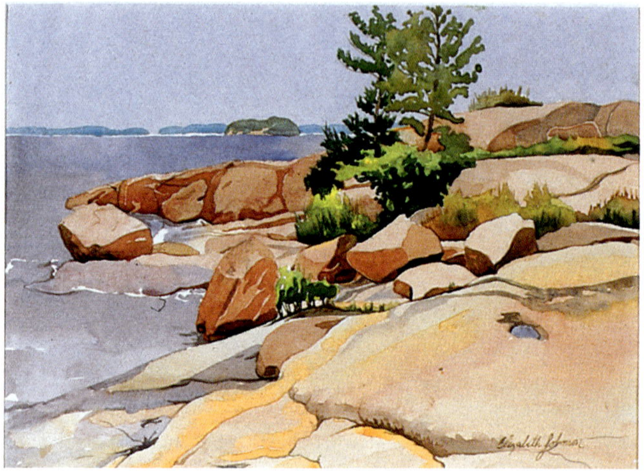

the site of a Greek temple. Draw a map of the Mediterranean while dipping your toes in its clear blue waters.

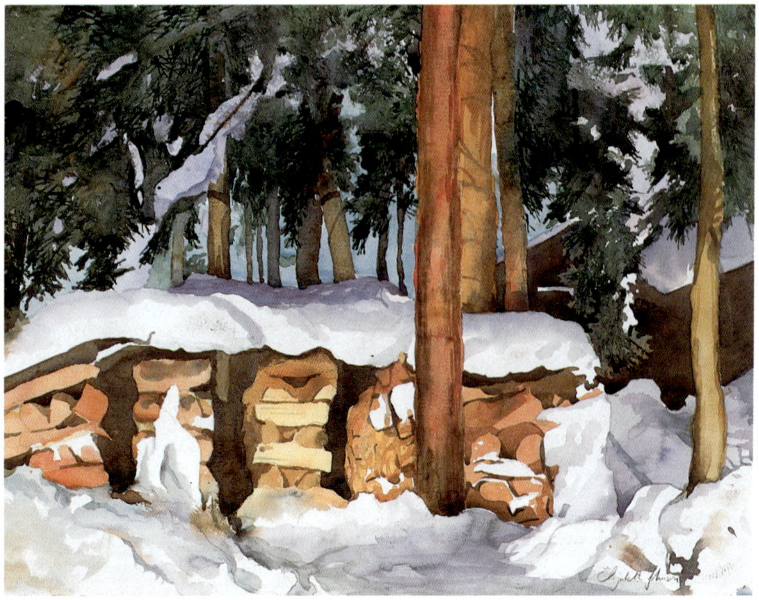

After the family returned to Canada, Elizabeth entered the more conventional learning environment of Port Colborne's public school system. Two years later, however, she could once again catch the scent of wild oregano and sage on a soft Mediterranean breeze. Elizabeth's father had accepted an offer to rehabilitate an experimental farm on Crete.

Every morning, Monday to Friday, Elizabeth slipped on a blue school uniform and matching hair band, stepped from the family's whitewashed house, and crossed through an olive grove and sheep pasture to join her school mates. Afternoons, she'd crack open Canadian textbooks to complete her high school education through correspondence.

When her father's contract expired, Elizabeth and her sister Beverley stayed in Europe. Finding work in Paris as au pairs, they studied at the Sorbonne, attended concerts and toured galleries.

Whatever Elizabeth's environment, art was always present. At age 10, she began painting on her own with an oil set given to her by her brother. While abroad, she painted the family's Christmas cards. In Crete, she took courses in sculpture and pottery.

Back in Canada at age 18, Elizabeth considered her options. "While art was a passion, it took me a while to recognize that it could also be a career."

Elizabeth chose instead to study modern languages at university. Toward the end of her first year, she met Brad Johnson. Elizabeth and Brad married two years later. They spent the summer working outdoors and decided, for a little while, to simplify their lives. They put off their studies and lived from October to May with innumerable field mice in a cabin on Shoe Lake owned by Brad's uncle.

The winter was bracing. "We had electricity but no water, so every second day we drew a supply from a hole we'd cut in the ice on the lake. We bathed in a big old galvanized iron tub. At night we slept close to the wood stove. On days when we weren't collecting and chopping wood, we'd pack a lunch and a compass, put on our snowshoes, and go for a hike. Sometimes we'd snowshoe into Dorset and warm up by the pot-bellied stove in Robinson's General Store."

In September, Brad and Elizabeth returned to university. Within two years, Elizabeth had completed her honours BA, graduated from teacher's college, and begun teaching French at Guelph Collegiate and Vocational Institute.

During Elizabeth's studies, art had taken second place. In the final year of her degree she squeezed in courses in drawing and colour theory, but in teachers' college the regimen allowed no time for personal interests. Again, Elizabeth put her art aside.

Then came the teaching job. "I was totally immersed in my lesson plans, and put everything else aside." At least, until the night Brad arrived home with an armful of art books. His message: "You've got to have time for yourself."

With Brad's ongoing support, Elizabeth took her art more seriously. She started spending her summers painting. Then came exhibits and, with the exhibits, prizes.

"Exhibiting and winning prizes gave me a tremendous amount of confidence. I liked teaching and always will be a teacher, but it wasn't enough. I had to do something else, and art was so much more fulfilling.

"I worked at it every spare minute, whether I was painting or taking a course or reading about art. It has always given me such peace that I just have to do it. I think becoming a successful artist is less about talent and more about love, drive and discipline."

With the birth of their two daughters in 1987 and 1989, and the sudden death of two close family members in those same years, Brad and Elizabeth began to reassess their lives. "Family and the pursuits of our dreams became very important. We thought maybe this was the time to head off in a different direction."

Brad was 33; Elizabeth, 30. Brad quit his job and they moved back to the cabin on Shoe Lake, which they had bought a few years earlier. Together they made the mouse-infested cabin semi-habitable, installing insulation, drywall, a shower and running water. The cabin was now winterized, and home for the next four years.

Although their tiny home was comfortable and cosy, Elizabeth had no room to paint. "If I don't have a creative outlet, I go crazy. Brad's wonderful at recognizing this, even before I do." Brad converted a boathouse into a studio, and they worked out an agreement. Elizabeth would slip down to the boathouse and paint from 6:00 a.m. to 9:00 a.m., then take over household duties from Brad.

After two years, Brad and Elizabeth began building their current home on the same property. The process took another two years. When they finished the house in 1994, the cabin became The Shoe Box, Elizabeth's main studio, showroom, and occasional classroom.

Once a teacher, always a teacher. From her own studio, from the Chapel Gallery in Bracebridge, from recreation centres and schools, Elizabeth has taught art, languages, resource management and Sunday school. Since her art courses at Guelph, Elizabeth has also continued her own studies – training under such artists as Charles Reid and William Schultz in the United States and John Leonard, John Bennett and Peter Kolisnyk at The Haliburton School of Fine Art.[5]

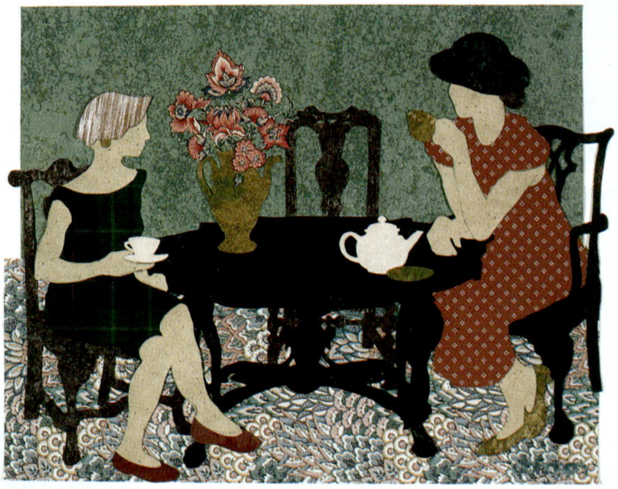

Among the many lessons Elizabeth has learned, in class and out: "There is so much delight in simple things." This applies equally to her life and her art.

In her studio on Shoe Lake, Elizabeth works slowly and in silence, capturing simplicity on canvas. It's a motif she and Brad also try to capture in their day-to-day lives. Since moving back to Shoe Lake, they've slowly pared away those things they feel are unnecessary. "We try to avoid being encumbered with too many material things. We also try to find time to go for walks or to read. Doesn't always happen, but we still try."

"I strive to achieve the goals of straightforward simplicity and honesty, through my family and through my art. They are my two major venues of expression. And part of that expression is a tremendous passion for life. I love life. Someone once said to me, 'If you were stranded on an iceberg, you'd just see it as an adventure.' I try to convey that passion and exuberance for life in my art.

"Having said that, I work at my painting almost doggedly. I don't have grandiose dreams or goals. My joy is just to do what I'm doing. I don't always succeed. I've had artwork rejected. But part of that comes from painting for myself. It's part of being an artist.

"Painting is a solitary occupation. There's also a constant battle against time. On one hand, there's this incredible desire to paint. I could paint all day long. But then, you still have to make supper or deal with dirty diapers.

"I'm always torn between the domestic world and my art, so circumstances will often dictate what I paint. People know me best as a landscape painter. I'm a real hiker and love being out

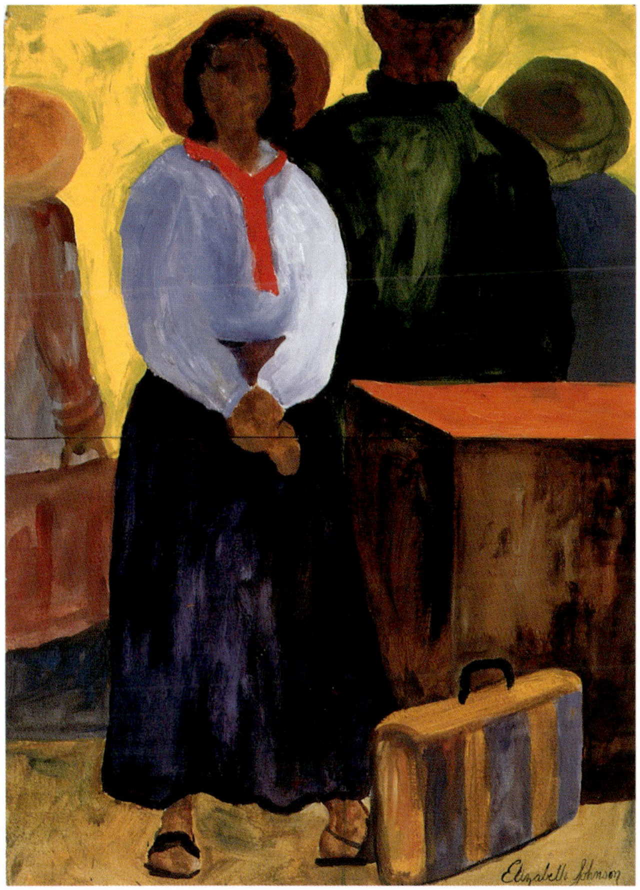

in the wilderness, but I also love to paint my children and family scenes. Since Graham's birth last year, I've looked closer to home. Now is not the time for landscape.

"When you start looking around, you can always find something to paint. It's here already, just waiting."

The Colour of Music

"Painting is like music. Colours are like notes, they harmonize. People talk about making colour in music. The terms we use to describe art and music are almost interchangeable.

"Both art and music are very important to us. We try to take Katherine and Sarah to art shows and concerts as much as possible, so that they can learn that these things are a part of life, a finer side of life. And at home we play a lot of good music, of all kinds. We also perform for ourselves. I play the piano, Katherine is learning the violin, and Sarah's learning the cello.

"We wanted to sensitize our children to the finer things in life at an early age. Art and music are so closely linked, and they enhance your appreciation of all the arts. Painting, dance, literature, music, they're all expressions of emotion, and they can deepen your understanding of emotions. They teach you how to observe, to listen carefully, to be a little more critical in your thinking.

"It's all part of keeping things simple and achieving my greatest potential as a person and an artist."

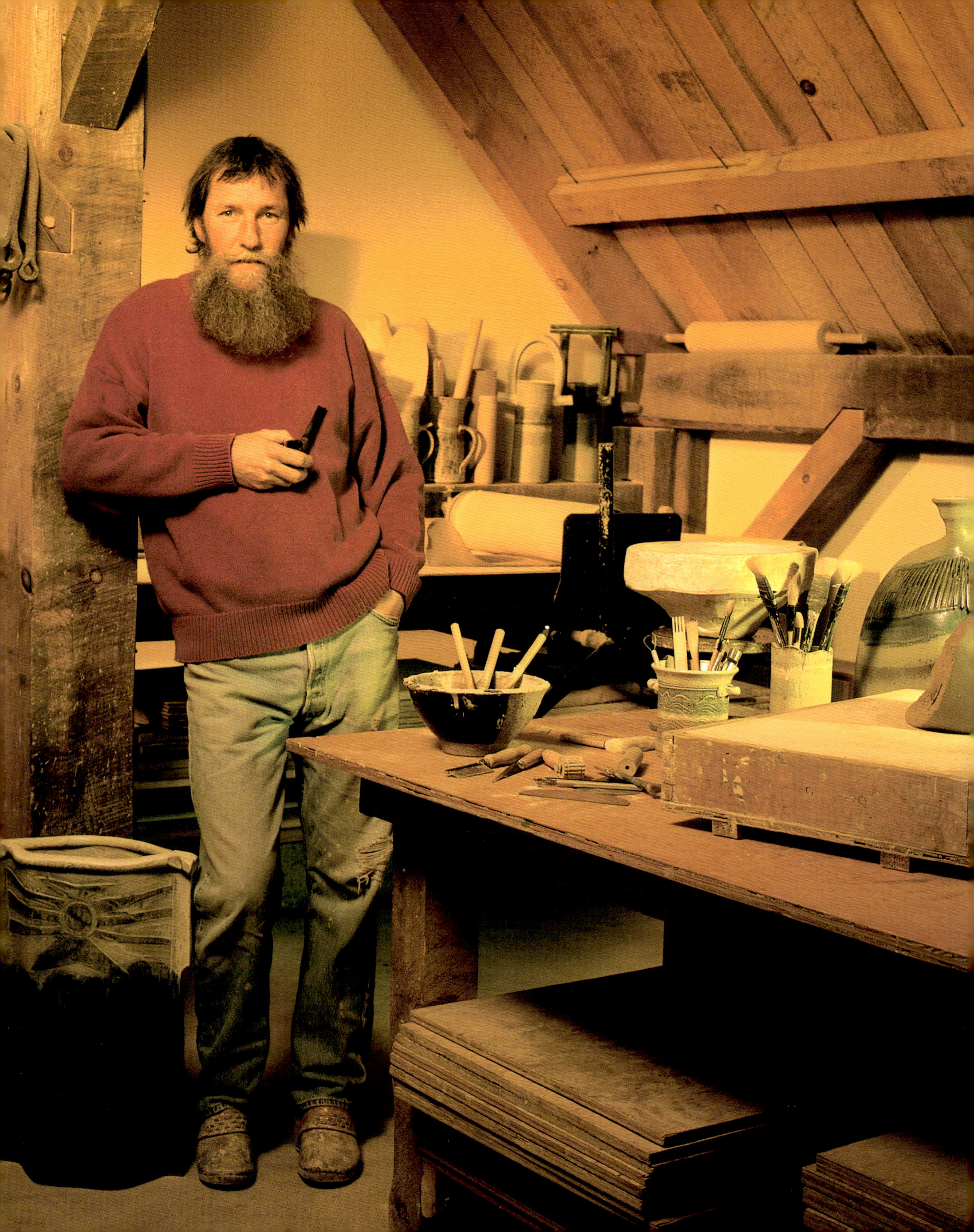

He who works with his hands is a labourer. He who works with his head and hands is a craftsman. He who works with his head, hands and heart is an artist. – St. Francis of Assisi

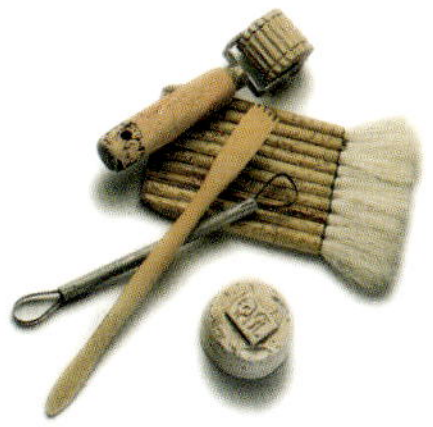

With These Hands

"I remember my father's hands and the way he worked with tools," recalls Jon Partridge in a moment of relaxation. Examining his own palms and fingers, he says with a touch of surprise, "They looked like mine."

Strongly boned, Jon's hands bear the callused marks of constant work. The hands may be unremarkable in appearance, but every piece of pottery that springs from them – whether one-of-a-kind sculptural vessels, decorative stoneware tableware or clay paintings – bears his signature of form, function, and spirit.

Jon's fascination with clay began in the late 1960s as a student at Central Technical[6] art school in Toronto, where he had followed in his father's footsteps and enrolled in a 3-year, post-secondary arts program. While at Central Tech, Jon met Suzann Sawyer, a vivacious art student whom he would marry in 1971.

"I was influenced by my father who was a commercial artist," says Jon. "Some of the same art teachers who taught my dad were now teaching me." After the second year, Jon realized that his artistic interests lay elsewhere. At the same time, Robin Hopper, the head of the ceramics department and a pioneer in the field of ceramics, was leaving the school to set up a new program at Georgian College in Barrie. With Suzann's encouragement, Jon, and a handful of other students, went with Robin.

Making It Happen

"The biggest joy or pleasure when you're learning happens the first time you get a lump of clay centred on the wheel, open the clay up, and actually make something.

"There's a moment where you realize, I can do this, I can make a big pot, or whatever it is you want to make. It's a skill that anyone can learn, and there's nothing more exciting. If you really want it, it will happen."

"He showed me something that was new to me, and that was making something functional with my own hands," says Jon of his experience under Robin's tutelage. After graduating in two years from the 3-year ceramics program, Jon taught in North Bay at Canadore College, then at Hamilton's Mohawk College before moving to Muskoka in the mid 1970s.

Jon and Suzann's purchase of a neglected 100-acre farm just west of Bracebridge was the beginning of a shared goal to live a creative life. Both had spent childhood summers at Muskoka cottages and loved the area. "This was the first property we saw and it was not what we had pictured," says Suzann. "We wanted a brick farmhouse with a porch and gingerbread trim," Jon explains. "What we saw was a house with corroded screens on the dormer, rust that had run in streams down the brick, and weeds choking the path to the front door. It had no plumbing, no insulation, and just 30 amps of electrical service. Most of the outbuildings had fallen down. We continued to look at a lot of other properties and eventually this place started looking better and better."

In October 1974, Suzann and Jon moved into the house with Clayton, their 25-day-old son. Over the years, Jon and Suzann have transformed the property into one of Muskoka's most popular pottery studios. The small 19th century red brick farmhouse has been nurtured back to its original condition. Behind the house, a renovated chicken coop serves as a rustic showroom for Jon's pottery. Next to the showroom is a spacious Gothic-gabled post and beam studio, built in 1983 to accommodate the expanding scope and size of Jon's work, and which now also houses studio space for Suzann. A huge vegetable garden tended by Suzann occupies the spot where a dilapidated barn once stood. Herb and flower gardens hug the showroom. "Looking back," reflects Jon, "it seems like a lot of work but at the time we were living our dream."

Since 1976, Jon has made his living entirely by his own hands. He's achieved this by dedicating himself to a simple philosophy – to make work he enjoys, make it well, and make it completely by his own hand.

During the summer, Jon is at work before the sun rises. He doesn't stop until it sets, around 8:00 or 9:00 p.m. With winter's shorter days, Jon works from 7:00 a.m. until dusk. The ease with which he throws bowls or mugs on the wheel results from years of repetitive practice. "During one studio tour, I was making serving dishes," Jon recalls. "Each dish took about four pounds of clay. In about a minute and fifteen seconds, I would throw a plate. Someone asked me why I would charge $40 for a plate that took only minutes to make. I replied that each plate required thirty years of experience." Throwing is just one of 18 stages in the production of a pot, from preparing the clay to putting the wares on display.

Given the amount of time that potting demands, why are there no apprentices to mix the glaze or unpack the kiln? It's a matter of preference and perception. "If other people do the work, then it's not mine," says Jon. "If apprentices are making my work using my shapes and designs, they will still put something of themselves into the piece and it no longer is my work. Everything I make is a part of me."

The forms and shapes into which the malleable clay is thrown or hand built, the clay's chemical compositions, the range of glazes, how the work is decorated, are singularly Jon's. Over time people have come to recognize his distinctive pieces. "Years ago, Roman Bartkiw, one of my instructors at Georgian said to me, 'It doesn't matter where you are. If you do good work, people will seek you out.'"

Many do. Jon now sells his work exclusively through his studio. One of the family's busiest times together is during the annual Muskoka Autumn Studio Tour, of which Jon is a founding member. As tour visitors come and go, the Partridges' two grown children, Clayton and Shannon, carry out multiple tasks of recording sales, restocking shelves, and carrying customers' purchases. Suzann's father distributes cups of hot apple cider while Jon's mother greets people entering the studio.

As visitors enter the studio or watch Jon demonstrate his work, he hopes they will look around with a fresh eye. "Nobody sees things in the same way and that's what makes us individuals," says Jon.

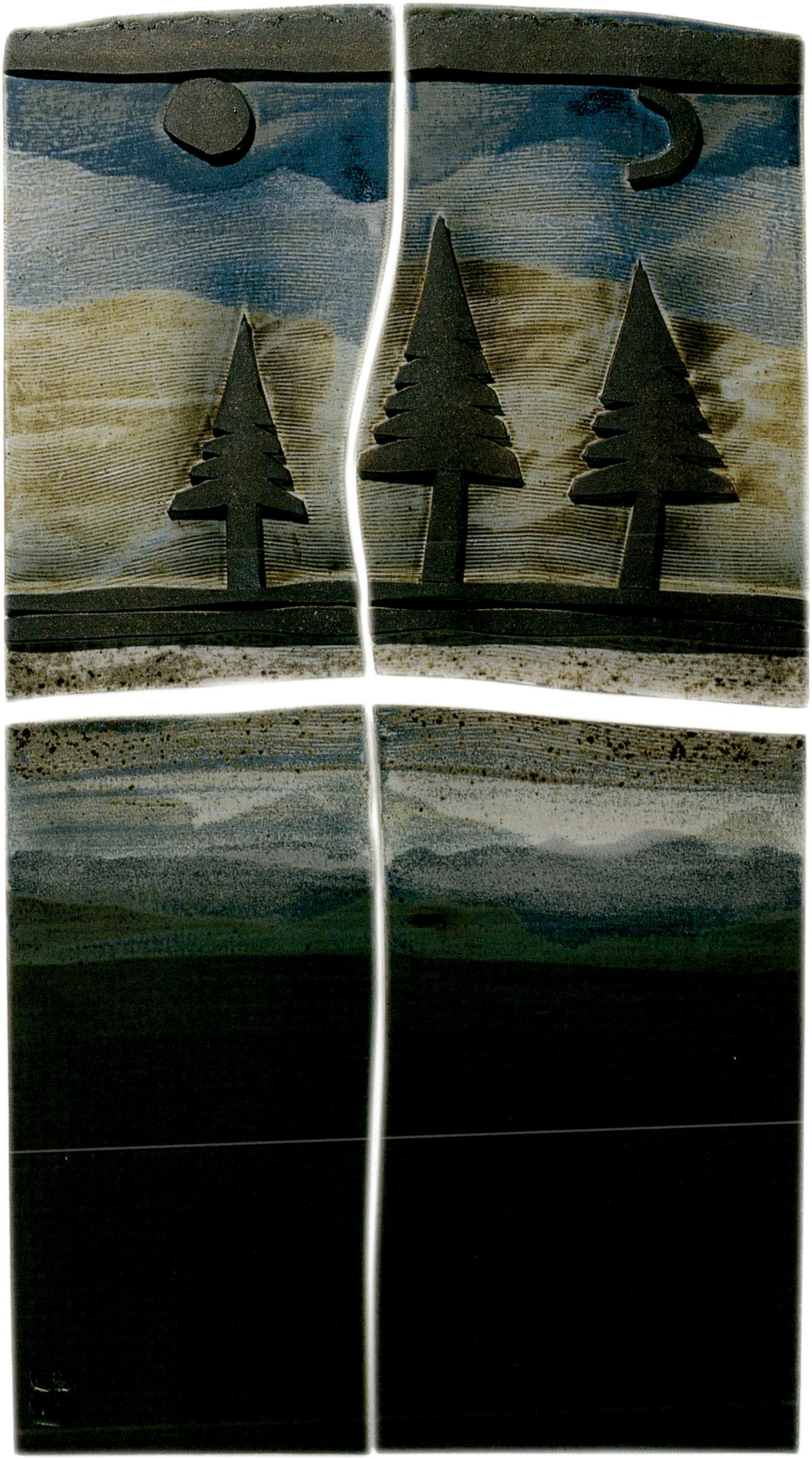

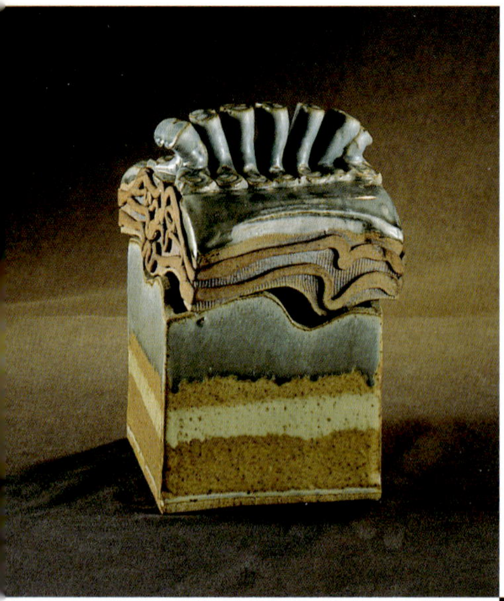

"I once taught pottery to someone who was blind. First, I made something. Then, to help him feel its shape, I had him place his hands on it." As Jon continues the story, his hands outline the contours of a pot in the air. "Next, with a new lump of clay I asked him to form the clay in that same shape. Working with him also helped me. It gave me another way to visualize and I now use this method as a teaching tool. Close your eyes and feel it."

Jon draws on many sources for inspiration. Sometimes it may be the profile of a row of mailboxes at the corner of his property. Often, it's the work itself. "The more I work, the more

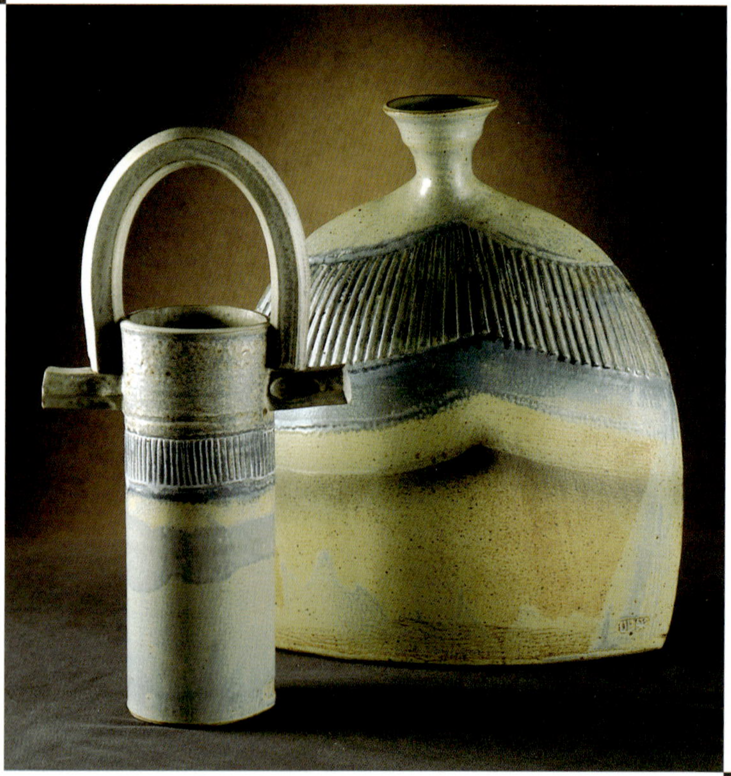

ideas I get. It's how you look at things," says Jon who can see the potential for a good sculptural vessel in a gas vent pipe.

After working with clay for 30 years, Jon has the same enthusiasm for the medium as when he threw his first mug. "It's ugly now," Jon says, "but it still holds coffee."

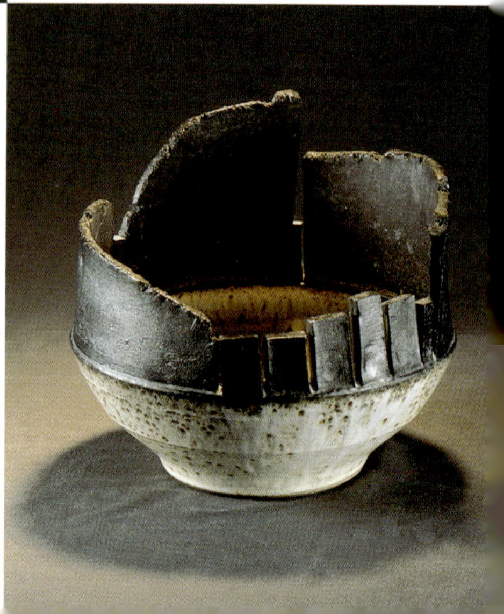

"It was the first thing I had thrown on the wheel. I didn't know if it would make it all the way through the different processes. In the end, it was the enjoyment of actually getting to the point where something I made could be kept rather than thrown out. And, that's part of the process which still excites me today. The exhilarating part is coming up with a concept, then visualizing how the piece will look when it's finished."

When Jon looks to the future, he sees himself always making pottery. "I want to be the best I can. I would like to have time to make more of the larger pieces, but I'll never retire. This is what I do.

"I don't know why I like clay," Jon says as he heads back to the studio. "However, I do like its soft, tactile quality. The only thing that holds you back in terms of what can be done is your own lack of experience."

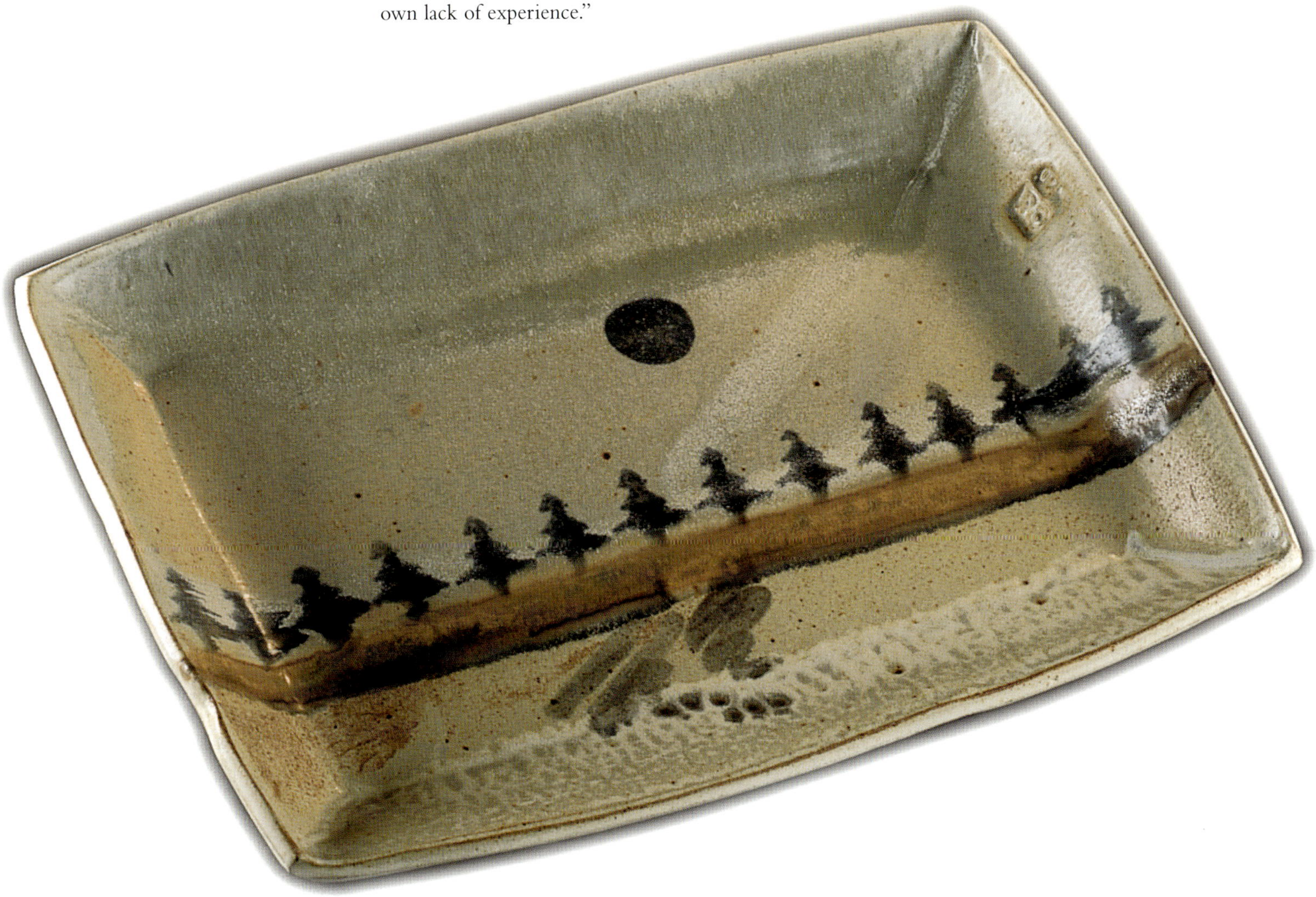

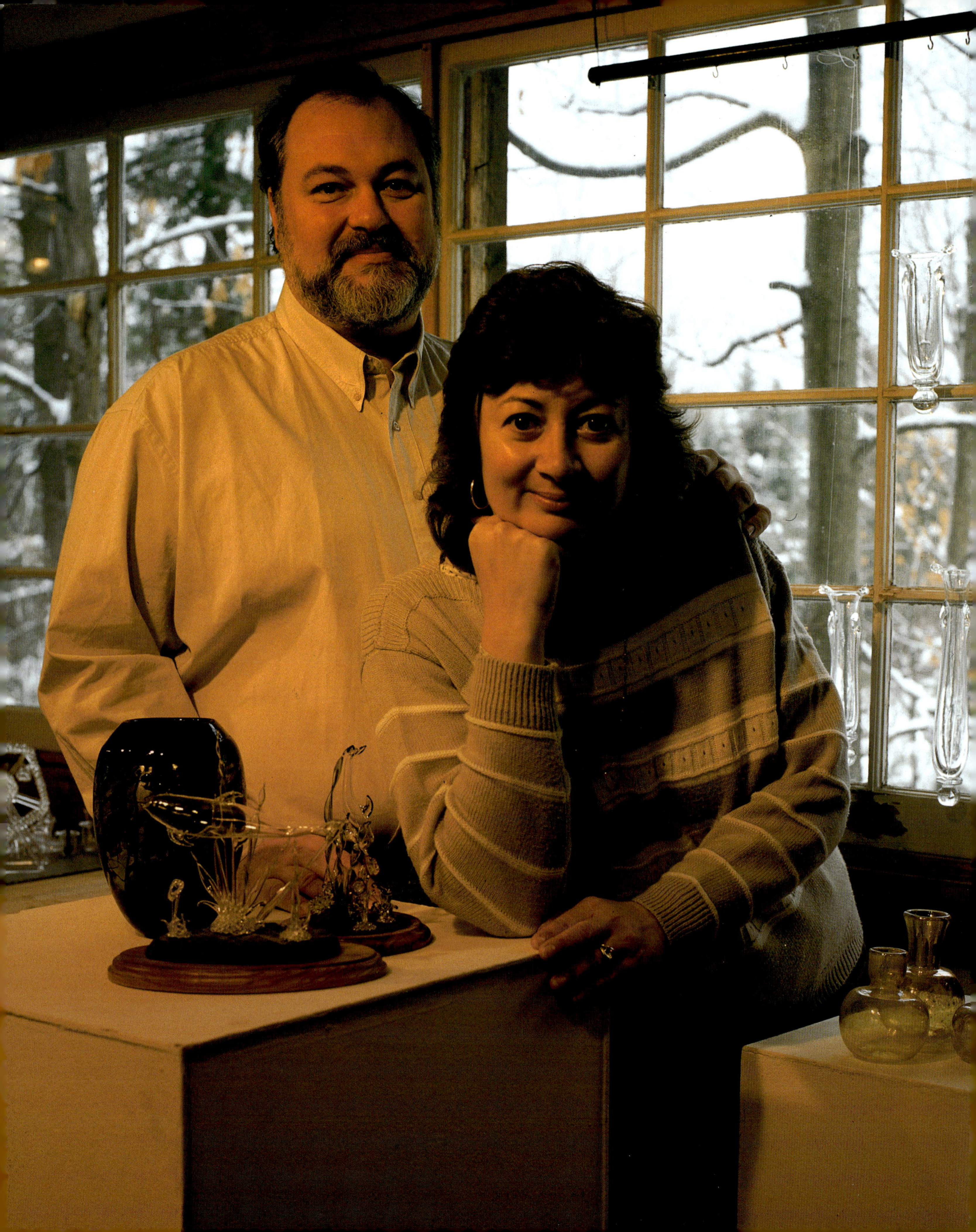

When love captures us... we make choices based as much on the good of what and whom we love – a child, a lover, work – as on what we want to do at the moment. – Carole Pearson

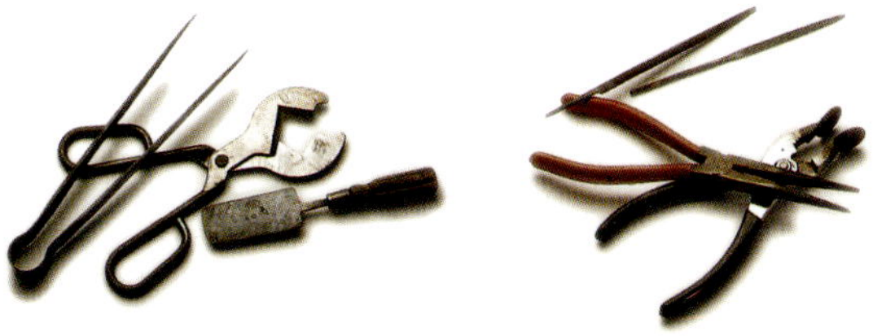

A Magic Combination

The elderly woman extends a hand to the earnest young man who will soon marry her granddaughter. "How you do," she says, exercising her limited English.

"Poljubi me malo," Brian replies in halting Croatian. Grandma Filipovic smiles, and standing on tiptoes, gently kisses his cheek. Giggles spill out from Brian's fiancée, Kathy, then laughter from family members who have gathered around the young couple. He's pleased and confused. "What did I say?"

" 'Give me a little kiss,'" answers Kathy, who had taught Brian the expression months earlier.

In 1998, Brian and Kathy Ashby celebrate their 25th year "together with glass." Kathy specializes in lampworking. Also known as torch work, it's an 18th century technique for creating delicate glass objects, such as scientific instruments and miniatures. Brian follows a 2,000-year tradition of glassblowing. Same love of glass, entirely different process and outcome.

Kathy, her petite frame alert, her dark protective glasses masking deep concentration, wields in each hand a bora-silicate glass tube or rod. With the heat of a torch and the fire of creative energy, she transforms the glass into fantastical miniatures of wishing wells, undersea dolphins and Cinderella coaches.

In Brian's hot glass studio, his imposing frame fearlessly advances on the glory hole of the fiery blast furnace. Like a dragon-slayer, he twirls a long steel rod dipped in soda-lime glass into the mouth of the beast. He retreats from the fire, allowing the molten glass to cool, then blows into the rod to create vibrantly coloured vases, vessels, and sculptures.

A devoted couple, instinct tells you: united in their exploration of glass artistry, their love for each other and their love of son Christopher. Nonetheless, Kathy and Brian have never walked in lockstep.

Brian Thomas Ashby, eldest of three children, was born in Toronto in 1950 and raised in

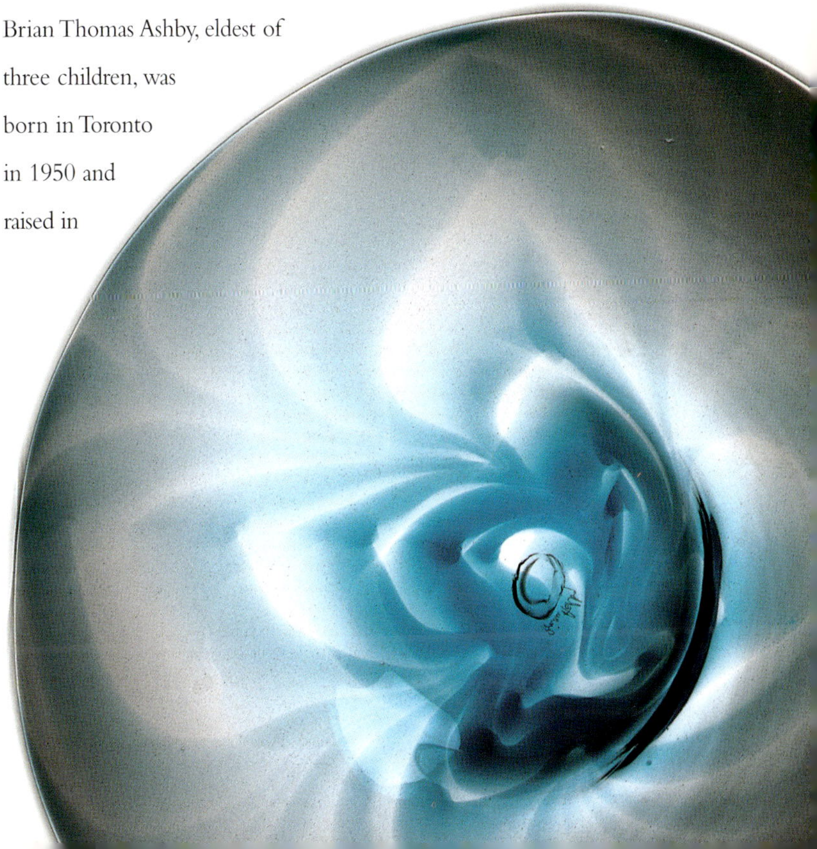

the suburb of East York, not far from the bustling Danforth strip. His mother, a physician from Croatia, and his father, a British transport captain had met after World War II while with a UN relief organization in Poland. They immigrated to Canada in the late 1940s.

Brian describes his upbringing as rich in creative encouragement. On his fourth birthday, he received a box camera. Thus began a lifetime fascination for photography. In Grade 3, he won an award for a papier-mâché puppet of a cowboy with wireframe glasses. At age nine, he sang in the choir at St. Paul's Anglican Church, rising to head boy until his voice cracked. He also played the violin and frequently let his born-to-be-creative fingers walk through the pages of his parents' visual arts magazines. Mrs. Wilson, a teacher at Oak Park Junior High, further nourished his interests, driving Brian and other students on Saturdays to the home of the McMichaels in Kleinburg, Ontario. There, Brian sat at the feet of Group of Seven artists Lawren Harris and Frederick Varley and lived, vicariously, their stories of artistry and adventure in Ontario's north.

The Glory of Glass

"Working with glass is an emotional experience you will come to understand when you can imagine the medium between 2,000 and 3,000 degrees Fahrenheit. It is the most fluid 3-dimensional medium an artist can work closely with. The sensual flow holds you in a kind of magic spell. The glass is only cold, hard and fragile when it returns to room temperature.

"For an artist, the process is a hot ballet of whirling and twirling, drooping and swinging the shape until at a precise spontaneous moment he or she decides to freeze it in time by taking it out of the fire. The dance ends, and the object quickly moves toward timeless suspension." – Kathy Ashby

"The glassy state is the magic combination of the primal elements and human intuition. Making molten glass is an experience that is simultaneously oppressive and liberating. Hot glass has an ephemeral quality that captures the imagination, giving the creative mind 'a turn on the dance floor.' Personally, I feel humbled by this fine and beautiful substance. I feel I have so many years of ritual and tradition to respect and maintain. Making glass art is a responsibility; creating with it, a privilege." – Brian Ashby

While Brian experimented with various media, Kathy Filipovic sketched, painted and sculpted 1,200 kilometres away. The second of four children, Kathy was born in Port Arthur (now Thunder Bay), Ontario in 1953. Three generations living under the same roof provided Kathy fluency in Croatian, her grandparent's first language. Local Croatian festivals and dances connected her to a rich ethnic cultural heritage and developed in her a strong sense of community.

Other girls played with Barbie dolls; Kathy, with a family of trolls. Her trolls lived in a house made of three shoeboxes. Every room had wallpaper, rugs and a framed painting on the wall. In the closets of each bedroom, an extensive wardrobe of handmade clothing hung on hangers the size of paper clips.

Kathy showed artistic promise at an early age, and was encouraged by family, friends and the community. Carefully stored in her memorabilia box are many early awards from contests, including a first-place ribbon bestowed in 1970 by the Croatian Fraternal Union for a watercolour of a parrot.

By the end of high school, Kathy knew her future lay in the arts. She left her family in 1972 to study 3-dimensional design at Sheridan College[7] outside Toronto. Accompanying her application to Sheridan was a box exquisitely wrapped in snow white paper and tied with matching ribbon. Inside lay a strawberry red sculpture of her hand that she had produced by pouring hot wax into a rubber glove, then moulding it into a life-like image.

At Sheridan, Kathy was drawn to glass and woodworking. Glass eventually won her heart. At the end of her second year at Sheridan, she applied to work on a project at Toronto's Harbourfront cultural centre. Five work studios were to feature artists demonstrating their techniques to the public. The project director, a Sheridan graduate, interviewed her. Impressed, he hired her as the project's lead glass blower. His name was Brian Ashby.

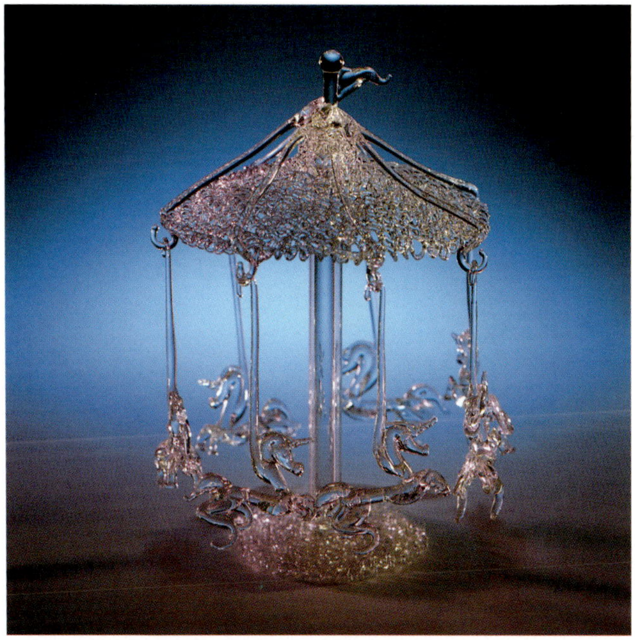

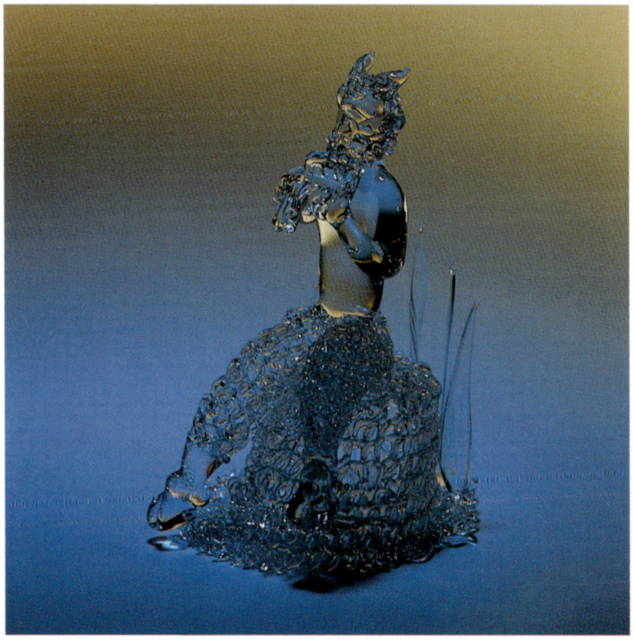

As for Brian, he had followed a more circuitous route to Sheridan. His early fascination with photography evolved from still to moving pictures. By Grade 8, he had earned a film projectionist license, and enjoyed immensely being summoned by the PA system to assist at school assemblies and other functions. Notoriety was nice but, more importantly, it freed him from the structure and routine of the classroom.

At 17, he helped out a troubled schoolmate and was rewarded by her father with an apprenticeship role in film editing. One of his projects involved cutting and splicing his way through film footage of the 1969 Russian invasion of Czechoslovakia for a National Film Board production.

At 19, the young film editor underwent surgery to remove a tumour on his wrist. On his return to work, Brian began to question his choice of a career which, although still gratifying, demanded that he work long hours at a gruelling pace. He decided to slow down and return to school for a formal education in still photography.

En route, he was waylaid. Arriving at a public glass-blowing demonstration, camera in hand, he was more taken by the medium than the photo opportunity. "It struck a chord in my past. I remembered the stained glass windows in St. Paul's, and felt a spiritual connection.

"I also saw connections with photography, moving images and glass. Glass is a moving thing, but then you freeze the image. It's also a transparency – glass depends on light in the same way photography does. There's something musical, graceful and

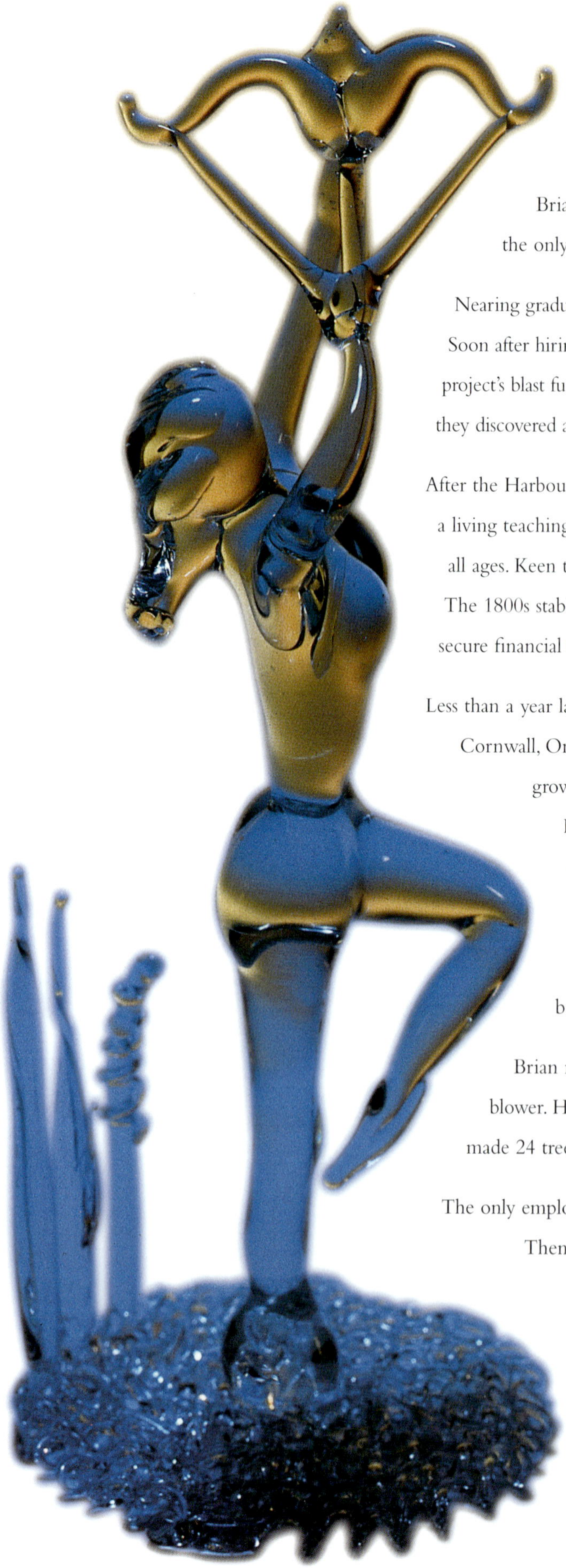

ephemeral about glass – same with photography. Art is like that. Moments pass, you get an inspiration, you've got to act on it, you can't let it go by. If you do, it just doesn't have the same feeling."

Brian was admitted to Sheridan's School of Design in 1971. At the time, it was the only school in Canada teaching the fine art of glass blowing.

Nearing graduation, Brian earned a 3-month contract to launch the Harbourfront project. Soon after hiring Kathy Filipovic, he invited her to join him on a 36-hour vigil while the project's blast furnace fired up for the first time. Camping out in the back of a pickup truck, they discovered a shared Croatian heritage, and Kathy taught Brian to say "Poljubi me malo."

After the Harbourfront contract expired, the two glass blowers remained together, eking out a living teaching Sheridan College extension courses from a 50-foot trailer to art lovers of all ages. Keen to open their own business, the couple moved to Alton, Ontario in 1976. The 1800s stable that housed Victoria Glassworks received a new roof and floor, but a secure financial foundation eluded its two owners.

Less than a year later, Brian accepted an assembly line job at Chalet Artistic Glass Inc. in Cornwall, Ontario. At $4.75 per hour, he worked alongside glass blowers who had grown up in the trade in Murano, Italy. "It felt like I was back in the 1700s. It was hot and dirty. We worked long hours. Every job was specialized – one fellow would just bring gathers of glass to the master glass blower."

Of the 20 glass blowers in the plant, none were women. Kathy pursued an interest in stained glass, producing hanging lamps, terrariums and lead boxes from a home-based studio nearby.

Brian moved quickly from line worker to lead hand and then to master glass blower. His team made Christmas trees in lead crystal. With his 5-member crew, he made 24 trees an hour, touching each tree 65 times for 10 hours a day, six days a week.

The only employee schooled in glass blowing, he faced daily ribbing for being an "artista." Then one day while he was at lunch, the roof collapsed on his workbench. His co-workers interpreted his escape from death as divine intervention. Brian became part of the family, and a member of a Venetian glass blowing fraternity whose history dates back many centuries.

Membership aside, the money was terrible. Worried about how to make a decent living, Brian received a call from his mother, then and now a respected social worker. Having just obtained seed capital to found a group home for men with brain damage, she needed resident staff. Brian and Kathy returned to Toronto to manage the home and teach its residents life skills and crafts.

Another year went by. The couple were restless away from glass work. Visiting Brian's sister in Gravenhurst sparked an interest in

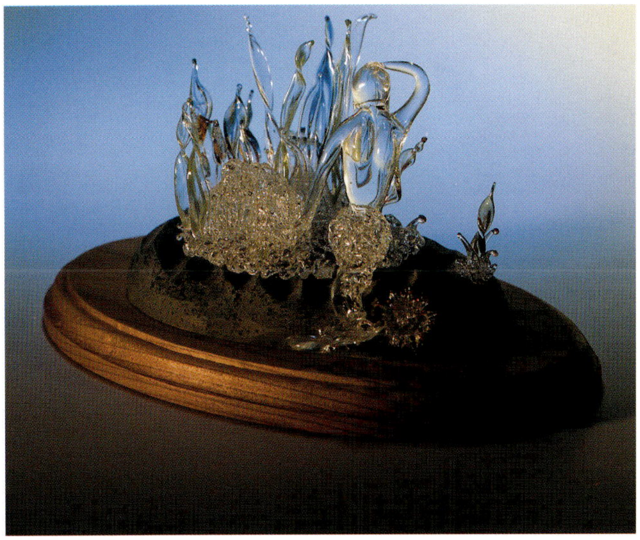

moving to Muskoka. Brian loved the natural beauty, Kathy felt like she was returning home. They purchased land and in October 1977 began building. By Christmas, they had moved in. The house was barely habitable.

Ineligible for bank financing, they took any job they could find. Brian made furniture in a factory. Kathy assembled car parts at Rockwell International and waitressed. By June 1978, they had cleared a workspace at home for Kathy's work in stained glass and finished Brian's hot glass studio. They finally convinced the bank to mortgage their home. After months of labour, Ashbys' Glass Studios are born.

Four years later, in 1982, Kathy gave birth to Christopher. Her interest in stained glass began to wane around the same time. Seeking a new creative outlet, she experimented with glass miniatures. She immediately felt at home, reminded of the miniature world she had created for her trolls. The following year, she became resident glass blower for Santa's Village in Bracebridge. For five years, she enjoyed perfecting her skills and demonstrating her technique to a youthful public.

Members of the Muskoka Autumn Studio Tour since 1979, Kathy and Brian have experimented over the years with different distribution methods. Both have been partners in co-op galleries, Kathy in Bracebridge, Brian in Gravenhurst. Brian exhibited for two years at the One of a Kind show in Toronto. For many years, they've packed up their wares for display at the summer and winter Muskoka Arts and Craft[8] show. It functions as both sales event and exhibition, recognizing and encouraging artists with awards in excellence conferred by a jury of peers. Brian and Kathy's list of awards is long.

While dedicated to excellence in their art, the Ashbys are no strangers to experimenting with unique commercial opportu-

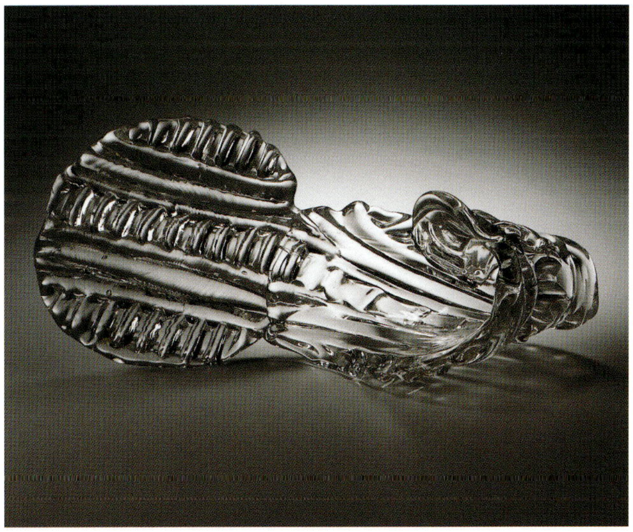

nities. For four years during the 1980s, they escaped the pristine but bitterly cold Muskoka winters to search the Caribbean for artistic inspiration and commercial adventure. They eventually came to the West Indian island of Bequia, whose native population, while rich in craft heritage and spirit, lacked formal training and job opportunities. "We felt a bit like craft missionaries," Brian says of the experience. Their efforts resulted in workshops with high school students in Bequia, St.Vincent and the Grenadines, as well as the incorporation of Studio Glass (Barbados) Ltd.

What madness possessed them to end this experience? Even artists have responsibilities – and it was time for son Christopher to start school.

Kathy and Brian will go back one day. In the meantime, they keep the entrepreneurial fires burning. Kathy recently forged an alliance with a local company, MacKinnon Tackle, concerned about environmental damage from lead-based fishing tackle. She has helped the owner design and produce glass lures that help preserve the environment and attract fish. Brian continues his passion for photography by helping direct commercial projects in association with a Toronto-based graphics design firm, MC² Design Lab Canada.

Both are active in the community. Kathy is drawn to working with youth, beginning with a grant in 1973 to establish arts and crafts summer courses for children at Sheridan College. More recently, she organized a glass blowing workshop for elementary school girls. During her 1987 stint as Muskoka chapter co-president of Canadian Parents for French, she advocated strenuously for her son's right to the bilingual education he enjoys today along with other children in the area. Brian has been active on the executive of arts related organizations, taking on such roles as chair of the Muskoka Autumn Studio Tour and director of the Canadian Glass Art Association of Canada.

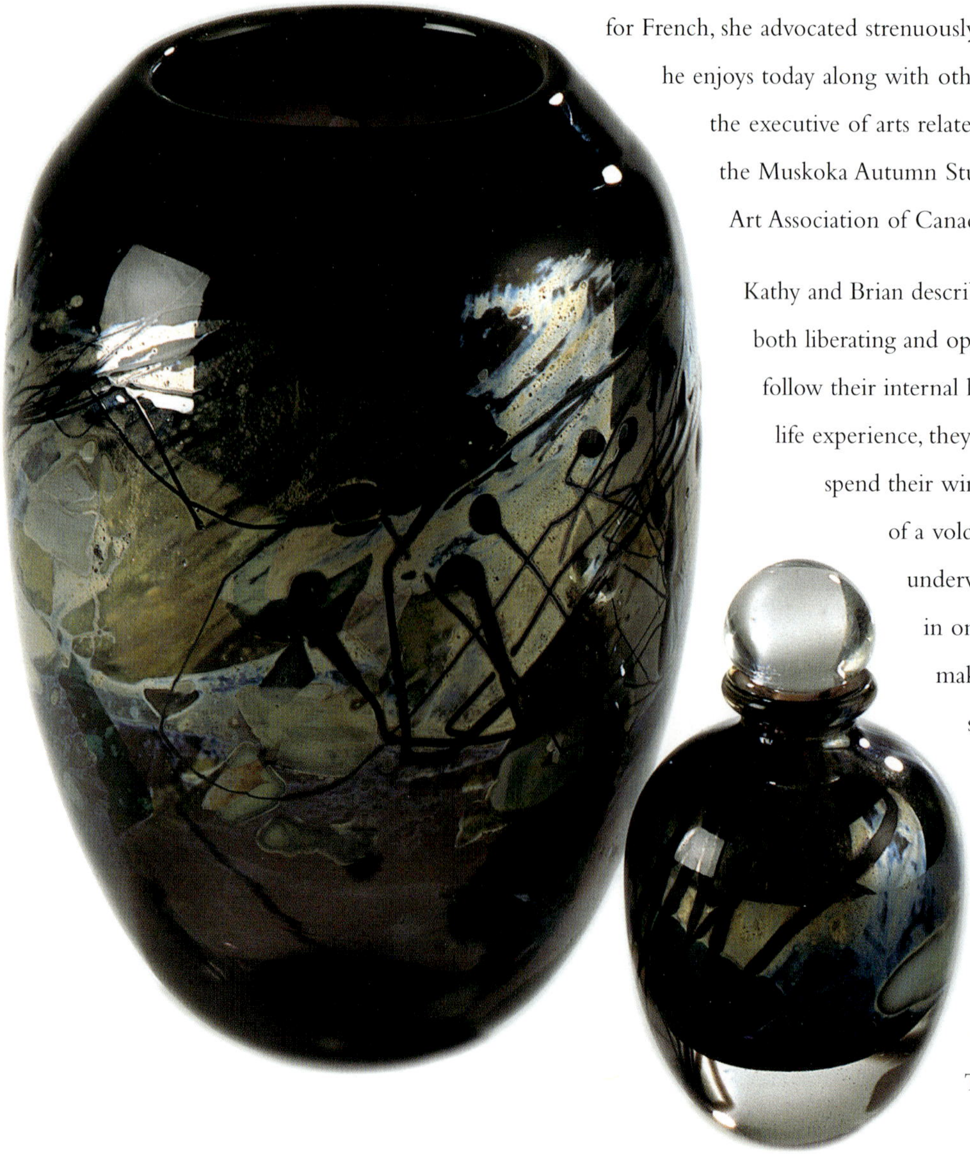

Kathy and Brian describe their work in glass and their life choices as both liberating and oppressive. Glass artists for 25 years, they're free to follow their internal leanings to do what they love. However, for rich life experience, they've traded financial security. At one time free to spend their winters in the Caribbean, they've made it to the top of a volcanic mountain and scuba-dived in a glassy underwater world of inspiration. But neither will cash in on a rich company pension plan at age 65, nor make it to the short list of a job interview process should circumstances prevent them from working in glass. Already well trained in the art of creative problem-solving, they'll survive.

After long years of hard work and sacrifice, Kathy encourages the would-be artist. "It's not easy. There are times of recession, times you don't get respect for your chosen profession. That's unfortunate because in any culture, it's the artists who reminds you of who you are, the musician who sings your song, the playwright who tells your story. Canada is a young country. It needs its artists to tell its history and dream its future."

Asked how he would advise others, Brian consults *The I Ching*, which he likens to a good cup of coffee when you're in need of an intuitive kick. "It gets you started." The book opens randomly at principle 53: gradual progress. He explains: "It talks about the wild goose who is faithful to its nature. It mates for life. Even after its mate dies, it doesn't go looking for another. It's the same with art. When you find something you love, you must be inwardly resolved to remain true to your own principles and your own nature. That's what makes you a strong person with character and substance. You don't act impulsively, you act with inner strength. And then like geese when they find food, you call out to others to share in the bounty you've found."

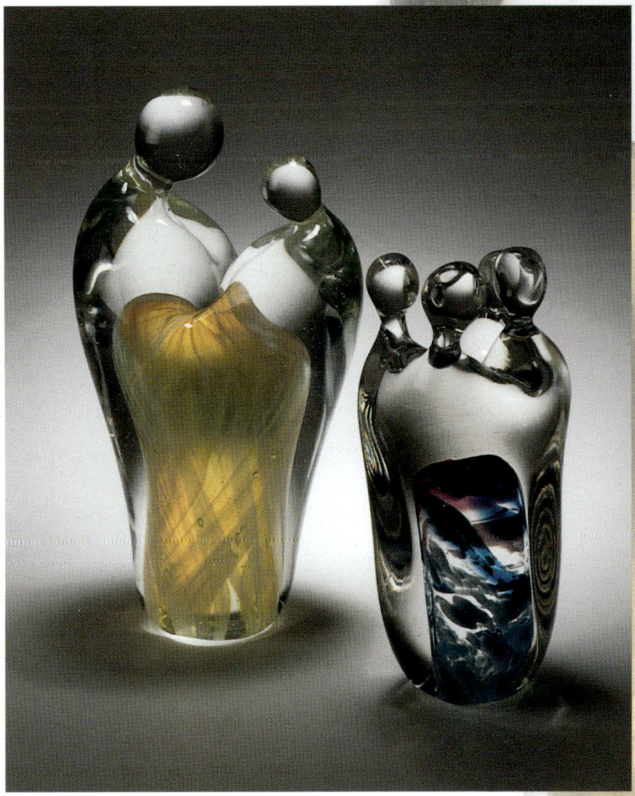

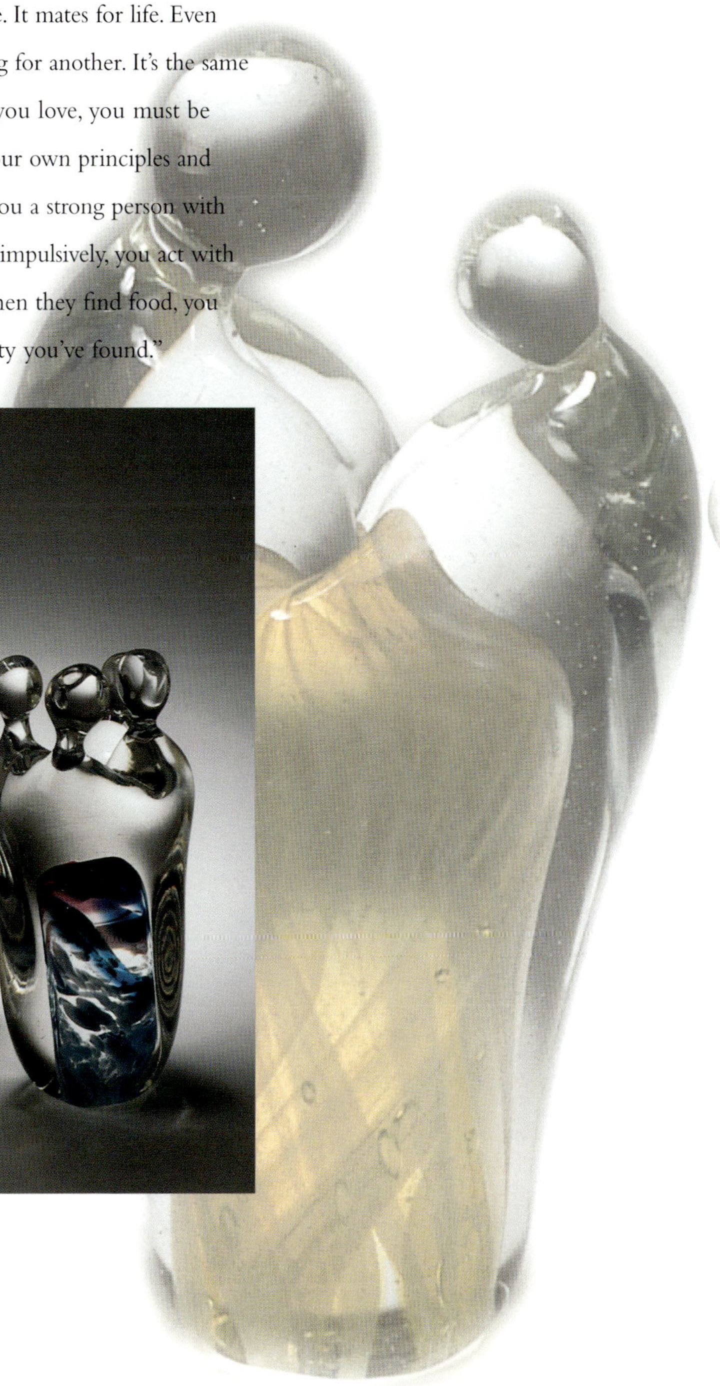

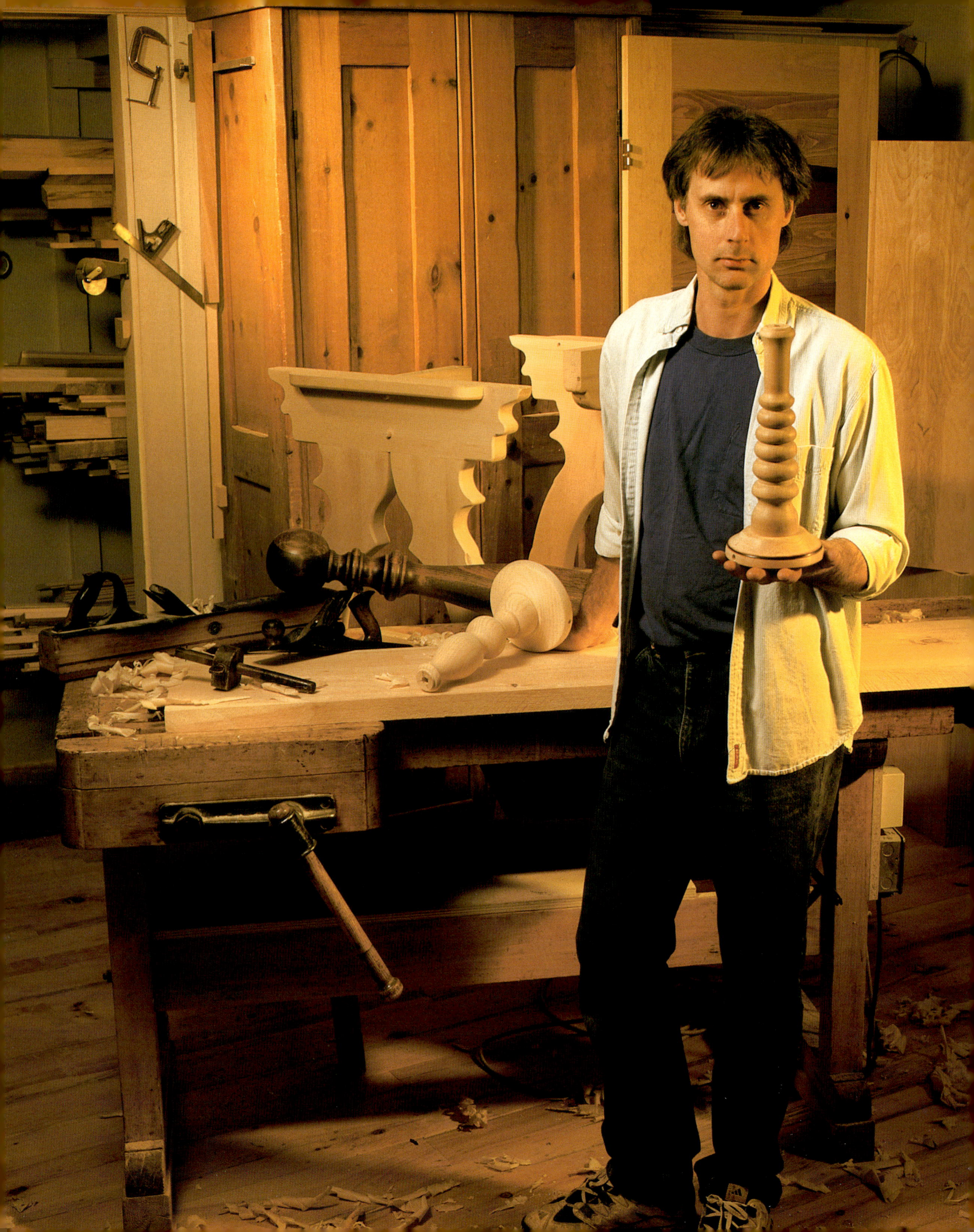

D I R K   W E H R M A N N

Talent develops in quiet places, character in the full current of human life. - Johann Wolfgang von Goethe

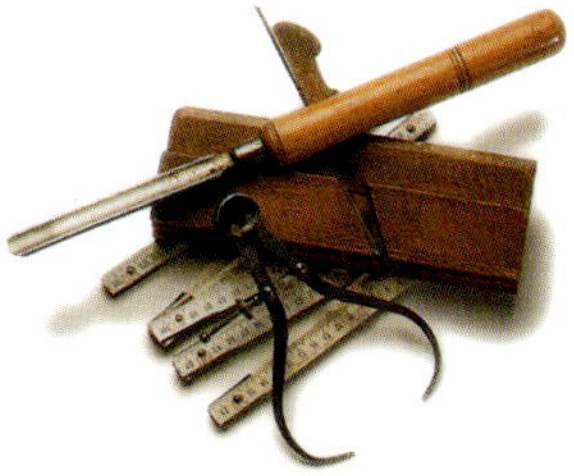

Phoenix Rising

In the 1960s, Caledonia Industries was a successful family-owned manufacturing plant in Caledonia, a small town close to Hamilton, Ontario. At one end of the plant, owner Ole Wehrmann made high quality, handcrafted wooden furniture. At the other end, 15 employees produced a variety of wooden brooms, scrub brushes and shoe polish handles.

Ole had learned his woodworking skills in Germany and brought with him to Canada a tradition of robust forms and simple, clean lines. Ole, his wife and three children – John, Dirk and Liana – lived above the plant until the summer of 1969, when the building burned to the ground.

Fast forward to 1998. Ole and Dirk, now business partners, oversee Wehrmann Furniture, a successful 2,600 square-foot workshop and showroom outside Huntsville. The family no longer lives upstairs. Three generations now reside, with greater peace of mind, several hundred yards away.

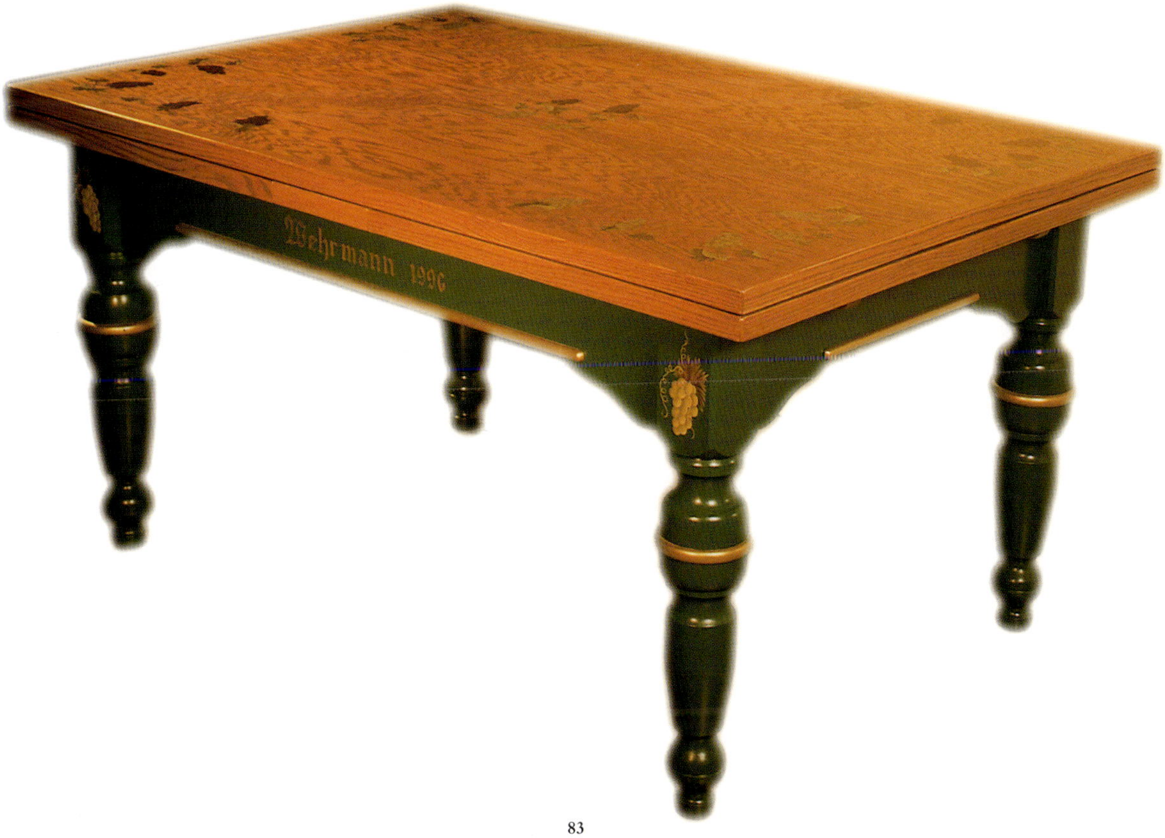

Ole is officially retired, though still puts in several hours a day at the shop. Dirk continues the family tradition, combining the quality craftsmanship of his father and the talents of his late grandfather, an oil painter and water colourist, with the independent spirit and acumen of both.

The family's rustic country chalet commands a hilltop view of Muskoka farmland and forest. Deer visit regularly. So do clients. Until recently, the chalet's main floor served as a showroom. The floor has since been reclaimed as family space, but still sitting in one corner are an armoire and arm chair, survivors of the 1969 blaze that saw an old way of life give way to the new.

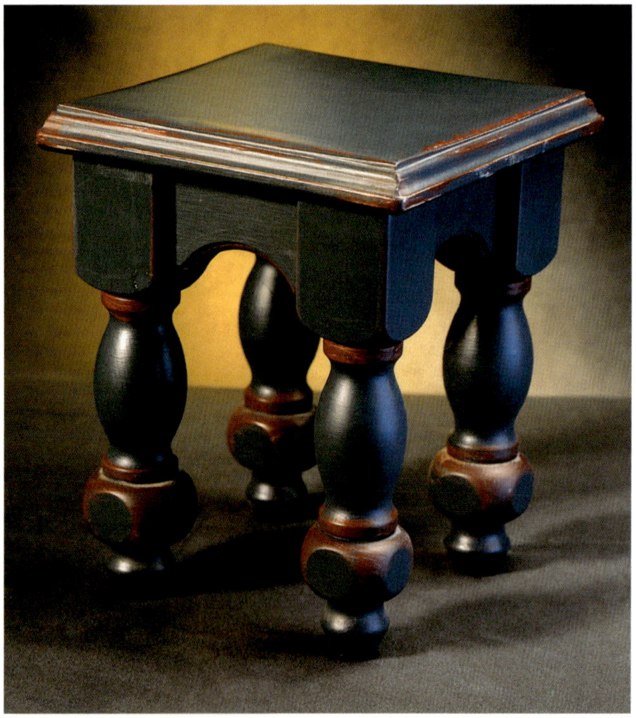

On that fiery night, a courageous team of neighbours who broke into the burning building managed to save only the two articles of furniture. All that could be salvaged after the fire were a few tools, some woodworking equipment, and enough lumber to start a small building.

Ole decided against rebuilding in Caledonia, and chose Muskoka instead. He had visited the area several times and taken the family there on holiday. Arriving in Huntsville with $2,000 in his pocket, Ole deposited half as a down payment on some acreage, and began the arduous process of reconstructing the family business.

The first winter they lived in a plywood shack hastily built by Ole and his two sons, and heated by a Franklin stove. No phone. No running water. "It wasn't much, but we got by," says Dirk. He doesn't waste words.

The following year they began building a proper home. As soon as the basement was completed, they moved in. However, converting the shack into a woodworking shop and generating business took priority over completing the rest of the house.

"Off to one side of the shack we built a lean-to roof, and under that roof we set up the machinery that we had salvaged from Caledonia. We'd do our machine work under that roof and do our finishing work inside, building the doors, doing all the joinery. We continued that way for at least six or seven years, winter and summer. Looking back now, I don't know how we did it."

The Wehrmanns specialized in custom-made rustic pine furniture for cottagers. The early days of the new business drew cottagers from the Hamilton area who already knew Ole's work. Their orders helped to re-establish the business and spread the Wehrmanns' reputation.

Dirk had joined the business full time while still in his teens. Born in Germany on July 27, 1955, Dirk was only two years old when he came to Canada with his mother and 10-year-old brother. His dad had found a job the year before as a steelworker with International Harvester. Soon after the family arrived, Dirk's father was injured at work. The injuries were severe enough that, despite two years of rehabilitation, Ole couldn't resume his job.

With a compensation settlement, Ole set up a basement woodworking shop specializing in broom handles, wooden brushes and other small items that wouldn't compromise his physical health. Dirk, still a child, helped out in the shop. While too young to run the equipment, he took on other tasks, such as painting kindergarten furniture in primary colours. "I'd do whatever my father let me."

The business grew rapidly. Within a few years Ole had 15 people working for him in a former lumber warehouse in Caledonia. The building also housed a 3-bedroom apartment for the family. By this time, his father had recovered enough to resume furniture making, an area of expertise he had brought with him from Germany. In the meantime, Dirk had graduated to lathework, packaging and clean-up.

Although Dirk was 15 when the family moved to Muskoka, he kept in touch with friends from Hamilton. Through them he met Lynda Robb. They married in 1975 and rented an apartment in Huntsville. "Other than a finished basement, the house wasn't much more than a shell. After Lynda and I got married, I finished construction on the upper level of the house, putting in walls, floors and a bathroom." Two years later, their son Andrew was born.

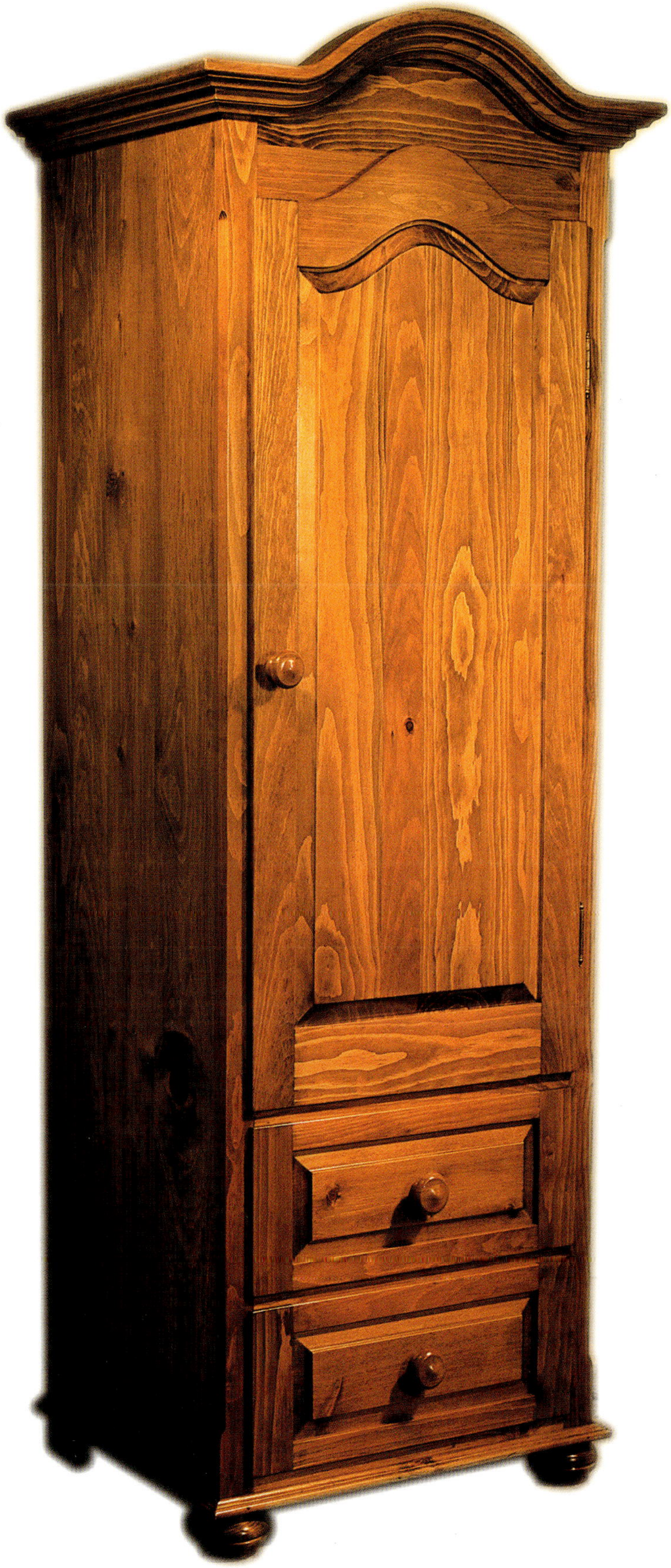

In 1980, Dirk saw his father off at Pearson International. Ole was returning to Germany indefinitely to care for his aging mother and left Dirk, now 25, in charge. "I had a lot of learning to do – how to design furniture, how to work with people, how to manage money, how to maintain a vehicle."

Dirk quickly concluded that, to meet his commitments, he had to teach himself how to make furniture better and faster. Along with his new responsibilities came freedom. Dirk began to introduce his own ideas into the work. In time a trained eye would note finer joinery in cabinets, drawers, and doors. A discerning eye would observe more pieces in oak, cherry and maple, featuring more contemporary lines.

Within months of his father's departure, however, a serious accident redirected Dirk's learning and added an entirely new dimension of adjustment. "I had been well trained, but sometimes you just don't concentrate. At that point the woodworking equipment was still outside. One very cold day, I had to wear gloves. My gloves were loose. They got dragged into the equipment."

Dirk lost four fingers on his right hand. It took a year for the pain to diminish, and for Dirk to recover enough dexterity and stamina to get back to work. "One of the side effects of pain medication is loss of appetite, and when you lose your appetite, you lose strength and mobility. But because I love woodworking so much, I couldn't stay out of the shop. A retired friend helped out by taking on some of the work that I couldn't, and this motivated me to get back on track. I can still do everything I need to do, but it took a lot of determination."

With that determination came growth and maturation. "My skills grew along with the business. I did rural home shows, continued to do work for repeat customers, developed some new customers. Times changed, and my designs changed. People tend to buy what they can see, and when they saw new designs and greater choices in wood, then they wanted new designs, they wanted those woods.

The Open Door

Creativity often lies in creating something original out of the familiar. "Lately I've really enjoyed doing doors. I recently made a door in my studio from different woods. Each piece of wood is a different colour, and the overall shape is rectangular, but all the inside lines are curved and gently flowing.

"To make it I cut all the pieces on a bandsaw. They're free-form so there were no lines to follow. I just cut them in the shape that I thought would suit that piece of wood, then made them all fit together. I didn't sketch it first. It's easier for me to picture in my mind what a piece will look like when it's done.

"This is the first time I've used a free-form style with a conventional form. It's not just a door, it's a piece of art."

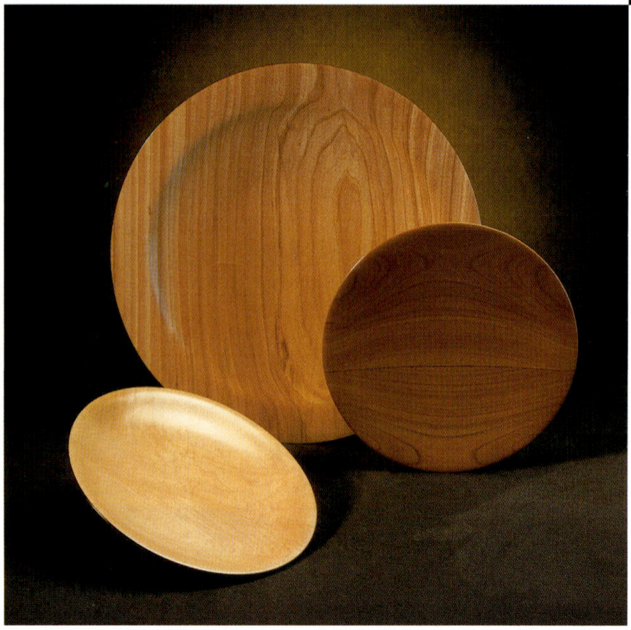

I always tried to stay away from the ordinary. If someone asked me to do something and I didn't know how, I'd go through books and find out. It gave me an opportunity to grow."

No longer content to work outside, he built a 2-storey workshop at the side of his house. Continued growth led to more changes. With his father, who had returned in 1990, Dirk drew up plans for a new workshop and showroom under one roof. The grand opening took place in September 1997, just in time for the Muskoka Autumn Studio Tour.

The building is down the road from the house, far enough away that the family is safe from dust and fire hazards. "I'm really happy with the new shop. It's nice to have the main floor of our home back. I have lots of plans for the future and, with our house finally the way we want it, hopefully my time will be freed up to work on new things."

Dirk now offers complete home furnishings in pine, cherry and oak. This spring, for the first time, he furnished a client's entire home. "It's always a challenge to give customers exactly what they like. My enjoyment comes from producing something unique to technically exacting standards. When my customers are happy, I'm happy."

Dirk loves being his own boss, but he's a demanding task master. "I'm up by 6 a.m., in my shop by 7. I put in a full day, then go back after supper for a couple hours. I still really enjoy woodworking, even after all these years. I haven't burned out. Must admit, things get pretty hectic, especially during the Christmas season – I'm lucky if I get to take a few days off."

With a steady six months of backlog, Dirk, Lynda, Andrew and his sister Amber, born in 1983, seldom take a vacation together. "Working at home, you get to see your family more than most others, so the need to get away with them is not as great." Dirk jokes about the stream of summer vacationers who escape the city to surround themselves with nature. "Every so often, we escape nature and get down to the city."

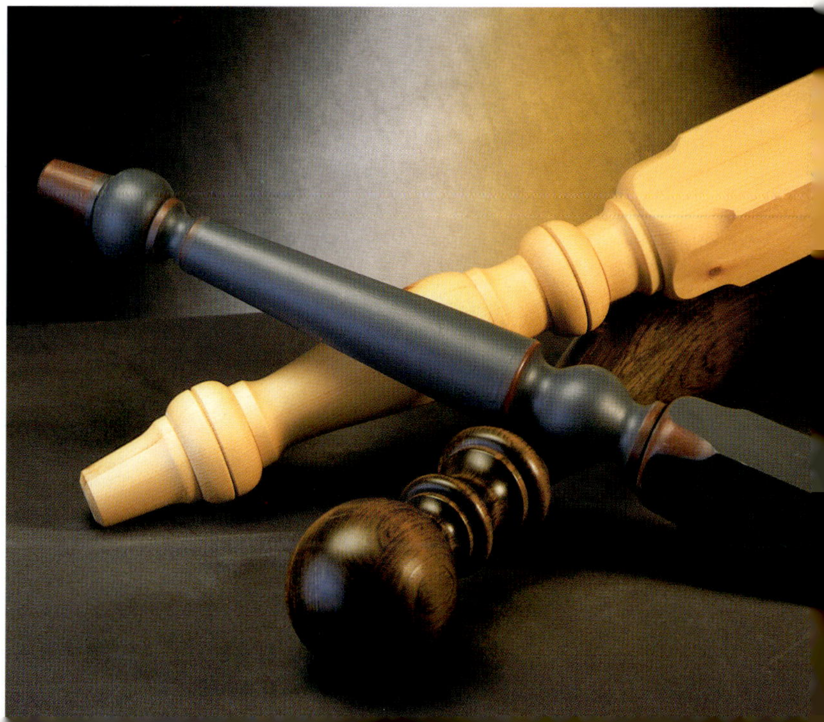

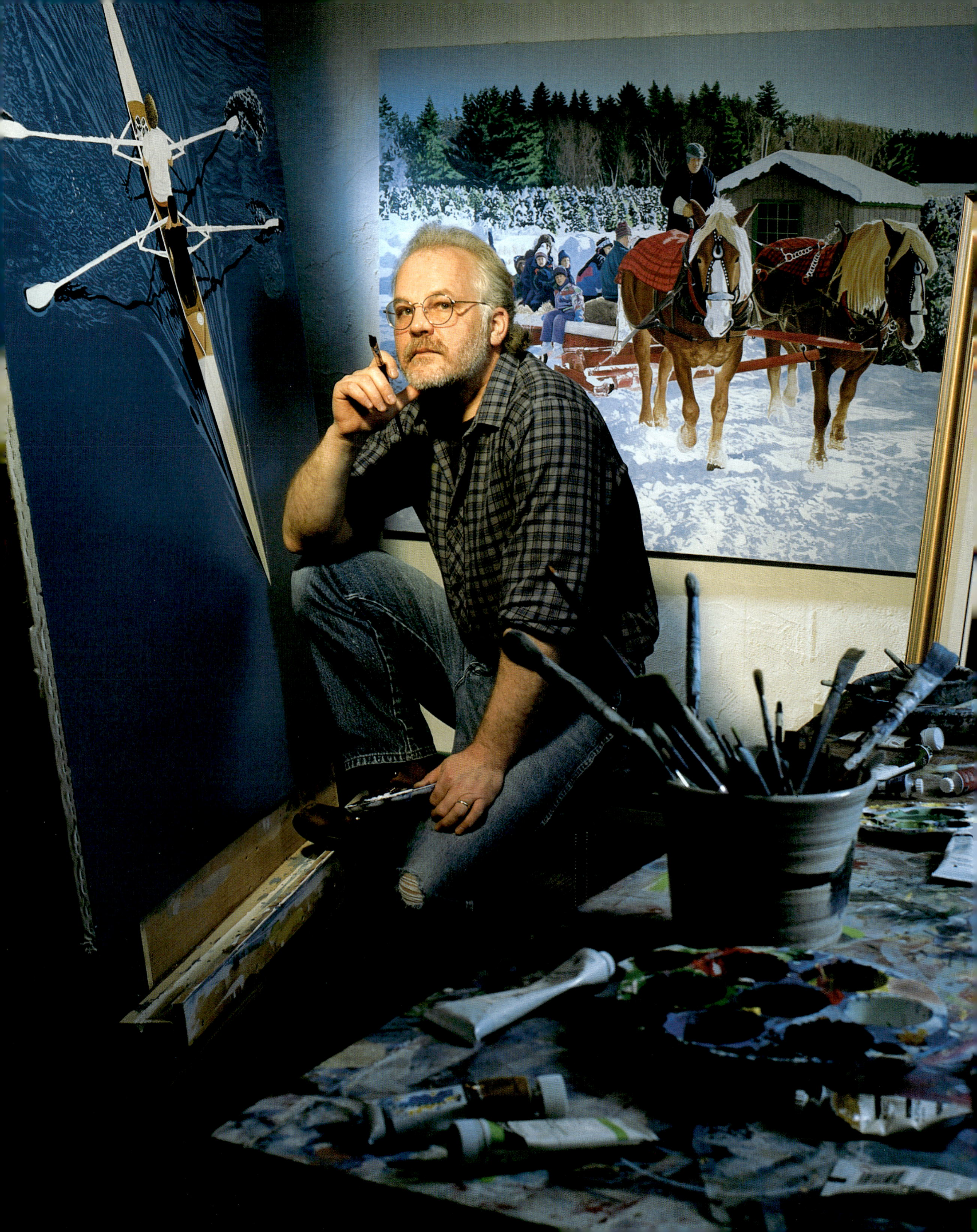

D . A . D U N F O R D

The return is seeing the radiance everywhere. – Joseph Campbell

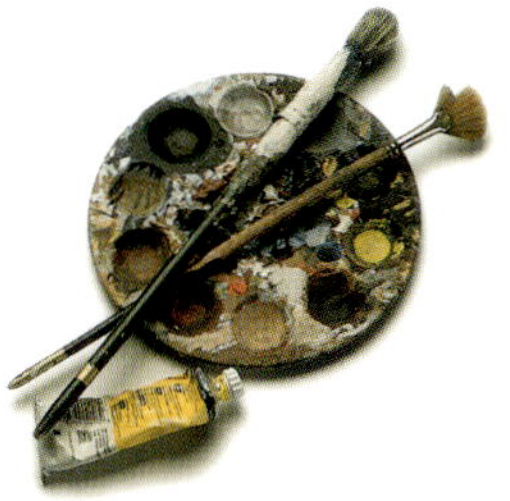

The Eye of the Beholder

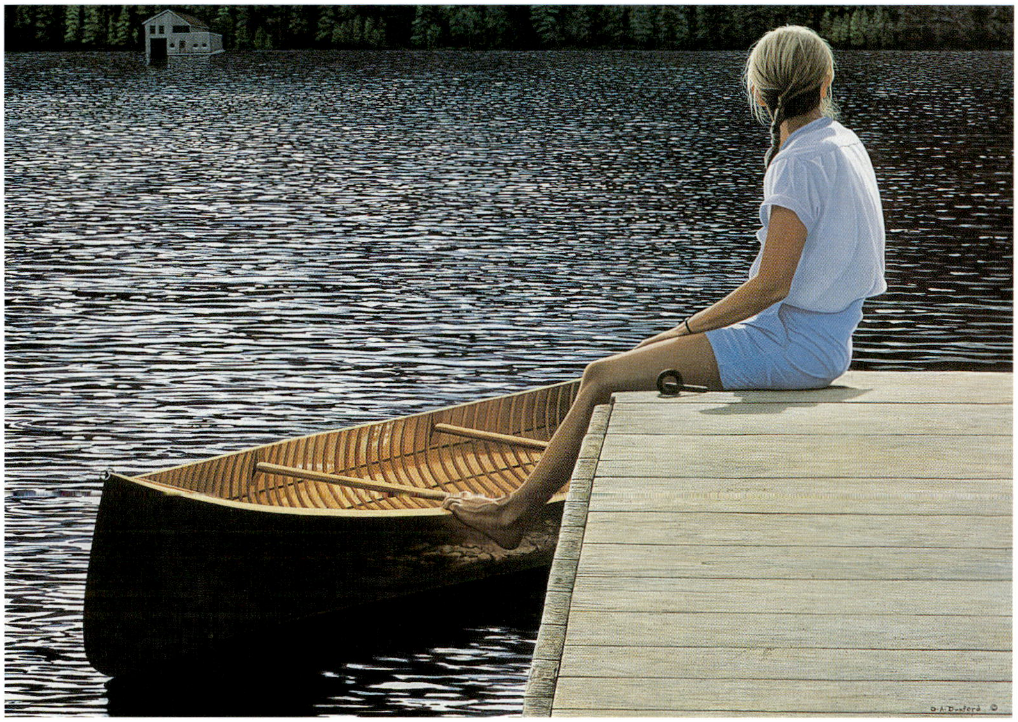

Summer Dreamer

A woman sits on the edge of a dock looking out across the water. Her toes curl over the rim of a canoe that bobs gently before her. Can you hear the music? The water music? A summer breeze lifts wispy tendrils of hair from her braid. On the far shore, just discernible on the water's edge, is a boathouse. What stories play out behind its windows and doors?

Two women stand before *Summer Dreamer*, hanging in D.A. Dunford's gallery just north of Bracebridge. "Look at that water," says one to the other. "It's so real, you can see it moving. It almost makes me dizzy."

A high realist, Dunford captures in his paintings the icons of Muskoka life – a blue heron, a worn Muskoka chair, a mahogany launch and, always, the water. His passion is water.

"As an artist, I'm trying to imitate nature as seen by the human eye, not by a camera. When I work on a commissioned piece, it's not just a moment in time I'm painting, but a study of life. I'll spend time at the clients' cottage, go for a boat ride around the lake, then talk to them. I ask a lot of questions about their life experiences."

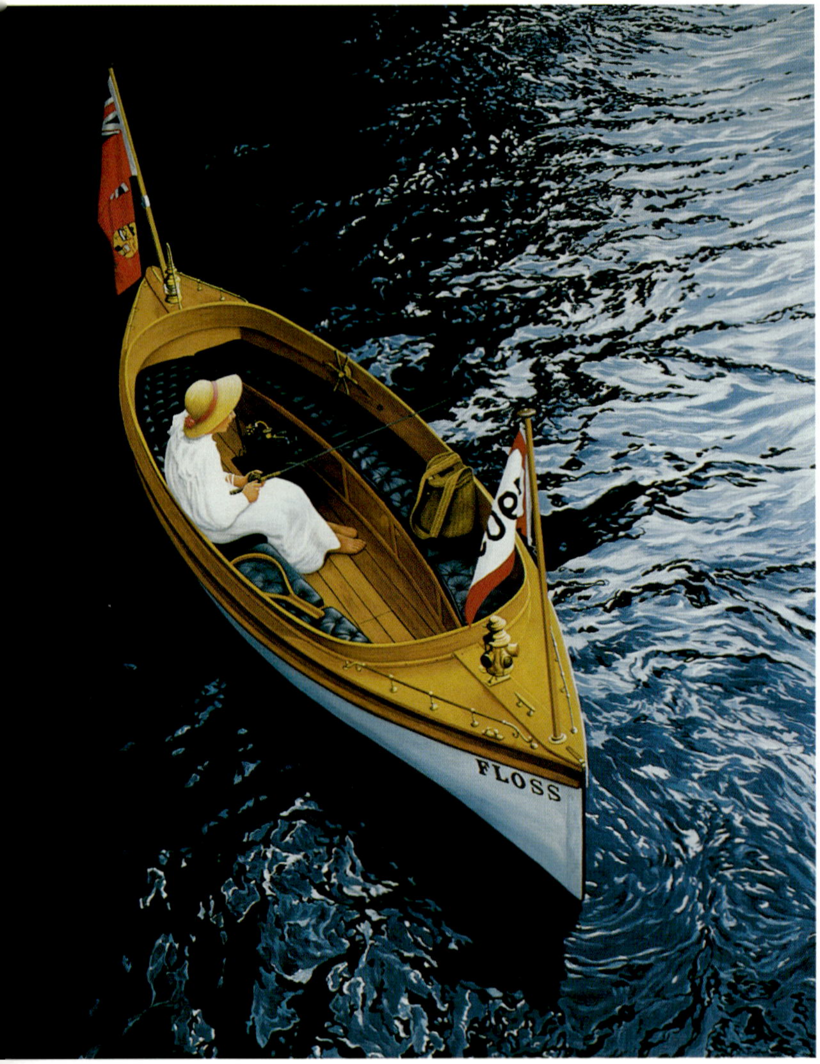

Heritage

We see only the back of her braided head as she paddles a canoe across the lake. Facing her is a young boy whose faded orange life jacket has drifted up around his ears and mouth. Off in the distance is another Muskoka icon, the steamship Segwun, its white plume rising high above the tree line. The blue water is calm, unhurried, its surface only slightly ruffled. Preserving the past. Honouring the present. Protecting the future.

We've all seen him, the new kid in school. He sports the wrong hair cut or the wrong clothes. Too short, too long, too something. He sits at the back of the room, shoulders hunched, eyes looking down at the surface of his desk.

This one's a little different. Oh, he's got a brushcut, while everyone else endlessly flicks bangs from their eyes. His shoulders are hunched, but one hand curves in front of his notebook, while the other layers the paper with image after image until, feeling the pressure of a pair of eyes at the front of the room, the pencil goes down and the head lifts. But soon the head slips down and the pencil picks up again.

For his first 30 years, Dunford stood on the outside, a boy apart, then a man apart. Whether his art was the cause or effect of his separateness, it is the strongest thread in his life story, and is today his primary connection to others.

Douglas Andrew Dunford was born in Owen Sound, Ontario on March 13, 1953, the eldest of three children. Soon after, his family moved to his grandparents' farm near Lakefield. There Doug's love of nature and open spaces took root.

Art fascinated him from an early age. "I remember when I was four or five years old, watching my uncle drawing objects – an apple, a square, a triangle. At first they were just flat images on the page, then he would shade them until they began to look real. In first grade I started doing the same thing."

Doug started to sense he was different when his family moved from the farm to Oakville. "I was in Grade 5. It was culture shock for me. All of a sudden you go from fishing and hunting and farm life, to kids having gang fights and breaking into homes for fun. I didn't fit in, so I withdrew to my room, to my drawing and painting.

"I was also academically behind in the new school. I had never learned French or advanced math, so most of the time I sat at the back of the class and sketched. I ended up in a school for kids with learning problems. I knew it was the wrong place, so I worked hard and brought my grades up enough to get back into the regular system."

By Grade 9, Doug again found himself in the wrong place, this time a trade school where he was supposed to study auto mechanics. He remained quiet and withdrawn, continuing to sketch, rendering anything that caught his attention – the back of a girl's braided head, a pair of scuffed sneakers.

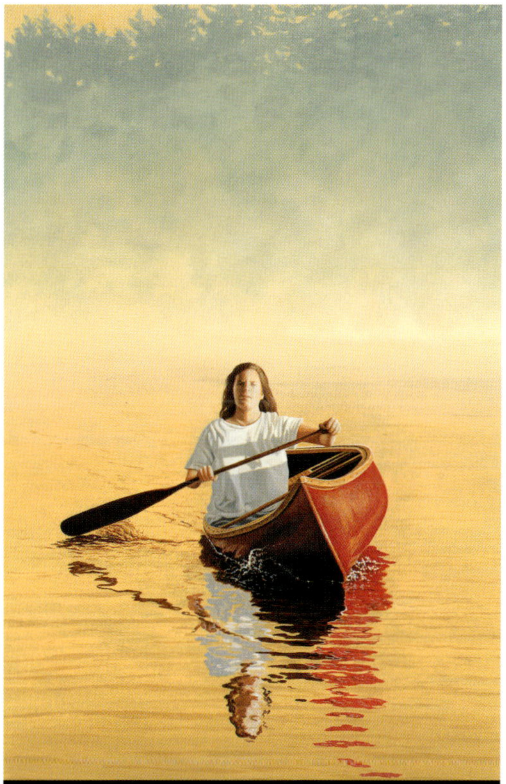

The Power of a Dream

Summer Dreamer, painted in 1989, became D.A. Dunford's first poster reproduction to raise funds for charitable purposes. In this instance, a women's shelter. Since then, his work has raised money for many causes. It's Doug's way of giving back. "To be an artist is a god-given thing, so how you use it is important. My art now has become less for my own purpose, more for the purpose of making a contribution to society."

Were it not for an astute teacher in the art department, Doug might have continued drifting. "After about two months, I walked by an art class. All these people were happy and excited about what they were doing. So I showed some of my pictures to the teacher. He marched me down to the principal's office and demanded that I be moved into his class." It was the beginning of Doug's formal education in art.

Doug's talent continued to draw attention. Among his enthusiastic supporters was naturalist painter Robert Bateman, then art director for the Halton Board of Education. Bateman used to call Doug "his student who was never his student," and encouraged him to pursue his art.

Evenings and weekends, Doug poured his energy into drawing and painting. At 16, he won a place in an evening life drawing class at the Ontario College of Art. By 17, with the help of his art teacher, he was granted early acceptance into Sheridan College's art program. The youngest of his peers, still living at home, still sporting a brush cut, he remained an outsider looking in.

After graduating from Sheridan, Doug supported himself by painting signs or selling the odd painting here and there. On a visit to his parents in Owen Sound, he stopped at Georgian College in Barrie to investigate course offerings and discovered a well established arts program. He spent a year studying sculpture and pottery, painting at home in his spare time.

At Georgian he met Richard Green, founder of the Muskoka Autumn Studio Tour. "Green owned a gallery at the time and invited me to do a show. Almost all of my paintings sold. That was really the beginning of my career. From then on, I never stopped. I just wanted to paint and sell my paintings." It was 1974. He was 21 years old.

The next seven or eight years were nomadic. From Barrie, Doug moved to Hamilton, then down to West Virginia, up to farm country outside Peterborough, and eventually back to Barrie where he shared a rambling old farmhouse with friends. For much of this time he painted barns. They sold well.

By 1982, Doug was ready for a change. "I was making a decent living, but I was bored. Technically the paintings were good, but the work had become mechanical. My first print, of Belgian workhorses, had just come out. I spent two months crossing Canada, selling copies along the way to galleries and stores."

After six months on British Columbia's Salt Spring Island, Doug returned to Ontario. He was still unsettled, still in need of change, but unsure of what or how.

Muskoka Solitude

A lone Muskoka chair faces out over the glassy surface of a lake, the distant shore a faint, hazy line. Mist washes colour from the lake, the sky, the dock, everything except a bleached planter full of crimson impatiens.

Doug was 30 years old when he retreated into Algonquin Park for five months. "I was not happy with what I was doing. I was born an artist, had always been an artist, but I had to find out who Doug Dunford was."

He moved into a cabin on Cache Lake. "I went in on Thanksgiving weekend, came out in March. It was lonely. Once a month I went into town for groceries. The rest of the time I painted pictures and tried to figure it all out.

"When the walls started moving, I knew it was time to pack it in. I hauled out a sleigh, loaded all my stuff onto it and dragged it across the lake. It was spring thaw. The water was up to the top of my boots. It wasn't until much later that I realized I'd learned something from the experience."

Mostly, Doug learned to feel at home with himself. "I was ready for the biggest experience of my life." The event: a boat ride on Lake Muskoka. "It was like a rebirth. I fell in love with the water.

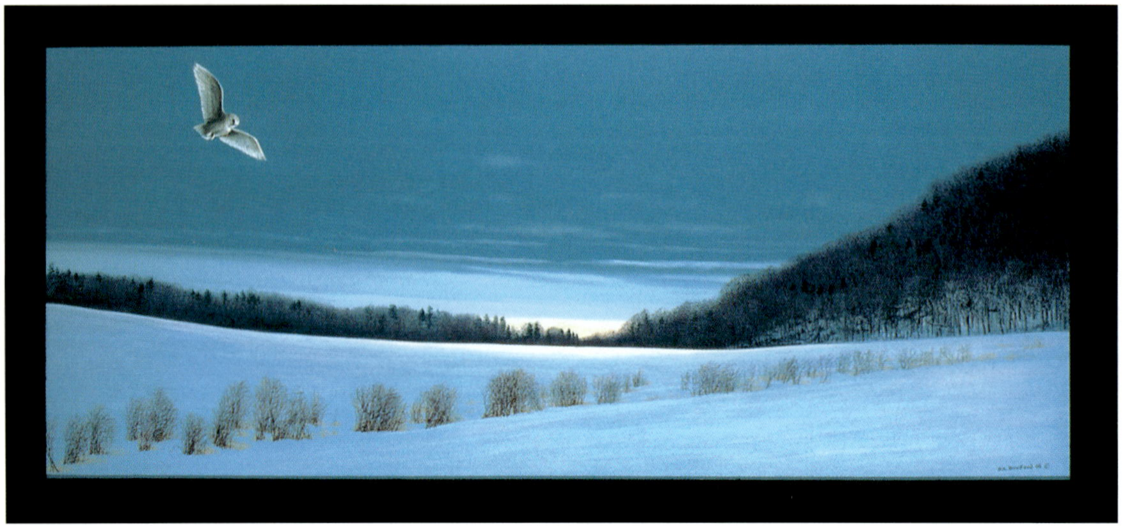

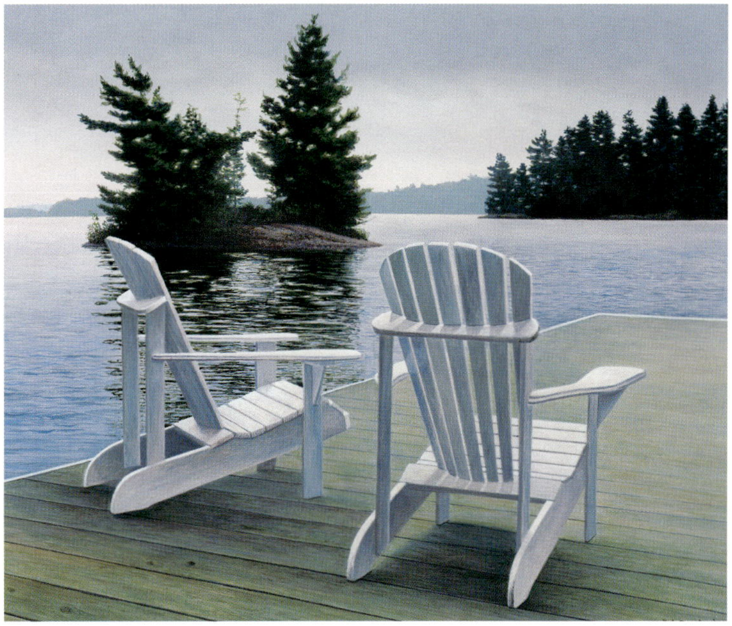

"The old boathouses reminded me of the barns I had always painted. Then I started noticing how different people are around water. Why do so many of us come here and dangle our feet in the water? People change personalities when they take off their suits and put on their shorts. It's a very inner thing.

"If you sit near water, you feel happy. If you walk in the rain, the air is fresher, you feel alive, it wakes you up. We have to have water, we need it to live.

"I study water to understand how it moves, how light reflects on it. I'm fascinated by the creatures that live in it, and the people who are drawn to it. I feel I could spend the rest of my life painting water and never get bored by it."

Old Friends

Two empty white Muskoka chairs sit side by side on a cedar dock, their arms nearly touching. Waning sunlight filters through the slats of the chairs. The view from the dock – a perfect composite of water, rock, tree and sky – is familiar and comforting.

Doug and his wife Judy Dunford now have three sons, Dylan, Jordan and Simon. Family has always been important to Doug, but he wasn't sure it would ever happen to him. "I didn't settle down and have kids until I was 37. I couldn't afford to get married and continue to do what I love. I felt apart from the rest of the world, but I knew what I wanted to do. I wanted to paint. I don't know why, it's just the way I am."

After a lifetime of commitment to his work, acrylics and watercolours by D.A. Dunford appear in private and corporate collections across North America. Limited edition prints and posters have made his instantly recognizable Muskoka scenes accessible to a larger and enthusiastic following. But financial reward and recognition for Doug are icing on the lake, not the lake itself. "Success to me is not fame or wealth. It's getting better at what I do.

"You have to have discipline and self-motivation to continue doing whatever you have passion for. If you don't have the skills, the passion gets lost.

"Most of us work hard to better ourselves, but what we work at isn't always what we want. The more honest you are about what you want, then the more comfortable you become with yourself, and the easier it is to be disciplined and motivated. And the better you become at what it is you really want to do. I want to paint."

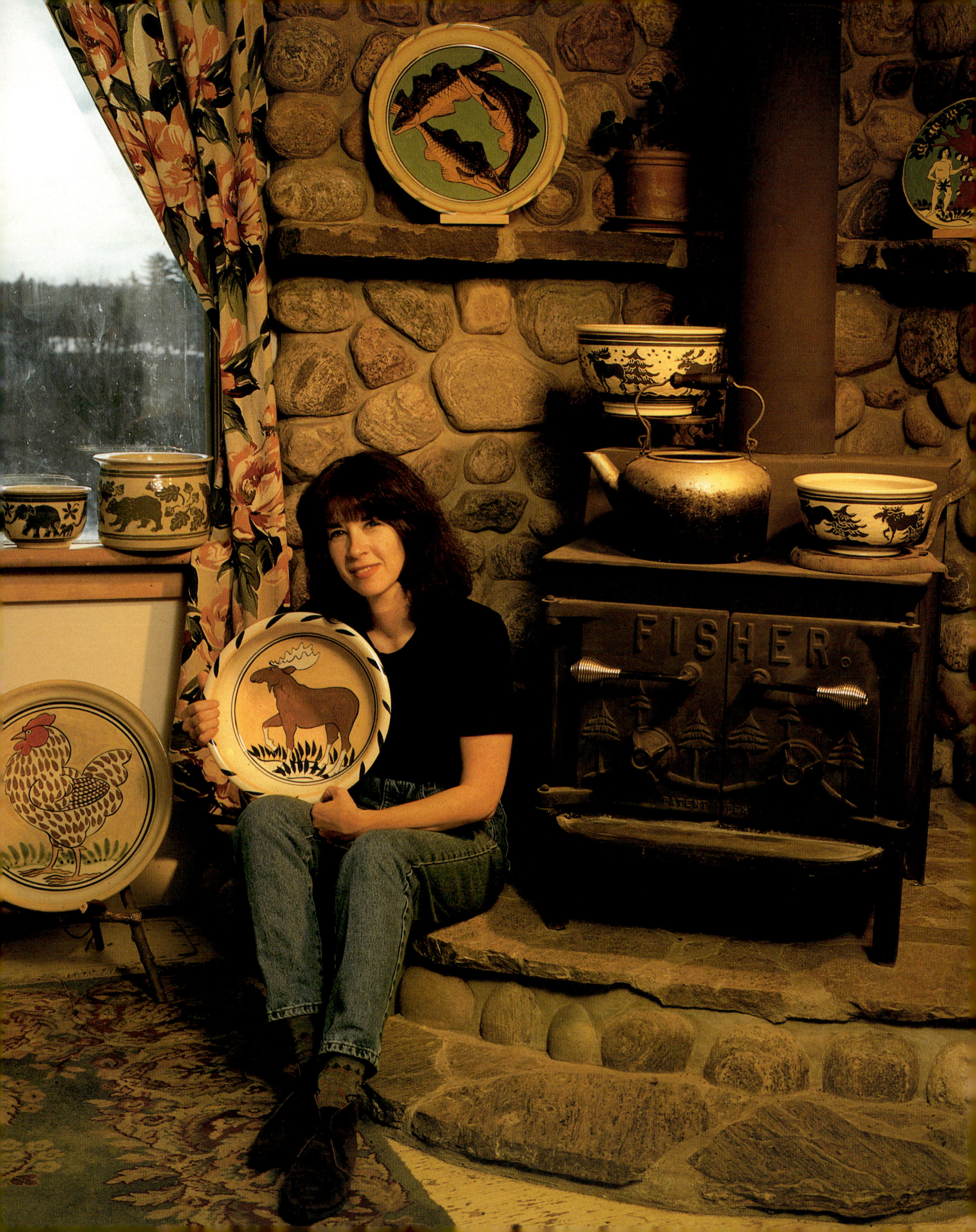
FISHER

Only with the heart can one truly see. – Lorraine Eidlitz

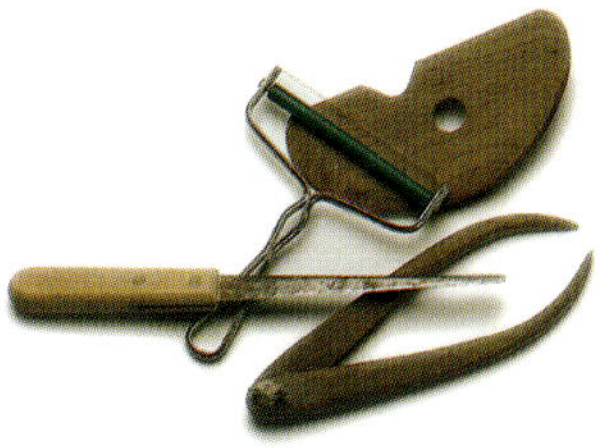

Connections

It's the annual Muskoka Autumn Studio Tour weekend. The curves in the road wend their way from Gravenhurst, through Bala and beyond, bringing you past a large road sign that reads: "Welcome to Port Carling – Hub of the Lakes." Next stop is Eidlitz Pottery & Paint Box, a 1914 farmhouse on Port Carling's main street.

Oak leaves from a rare white oak crunch beneath your feet as you make your way to a pottery workshop at the back of the cottage. Lorraine Eidlitz sits at her wheel, surrounded by wide-eyed visitors. She talks and works at the same time.

"Once upon a time, I wanted to be a children's book illustrator. But then I became a potter. When I started out in pottery, I experimented with different techniques. At one point, I was doing this Japanese stuff that everyone else was doing. I thought, 'I don't want to be like everyone else. What can I do that's unique to me?' I began looking through history books and discovered 17th century English majolica, an earthenware technique."

She looks up and gestures to a young woman standing at the door. "Can you hand me that big platter?

"Earthenware techniques, that's where I was. Now, I was working in stoneware, not earthenware, but I thought I could translate the look."

She brings attention to the platter in her hands. "I mark the top of my platter before I draw a picture on it so I don't end up with an upside down chipmunk. I have a great tool, a grip to help me centre my pots. I used to centre by hand, which can be time consuming. You wiggle the pot around, and push here and there. The centring grip locks it quickly in place.

"This little piece of plastic has saved me so much time. I resented buying it at first. It cost $100 that I didn't have. So I waited another year or two and it went up to $200. I bought it at $200 and it's speeded my production by three times, paid for itself in a week. It's invaluable, because I really don't think I was put on the planet to centre pots.

Waste Not Want Not

Deer were once frequent visitors to Lorraine's backyard, usually foraging for food in the long grass. Not always. On one occasion, a deer hit by a car dragged itself through the grass toward the forest to die. Borrowing from First Nation traditions, Lorraine enlisted a friend to help carve up the animal. They preserved what they could for human consumption and gave the rest a proper burial. "In native spirituality, it is believed that all in nature is connected, that it's a mistake not to honour the connection. The deer was so regal in life. I just didn't want it to die for nothing."

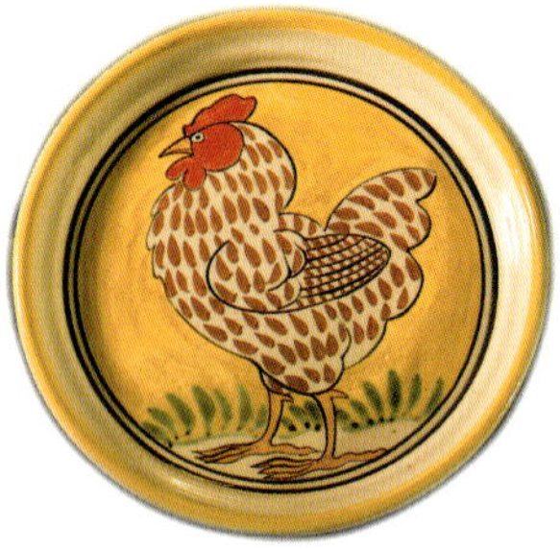

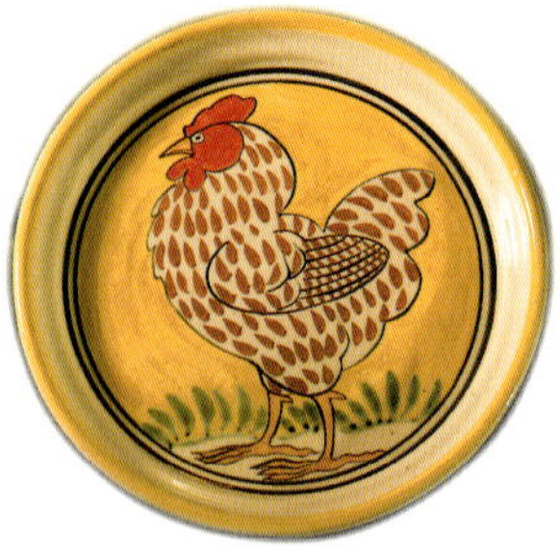

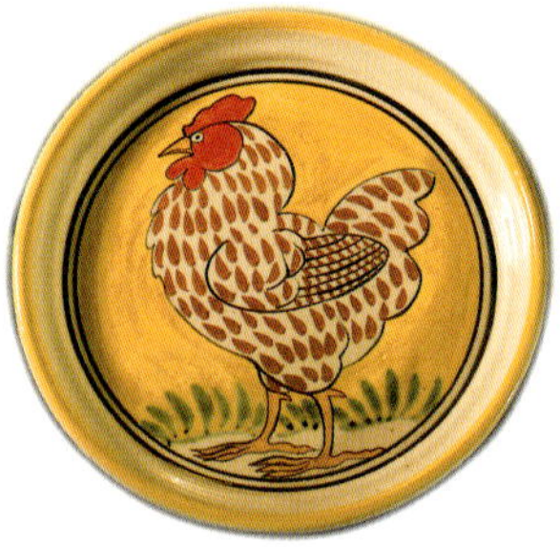

"Next I map out the area I want to illustrate." Paint brush in hand, she starts the potter's wheel spinning, holding the brush in place as it trails a circular frame on the platter's surface.

"So, I really liked the look of English majolica. The drawings had a cartoon quality that appealed to me. I didn't want to do shadows or things that were too complicated. I just wanted to draw pictures of animals. My style is very simple. I colour in rather than splash colour on, so it's not as spontaneous as others. I like the splashed-on look, but what I do is more illustrative.

"In the end, by looking for something unique to me, I found a way to channel my drawing ability, a love of animals and an early interest in becoming a children's book illustrator."

She looks up from her platter at the audience. "And now I need someone to suggest an animal for me to draw."

"I saw a beautiful heron on the way here," offers a muffled voice at the back of the room.

"I don't think I can do a heron from memory. I'd need a picture. How about a crow? If you don't mind, I'll just do a crow."

The screen door whines as more curious spectators enter. Otherwise, the air is still as she outlines the crow, then colours it in with dark blue.

"I don't know if everyone was here when I talked about the concept of perfection and how damaging it can be to an artist. This stage of pottery is porous. It's called bisque ware, and it's like a sponge. Already, my colours are deeply stained onto the platter. Once you put the stroke down, it's there forever. If I don't like it, I'm just going to have to live with it. So to be a perfectionist would be counterproductive."

Art and the philosophy of art have been a big part of Lorraine's life since learning "something from nothing" at the side of her Lithuanian grandmother. A doll her grandmother made from a cracker box, the face a stuffed nylon stocking with embroidered eyes, nose and mouth, has a special place in Lorraine's living room. More than a souvenir of the past, it represents her grandmother's gift of imagination.

For many years, Lorraine has drawn on her imagination to create a wide range of folk art stoneware. Her platters, bowls and cups delight the young and the young at heart, revealing at the end of a meal a grinning barnyard cow or a strutting rooster.

Lorraine's imagination doesn't stop at stoneware. Exploring other media and techniques is as stimulating to an artist as undiscovered territory is to a world traveller.

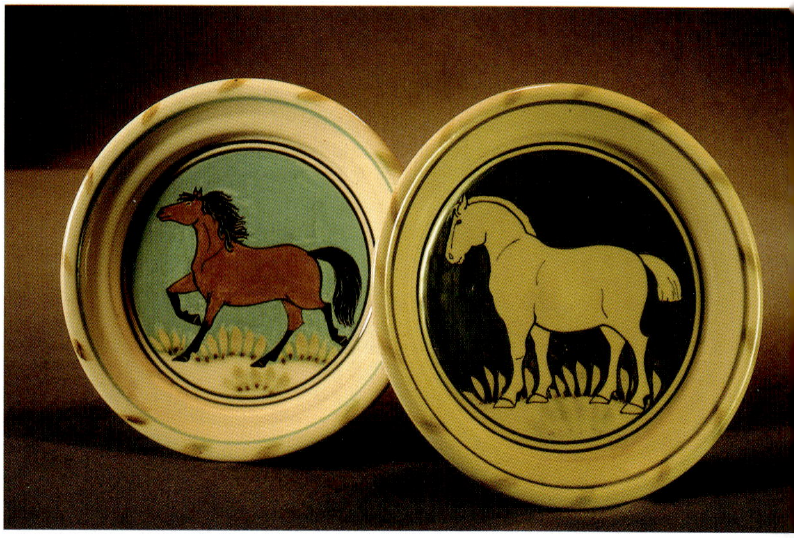

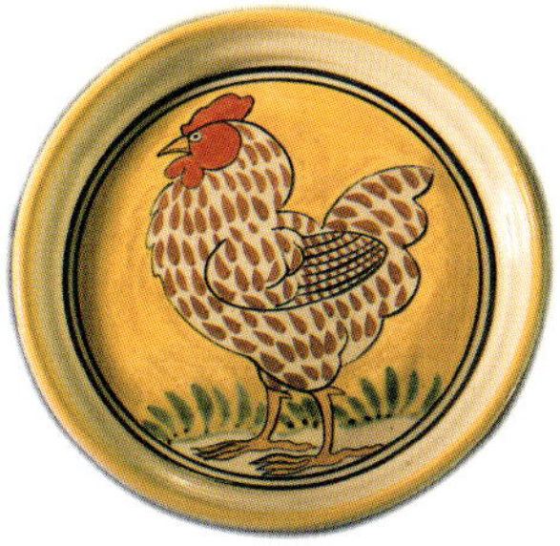
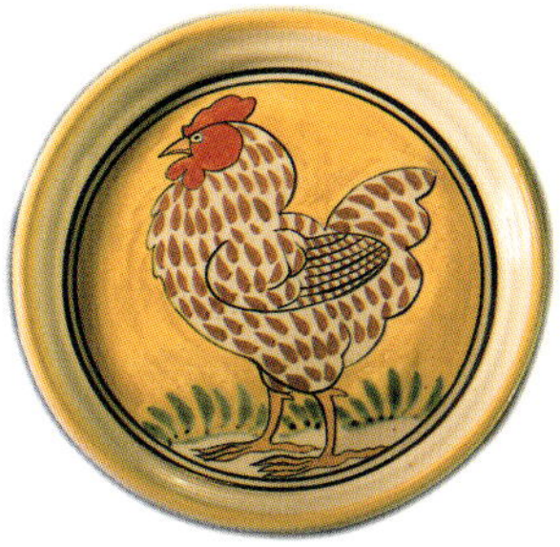
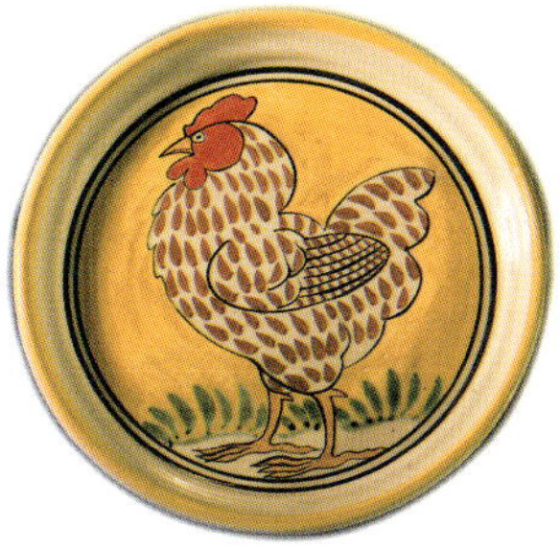

A packrat, Lorraine rarely throws anything away and often digs into her treasure chest for inspiration. She creates 2-dimensional collages using found objects and has occasionally explored 3-dimensional sculpture. Beyond Androgyny is one such piece. Mounted on a weathered bocci ball are mismatched body parts – a head sculpted in clay and covered in goldleaf, a piece of driftwood for the torso, wooden wedges taking the place of arms, rusty nails of fingers. "The sculpture is about spirituality

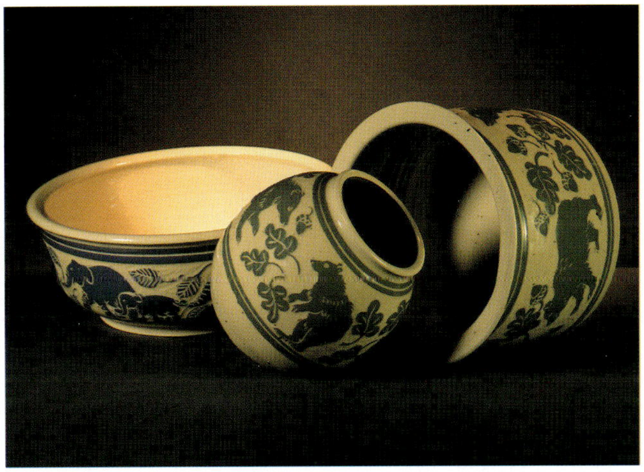

and transcendence over our physical selves. We have to get beyond this perception of ourselves as male or female, beyond our corporal body, and recognize a higher order."

Oil paintings of fantastical animals have also provided a satisfying creative outlet ever since she studied illustration at Sheridan College. She never did become a children's book illustrator, disenchanted after her first year by a curriculum that did not allow her enough creative elbow room.

It got worse before it got better. She lasted 9½ months at her first and only full-time job. In 1973 she worked as a receptionist for a pension management firm. Some might say imagination was a prerequisite. Lorraine tried to imagine herself elsewhere.

"I had to wear a headset. I resented that. It felt like I was being automated. I had to press all these buttons and remember whose name belonged to which button. Me, the girl with no memory. I begged for other work, so they had me open envelopes and copy social insurance numbers from one page to another."

Deciding the world was divided into goods and services, Lorraine concluded she wasn't cut out for the services sector. She explored a range of "goods" at Toronto's now defunct Three Schools of Art. Flowering under the opportunity to design her own 10-week program, she studied macramé, photography, bookbinding and ceramics. She connected immediately with clay. At the end of her program of study, she discovered that she could practice her pottery skills for $1 a day at a craft centre in Etobicoke. That's where she met Molly Moss.

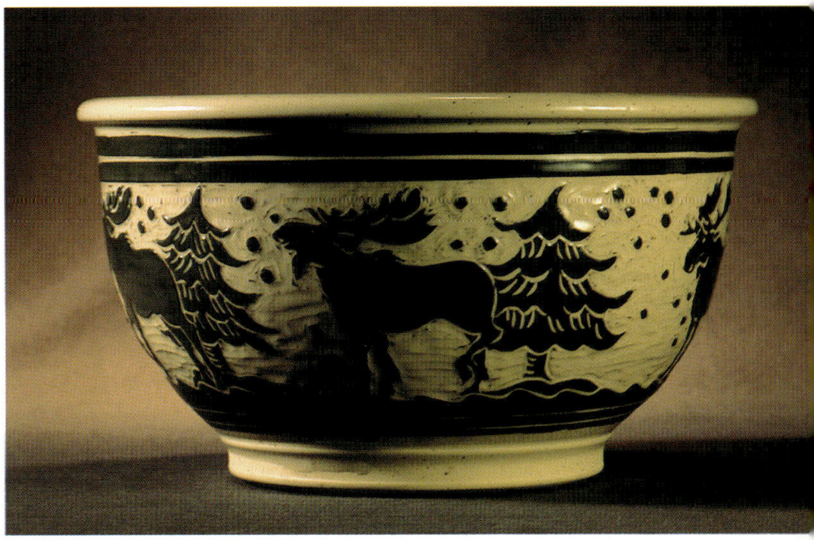

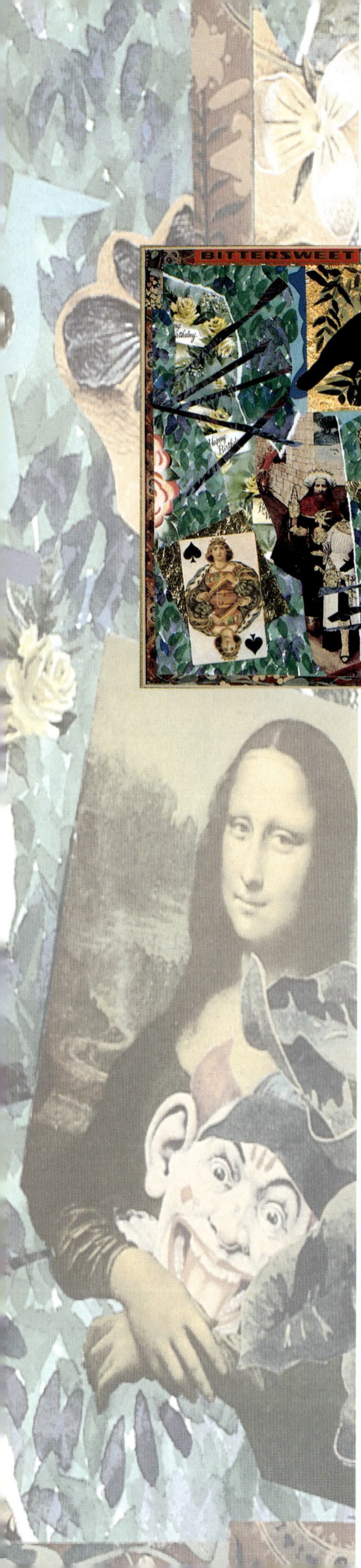

"Molly was a member, not a paid teacher. She wasn't paid to teach. But she ended up teaching because she was more advanced than everyone else and loved what she did. But it wasn't just technique that she passed on. She was more a spiritual guide. She taught us to be mindful about what we were doing, to be aware that in centring your pot, you also needed to centre yourself."

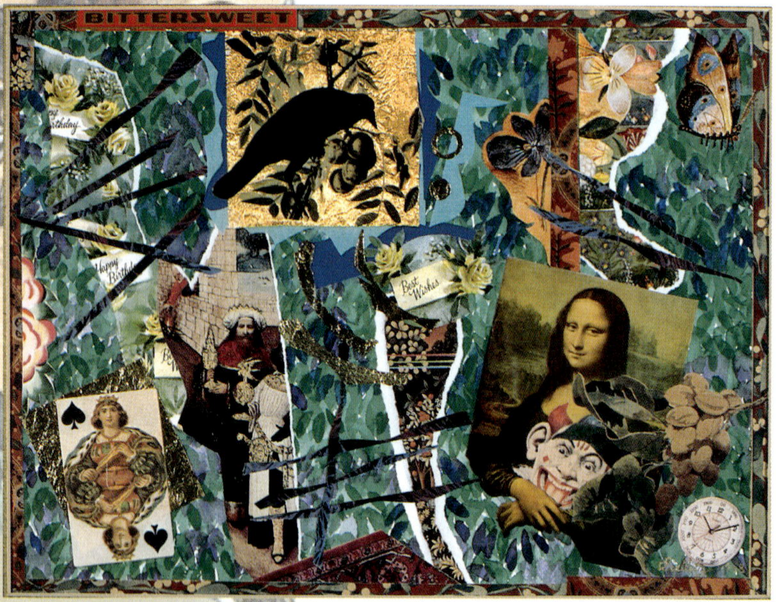

One personal centring device Lorraine used in the early days was a message she scribbled on the wall in front of her potter's wheel. "Remember, your work is not the measure of your worth." Her challenge then became to put her work out in the world, while staying true to herself.

Today it all seems clear to Lorraine why those early years were so tough. "It takes years to perfect a skill. And while you're learning, being tied to the opinion of others can be insidious. You need to baby your talent, not the product. The product is just the shell of the experience."

When Lorraine began selling her pottery in the mid 1970s, she put little clay mice on butter dishes and cups. "I camouflaged my work with cute. I swallowed my pride in the process of learning." The mice became her signature. She then experimented with loose brushwork that evoked Japanese designs. In her spare time, she produced oil paintings of whimsical animals – the White Knight's horse from Alice in Wonderland, a hippo on his hind legs, strutting with a cane.

Recession hit in the early 1980s. "Sales were so poor, I was afraid of going out of business. I'd been doing functional pottery with a Japanese look. It seemed everyone was doing the same thing. So then came the question, 'What in my work is unique to me? What is personally satisfying?' I really liked to draw animals and work with more colour. I began to incorporate these in my pottery. Sales tripled. It's as though I created space for a miracle."

A few days into the new year of 1987, another miracle came her way. Marisa, a friend since grade school, asked, "What's your New Year's Resolution?"

"I don't know."

"Well, what would you do if you could do anything you wanted?"

Lorraine pictured herself waving a Gitane while passionately debating art and life on the Left Bank. "I suppose I'd go to art school."

"How much would that cost?"

At the mention of money, Lorraine became suspicious, but continued to play along. "I don't know, around $8,000."

"It's yours."

Having seen her friend struggle for so many years, Marisa believed a financial boost could make the difference. In the end, Lorraine didn't go to art school. She decided to open a studio and gallery instead. Her angel's interest-free loan helped.

Bruce Gallagher and Beth Barry are potters in Muskoka, former members of the Muskoka Autumn Studio Tour. In 1988, they encouraged Lorraine to open her studio in Muskoka. With a real estate agent she visited a ramshackle house set back from the main drag of Port Carling. She sat in the car at first, hesitant to step out. The house was brown and green. What nasty surprises lurked behind those boarded-up windows?

Pleasant ones. Today, Eidlitz Pottery & Paint Box invites visitors with its picture postcard yellow and lavender exterior. She operates a busy summer retail business from a showroom in what had once been the house's front room, selling her own and other artists' work. Both a walkout basement, which doubles as an airy, well-lit pottery studio, and her main floor living room overlook a lightly forested lowland and the river beyond.

When Lorraine first moved in, the scrub thicket and surrounding meadow of long grass were home to the inspiration for her wildlife designs – moose, bears, beavers and chipmunks whose images appear on her platters and bowls. Donating proceeds from the sale of certain items to a nearby wildlife sanctuary was one way for Lorraine to give back. "I figure I owe them, making my living on the images of animals as I do."

An incurable animal lover, she finds it hard to turn away the strays that no one else wants. She currently shares her home with a dog, Archie, and two cats, Axel and Elmo. Stray artists are no less important to her. Having received much encouragement and support over the years, Lorraine opens her doors generously to others in need. She responds to words of appreciation with "Just pass on the good luck."

It's a question of faith in herself and others. "I still have the artist's fear of looking at an empty canvas, and have to coach myself to make my mark. I figure, 'Try it, you can only get

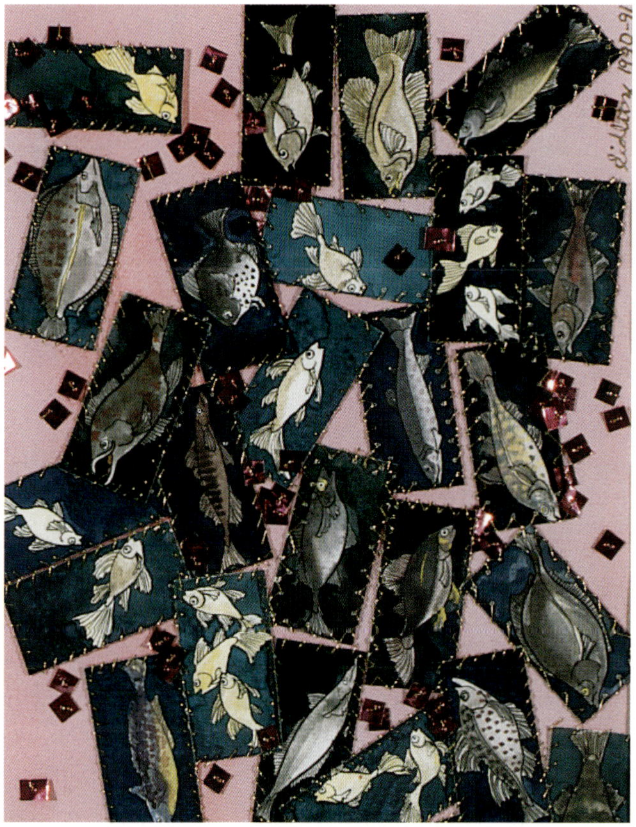

better.' Each step we take beyond the path of our knowledge and skill becomes an act of faith. There's an exhilaration to challenging our fears and preconceptions that's every bit as tangible to the artistic adventurer as a new slope is to a downhill skier.

"On one of those quiet days when you're alone, dare yourself to pick up that creative project you've been sidestepping. Throw away your self-critical perfectionism – we all share it – and give in to your feelings just this once, while no one is watching. And remember what jazz stylist Miles Davis once said, 'Do not fear mistakes. There are none.'"

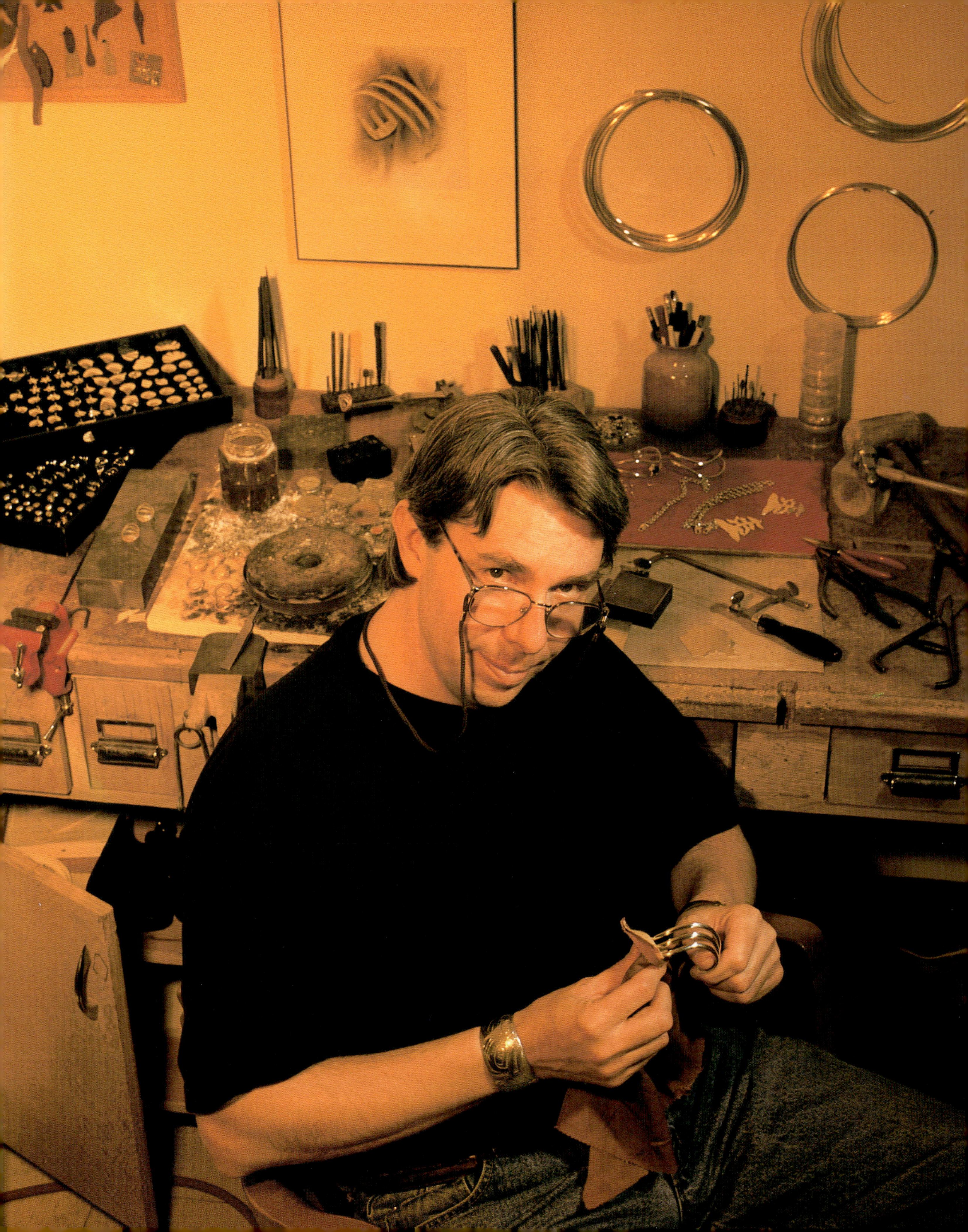

Never fallen into formula / ...never fallen into the arms of an employer to feed myself / fallen into the arms of life is what I've fallen into / life has never ever ever let me down / life has given me every lesson I've needed to learn / every smack in the face I've ever deserved.
– Stan Tait (spontaneous lyrics from an August interview)

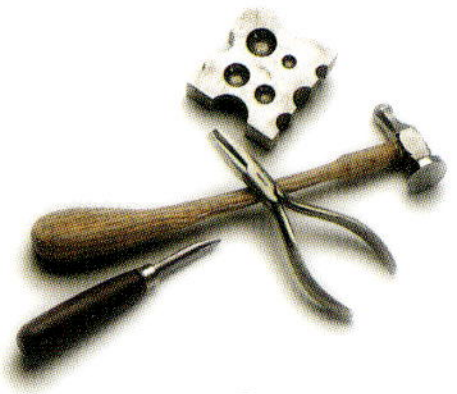

The Wealthy Jeweller

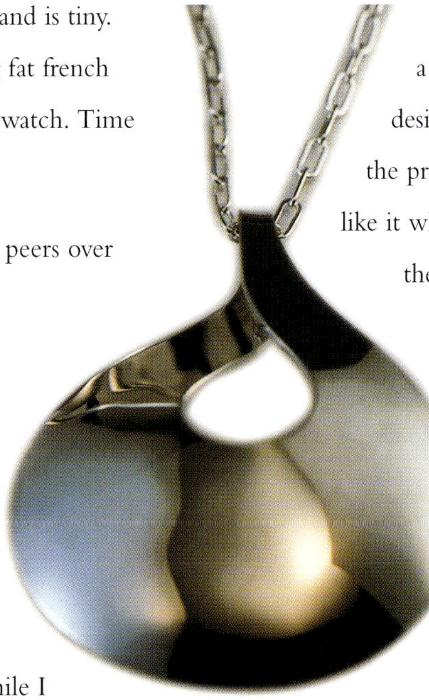

The salad I piously select at the lakeside stand is tiny. I return to the counter for an order of big fat french fries. I gobble them down then check my watch. Time for my next interview.

Stan Tait greets me as I enter his store. He peers over his glasses. The look is friendly but weary, like his voice.

"No chance to take any time off this summer, Stan?"

"Well, I did take the '60s off," he says without missing a beat.

I grab onto his opening and we're off. While I settle in, I recall for him the theme of our interview – something philosophers call "right livelihood," making a living doing work that is personally meaningful.

"I know what you mean. I've lived my entire life – until I discovered credit cards – doing exactly what I want. I have a Grade 10 education. I've never had a real job. I played music until I was 26. And for the last 23 years, I've chosen to do what I'm doing right now.

Twenty-three years making jewellery. "You must love your work."

"I used to. So much that I could do it 24 hours a day. But I'm getting burned out. I still love to design jewellery. It's probably my favourite step in the process. That and cashing the cheque. I also really like it when customers buy a piece of jewellery, put it on their body and say, 'God I love this.' That's a thrill. Money can't buy that.

"It's all about connecting. I tune into a frequency when I make the piece, they tune into that same frequency when they see it."

"Tune into a frequency?"

"The energy comes right out of me, straight, honest and clean, and comes on to them. Take my tree, for instance." Stan selects a silver brooch from the display case. "I love this tree. It has that windswept Georgian Bay look. I wanted to make a tree because I come from a long line of west coast loggers. So I went to the universe and said, 'Universe, I need a really great tree.' And the universe responded, 'Okay, Stan. Can you draw this?' I said, "Yeah, I can.' And Universe said, 'That's your tree.'

"It's like we're in partnership, me and the universe. I had to be open to get my tree. When you write a song, you've got to be open to allow a great line to come through. But you also have to be present in life. You have to be present when the line comes into your head. You have to be present to write it down. You have to be present to repeat it. And you have to be present in order to put it out there for public consumption.

"Life wants to dance and it wants to dance with you. If you don't want to dance with life, you both lose. But if you stand up and get on to the floor with life, it'll be there for you." He pauses to take up a tool. "It's an interesting way to live."

"Do you meditate?"

"I think I am a meditation."

"You're so positive. Hasn't life ever let you down?"

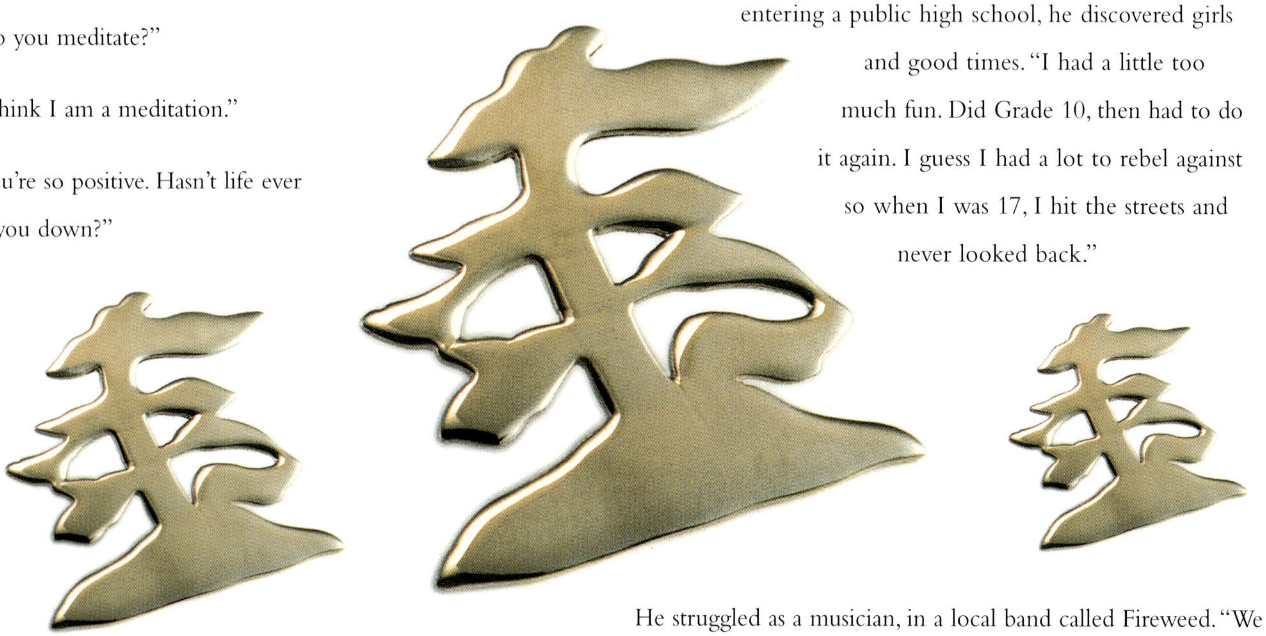

"Life is life. It's all the colours of the spectrum. It's Christopher Reeve falling off his horse. I have a real appreciation for wholeness and for those who become whole. And I have a tremendous soft spot in my heart for anyone who shows the kind of courage that Christopher Reeve has shown. But I digress. Are you getting what you need for your interview? You better take control soon or you won't get the information you want."

I ask about his roots.

"I was born and raised in White Rock, BC, a beautiful coastal village on the US/Canadian border about the size of Port Carling. We moved to Vancouver when I was nine. Then I went to an all-boys boarding school for junior high. I was the youngest of five children. Two brothers and two sisters."

"Me too. How was it for you?"

"Confusing. My father died of cancer when I was nine, and I'm the only surviving son. One brother drowned at 11. My other brother died in a car accident in Germany."

In junior high Stan explored a love of music in the school pep band, playing drums at school basketball games. After entering a public high school, he discovered girls and good times. "I had a little too much fun. Did Grade 10, then had to do it again. I guess I had a lot to rebel against so when I was 17, I hit the streets and never looked back."

He struggled as a musician, in a local band called Fireweed. "We were 13 or 14 crowded into a one-bedroom house in Kitsilano. We wrote all our own music. They called us hippies in the '60s. Today, we'd be called street kids. A lot of them were from abusive backgrounds. They were fabulous musicians, gifted and wonderful people, but for the most part profound alcoholics and drug addicts, seriously into hiding their pain. I used to stand with my mouth open a lot, an observer. You wouldn't dare intervene, it was their right to self-destruct."

Ten years passed. By this time Stan was a successful musician with a house, a mortgage and a Mercedes. Exhausted by the pace and frenzy, he had reached a point where he no longer wanted to play music. It was the early 1970s. One day he acquired a box of jewellery tools from a friend who had taken a course and then lost interest. Stan picked up a pair of pliers he still works with today and poured his creative energy into crafting jewellery.

"I had 20 minutes instruction with Native Indians and looked over a guy's shoulder who was trained through the jewellery trade in the United States. So I had like an hour and a half of instruction and have been going on for 23 years. I'm a hard worker and had a lot of healing to do, so I sat down and made a lot of jewellery. I worked and worked and worked, working through the demons.

"Designs kept coming. I would honour whatever came in my head. I would make it no matter how weird. And if I didn't know how to do something I would figure it out.

"Being self-taught has its pros and cons. For 10 years I polished standing up, then realized I could sit. Six years later I discovered that listening to music with headphones would drown out the sound of the polisher. It's not always the wisest route to learning your trade, but it turned out okay for me."

All through the 1970s Stan built his business by selling to quality stores that promoted handmade goods. When he moved to Ontario, he discovered craft shows.

"Was that what brought you to Ontario?"

"I came to Ontario to get back into the music business. My second wife, Dorothea, comes from Muskoka and that's where we settled. Originally in the bush, then we built a log home just

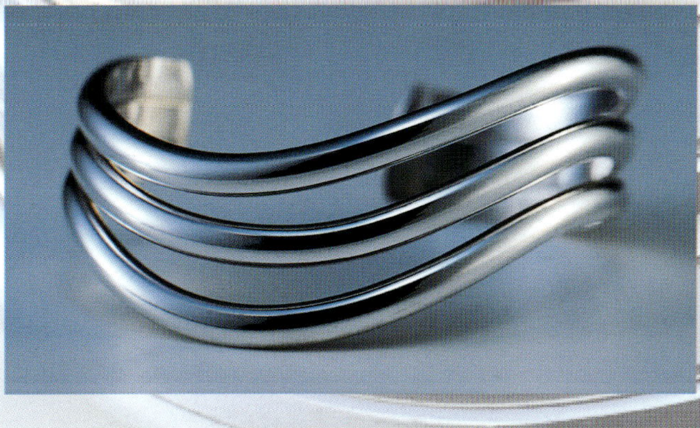

The Music Man

"I design and make jewellery. I'm also a musician. I was born into a musical family and I've had music in my life all my life. But when I stopped performing in Vancouver, back in the '70s, I put a tremendous amount of distance between myself and my music. I still played with friends. I've always done that. But I had to take a hiatus from that creative process.

"It's an ebb and flow. I think I needed a quiet place to be contemplative, and still be productive creatively and economically. Jewellery provided that. Now I'm creating and performing my music again.

"Music and design both have a creative integrity. They're a personal form of expression. In music, it's rhythm, harmony, melody and structure. In jewellery, it's shape and form.

"I have respect for what I'm able to do with jewellery, and I enjoy the work that I'm doing. I see it as being something that I will always have respect for. But how I create it will change. I can't say yet what form it will take. At this point I make everything by hand, but I may choose to share the process with others who have a like mind and the skills to complement my designs.

"You know, I also respect the process of jazz, as a spontaneous and creative approach to living in the moment. That's how I live my life, creating forward into the moment." – Stan Tait outside of Rosseau. When we decided to have children, I went back to making jewellery because I was realistic enough to know that a singer/songwriter on the road couldn't support a family. The artists in the community were great. They encouraged me to get into craft shows, like One of a Kind, and to open my own shop. So I stopped doing wholesale and got into retail, which I've done since '92."

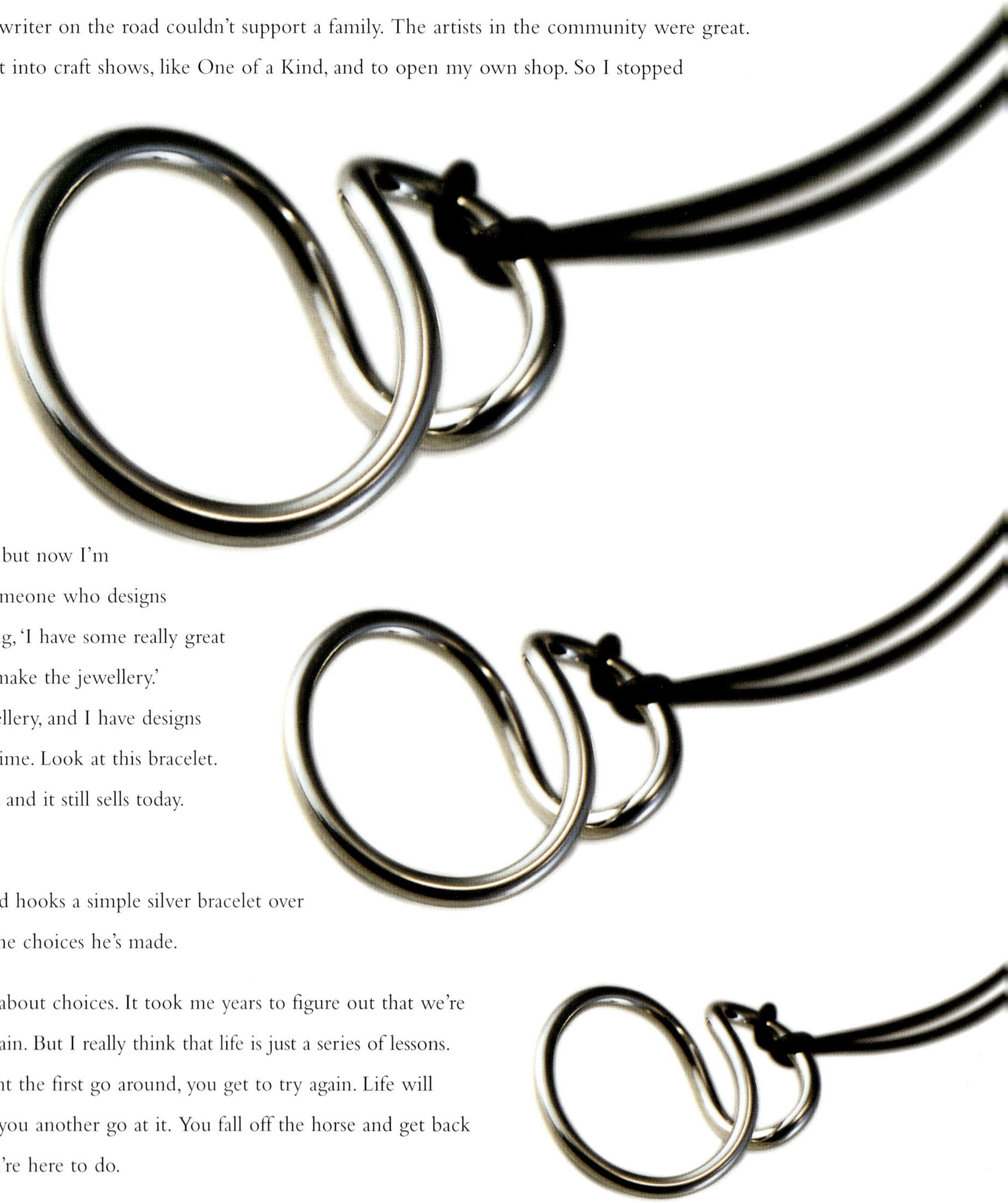

"You mentioned earlier that you were burned out."

"Well, since moving here, I typically work from 9 to 5, five or six days a week. Sometimes, I couldn't get enough of it, but now I'm ready to leap from being someone who designs and makes things to realizing, 'I have some really great designs. Someone else can make the jewellery.' The world needs great jewellery, and I have designs that have stood the test of time. Look at this bracelet. I designed this 23 years ago and it still sells today. It's timeless."

Stan reaches for my arm and hooks a simple silver bracelet over my hand. I ask him about the choices he's made.

"I learned a lot in the '60s about choices. It took me years to figure out that we're all trying to work out our pain. But I really think that life is just a series of lessons. Even if you don't get it right the first go around, you get to try again. Life will always set you up and give you another go at it. You fall off the horse and get back on to achieve whatever you're here to do.

"People don't have to live by rote. They can be free, original, spontaneous and creative. It's partly about choice, but mostly it's about recognizing that the gift of life is so precious. Life is short, and this is no dress rehearsal. Here in the heart of Ontario's richest resort community, I meet people every day who say they want freedom, but really they like to be safe."

He lowers his baritone voice to a whisper and performs a dialogue with an imaginary visitor.

"Oh God, you're so lucky, I'd love to be doing what you're doing.

Why don't you then?

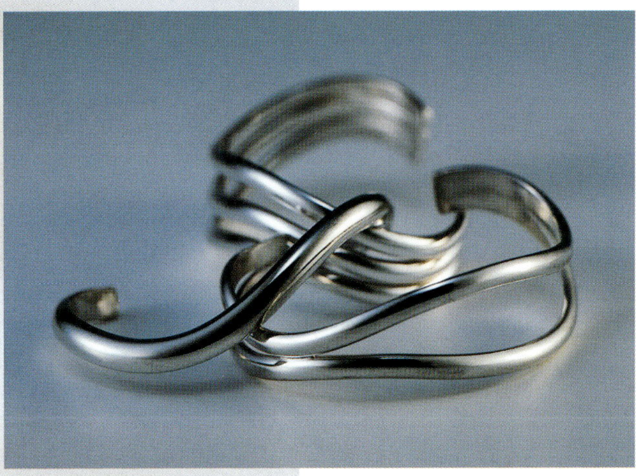

Well, I don't know exactly what I'd do.

What do you like to do?

Well, I like to paint.

Why don't you paint?

Oh, I could never paint.

Why couldn't you paint?

Oh, I just couldn't. I'm not good enough.

How would you get to be good?

Well, I'd probably have to work at it.

Why don't you work at it?

Oh, because I don't have the time, we need the money. But, oh I'd love to be free.

Then open the door to your cage.

Oh, I couldn't do that.

Why couldn't you open the door to your cage?

Because then I'd be free.

And what would happen if you were free?

Well, I'd really be on my own and it would be up to me.

And if it were up to you, what would happen?

Oh, I'd probably fail.

Well, then you probably will.

Well, I think I'll just stay in my cage."

Stan rises and reaches for his jacket, guitar and keys. "Sorry I have to quit now, but I'm late for an appointment with the local cable TV station. I'm going to perform a few of my songs."

I ask one more question. "What do you do when people choose to stay in their cage?"

"Most people want to be free, but it's hard to break out of a mould, to believe it's possible to have what you want. All you can do is make the offer.

"Allow me," he says, opening the door on a sunlit August afternoon.

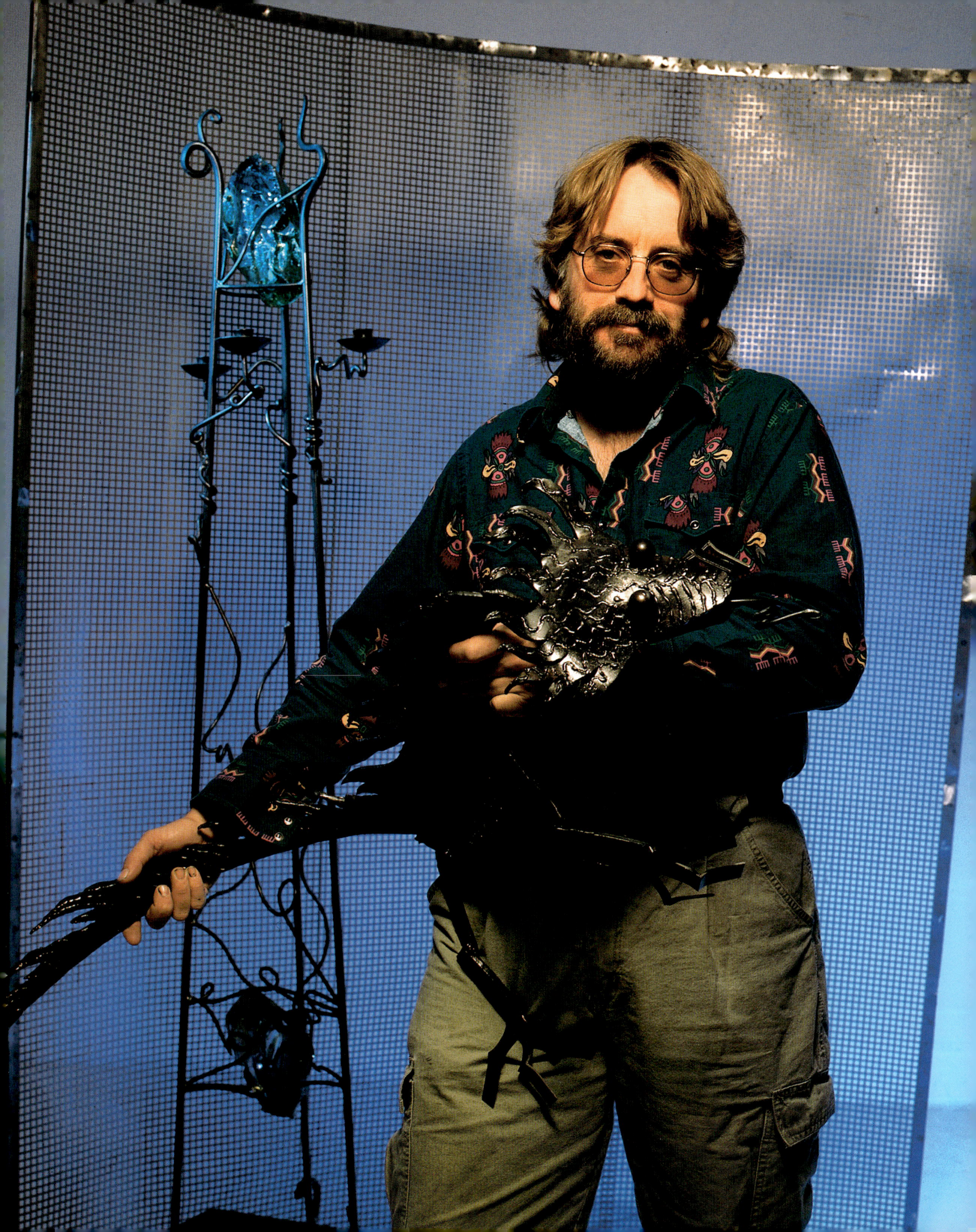

The world would have you agree with its dismal dream of limitation.
But the light would have you soar like the eagle of your sacred visions. – Alan Cohen

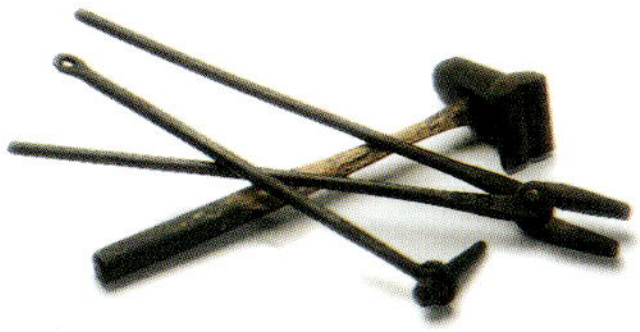

Iron Maverick

An 18-year-old high school student listens with scarcely contained amusement as the school's guidance counsellors bombard him with advice. They fear for the future of this Ontario scholar who is about to trade in his round-trip paid university education for an untried and, worse still, unconventional college program. The school year ends. Grades in hand, the student initiates a school-wide water fight. It's a parting gesture to the institution that failed to dampen his resolve.

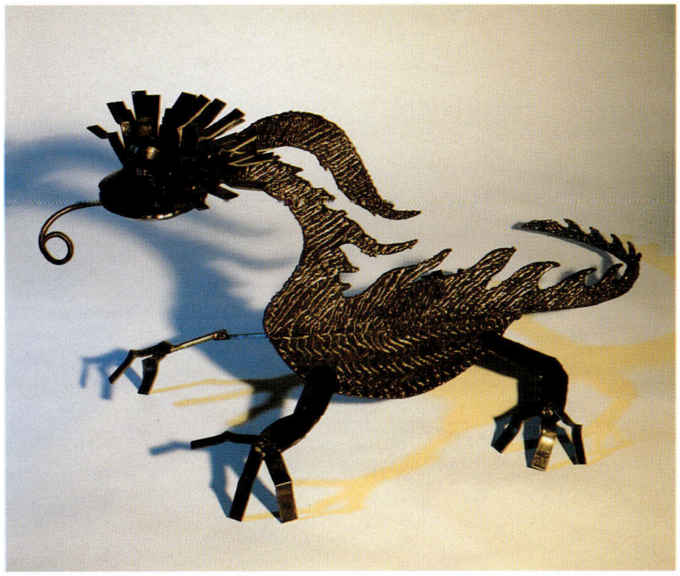

Don Pell tells this story from the porch of his studio outside Port Carling, Ontario. Leaning back in his chair, he hooks one leg over his knee. A reinforced steel toe gleams through the aged leather of his work boot. His fingers rake the hair from his eyes, leaving a black streak across his forehead and completing a picture of a man totally in his element. In the background, his wife Jane strides back and forth, armed with ironwork as she helps clear the studio in preparation for two upcoming events: the Muskoka Autumn Studio Tour and a family sabbatical leave that will begin soon after.

Don jokes about the first time the family took a week off in the late 1970s. After three days, he went into withdrawal and had to get back to his shop. For a man who deeply loves his work, a year away is a daunting prospect. What possessed him to take this step?

A need, both personal and professional, to keep on growing.

Artist blacksmith for over 20 years, Don has fashioned his own career. He's taken on leadership roles in the art community. He's witnessed firsthand the fear caused by financial uncertainty and its toll on creative expression. He is determined not to fall into the same trap. "I fear falling into complacency. I fear not being able to change or do things differently all the time. But most of all I fear the fact that artists pull back and do conservative, staid work out of economic necessity. If we don't push the limits, we'll never grow as artists."

Don's year away will provide the time and space to reinvent himself, his art, his family relationships. It will open up a new world of opportunity, enabling him to roam the continent in

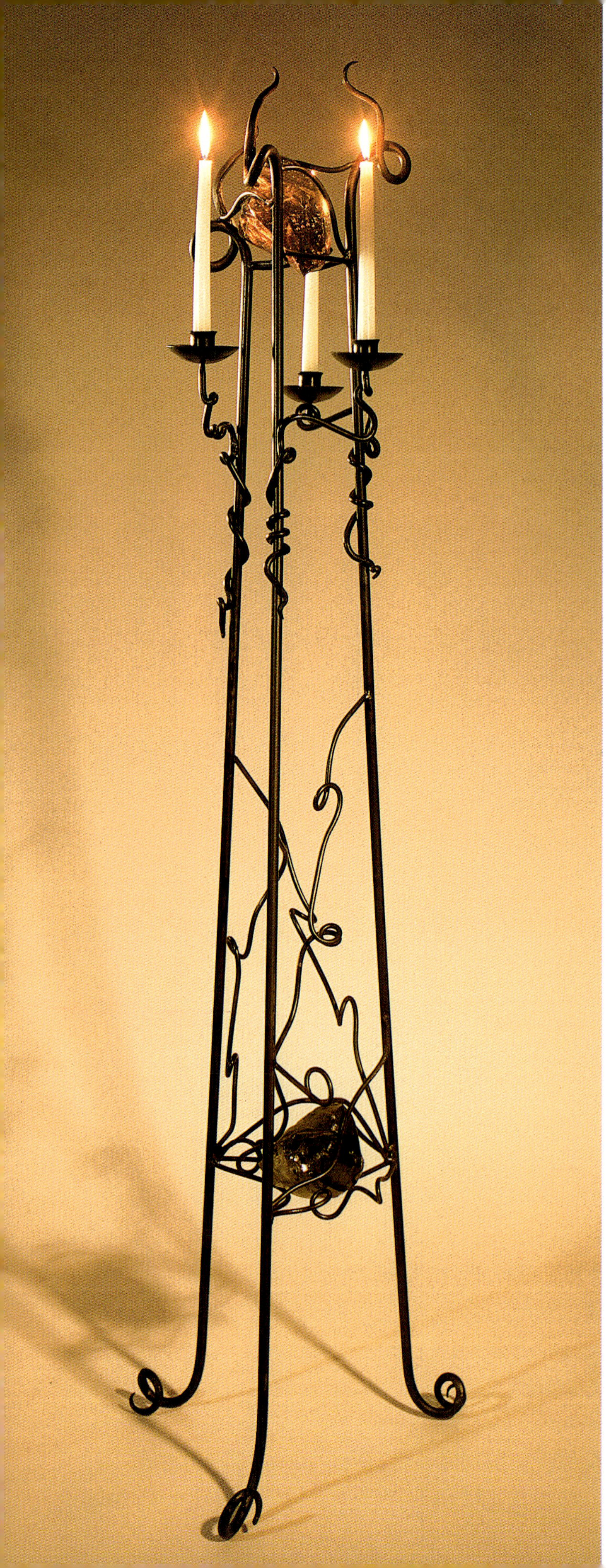

search of unique materials, find inspiration in the works of other artists, learn new skills, and push creative frontiers.

Don Pell began pioneering early in life. Born in Milton, Ontario in 1953, he spent his first seven years on a farm. Then as now, he loved to explore the woods near his home. "I was never satisfied to stay in one place. I always needed to know what was out there." When his father developed farmer's lung, the family moved to nearby Oakville. Don felt separate from his new classmates. "I was the only kid from a farm. I just knew my sensibilities and my family's were different from their's."

The youngest of three children, he saw himself from an early age as the daredevil in the family. If told he couldn't do something, that he was too young, or too small, or not allowed, he would quickly find a way to prove you wrong.

Don's first test of mettle as an adult occurred in Grade 13 when he decided to enter Sheridan College's new program for people with an interest in 3-dimensional design. He knew already the rewards of working with his hands, influenced by his father who was a farmer and agricultural blacksmith, by his mother who taught him leatherwork, and by a friend's parents who taught him weaving and pottery. An excellent student overall, Don's choice of college meant turning down university scholarships for his other two passions: history and forestry.

The school's guidance department took on Don's case with missionary zeal, trying to convince him that he would ruin his life. While some might bend under the pressure, some melt under the heat, Don's iron will sustained him. "I just knew I wanted to make things."

The first two years at Sheridan introduced him to five media: glass, clay, jewellery, wood and fibre. Glass blowing became his preferred medium and he quickly gained a reputation for creating the wild and zany. His work earned the respect of his peers and attention from professional circles. One early set of goblets earned Don an award for best student work and toured in a design exhibit.

Highlighting the modern glass movement, the exhibit opened in New York, then toured Great Britain and Europe.

In his third year at Sheridan, Don was finally introduced to metal. Immediately taken with this new medium, he began in his spare time to learn blacksmithing techniques from his father. That same year, the college cancelled classes due to a government funding shortage. Students had eight additional weeks of free time on their agenda. Not one to waste time or momentum, Don approached metal sculptor John McEwan, and asked to be his apprentice. John responded that apprenticeships were a waste of time and money, but finally relented under Don's persistence and his proposal of a 1-week trial period. "I learned more about metal sculpture from John than I learned in my entire three years at Sheridan." In return, John had an energetic assistant who stoked his wood stove at 7:30 a.m. and made coffee while the room heated up.

Sheridan College was for Don a formative learning experience in the art and business of design. It also laid the foundation for his family life. Early into the program, he met Jane McLellan, who was studying weaving. Today Jane is his business partner, wife, and mother of their three children, Erin, Michael and Alex.

The Ontario craft show landscape in 1975 was relatively barren compared to today; galleries that accepted crafts were rare and highly competitive. Diplomas in hand, Don and Jane headed east in search of a supportive arts community. They spent the first few months with family in Jane's native Prince Edward Island.

On learning about the start-up of a new art and craft village, they crossed the strait to New Brunswick and joined Opus. On a large acreage north of Fredericton, the Opus co-op included a candlemaker, leatherworker, glass worker, potter, jeweller, weaver and Don, the artist blacksmith.

Within a few years, Don had established a business in custom work that did not rely on Opus' showroom traffic. He had also learned that cooperative decision-making went against the grain of his individualist nature. Don and Jane parted company with Opus in 1980 to set up their own shop 80 kilometres away in Lakeville Corner. While Don wrought iron into functional tables, chairs, gates and wonky sculptures, Jane juggled the technical aspects of painting the final products with day-to-day business activities, such as accounting, banking and deliveries. Their business continued to grow through craft and trade shows, custom work and wholesale channels such as restaurants and hotels.

By 1985, the couple had two years of backlog before them. In the 10 years since they had arrived in New Brunswick, they had rarely taken a vacation, working long hours first to get the business off the ground, then to keep up with demand. They began to consider moving back to Ontario, if for no other reason than it would enable them to slow down while they rebuilt their customer base.

E-Mail Greetings

"Here we are in Palm Springs. We came here in November from central California to find somewhere warm. Last month, while out exploring we came across the area's oldest nursery. It also happens to be an artist colony, and after talking with the owner a few times, we were invited to join them for as long as we could.

"The campground we're staying in is fabulous. I work outdoors in a beautiful nursery with only a roof over us, looking at snow capped mountains while surrounded by palm trees and an amazing variety of plants in bloom.

"I've been able to blow glass again, and do some bronze foundry work. It's been rewarding to share knowledge and ideas with a supportive group of artists – a glass blower, four painters, two metal sculptors, a potter, a clay sculptor, two stone carvers, two stained glass workers, batik artist, basket maker, and others. We've met amazing people from all over, and made life-long friends.

"In all, being here has fulfilled a long-term dream." – Don Pell, *January 30, 1998*

Two months before their planned departure for Ontario, their backlog of orders almost filled, they received a call from John McEwan, the sculptor with whom Don had apprenticed. Having no knowledge of their plans, John proposed that Don take over his blacksmith shop in Hillsdale, Ontario, a small town west of Barrie. They accepted.

The next few years were nomadic for Don, Jane and family. Their first house, in Barrie, required a 7-mile commute to John's shop. After years of working within walking distance of his home, Don found the drive intolerable. They soon bought a house in Hillsdale, but it became subject to zoning restrictions that limited Don's ability to work from home. Exhibiting at the Muskoka Arts and Crafts summer show, they toyed with the idea of yet another move. In the end, moving was more appealing than continuing their battle with the municipality. By 1989, Don and Jane had set up a studio in Port Carling and joined the Muskoka Autumn Studio Tour.

As for Don's work during this time, it also evolved toward a more comfortable niche. Considered a wacko in the Maritimes for some of his more outlandish sculptures, Don attempted to tame his style to suit a more traditional Ontario market. Following a project in the early 1990s with an Arizona designer, the family went on vacation to New Mexico, visiting as many art galleries as possible in their 2-week tour. Don quickly noticed more humour and whimsy than in work he had seen in Ontario.

"I can't be conservative any more," Don announced on his return. Friends laughed: "When have you ever been conservative?" Others warned he'd never make a living on the weird stuff he was producing. "It can't be done" only fortified his conviction.

Don's new work abandoned straight lines, angles and simple, predictable casts for more free-flowing and experimental forms without structure or order. He began incorporating unusual material from nature that he sourced in his travels. Chunks of raw glass embedded in free-standing metal sculptures. Stone slabs set on ornate wrought iron table bases. Purple slate from North Dakota that forms

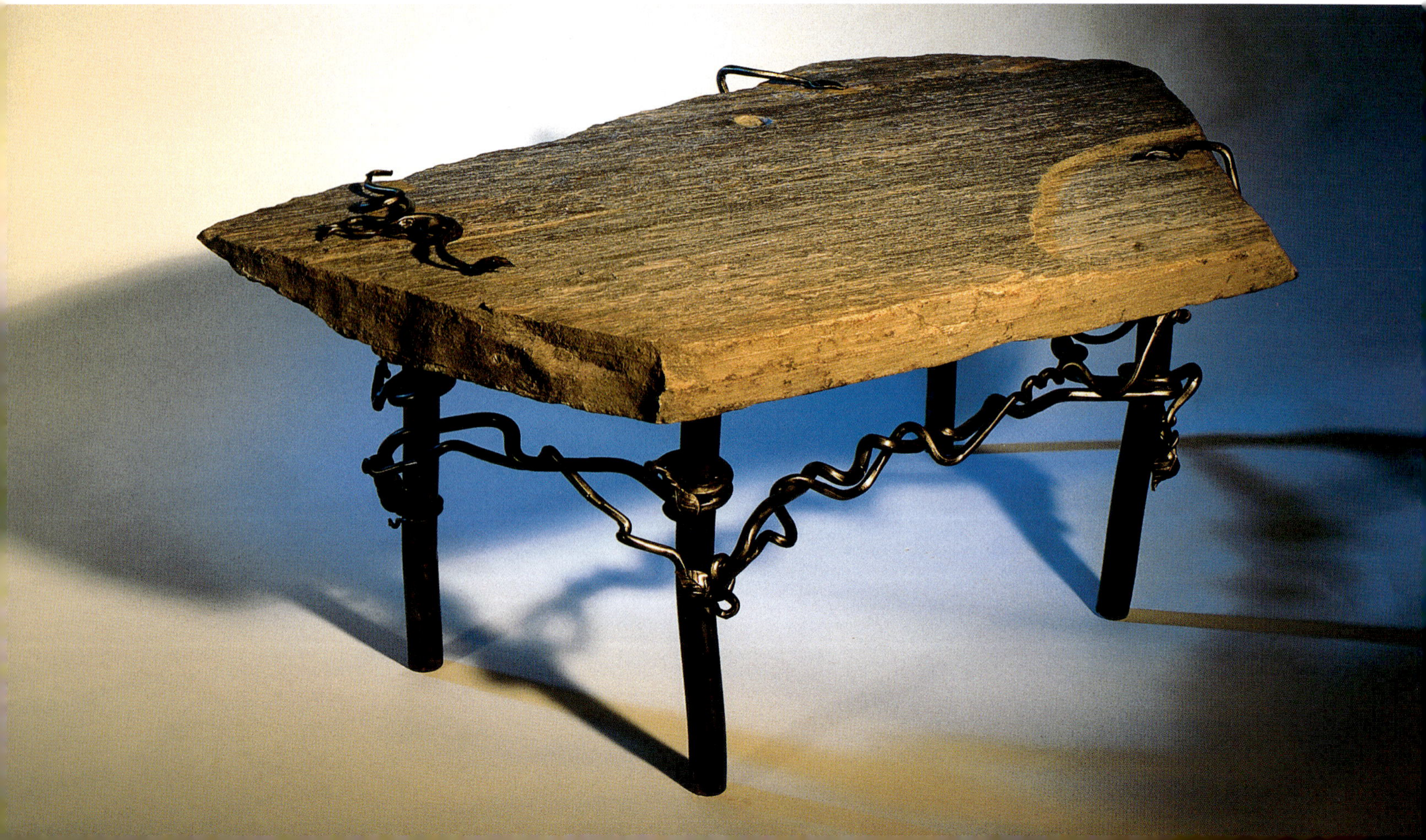

a colourful backdrop to the light from candelabras. Whimsical earth men with found objects for body parts.

Don's change in approach affected more than his work. "I became a much happier person. I also attracted another type of clientele, people who express their individuality by what they surround themselves with. They're not trying to look like the guy next door, and I'm not competing with Canadian Tire, Sears, and Home Depot."

Today, when asked to do custom work, Don encourages customers to hand-pick their own materials, to carefully select a geode or stone slab that calls out to them. "I want people to react to my work. Either good or bad, I don't care, but I don't want ho-hum." Indeed, not everyone appreciates his work. Recently, one woman walked out of his studio within seconds of entering. Intrigued by her about-face, he followed her out and asked why. "There's not enough structure in there. I just can't deal with it," she exclaimed.

In over 20 years as an artist blacksmith, Don has never accepted that an artist cannot also be a business person. Neither traditional in his work nor his approach to business, he nonetheless respects both his artistic and his financial bottom line. He has chosen to do one-of-a-kind, whimsical pieces, trading conservative clients for those who seek the unconventional. Keeping forms intact without trying to smooth their raw singularity maintains his respect for nature. His avoidance of reproducing identical items ensures each piece's uniqueness. Though he hasn't stepped inside a bank for 10 years and occasionally engages in water fights with customers in view, he made a promise long ago that his children would never suffer financially for his decision to become an artist. He's kept that promise.

He has also remained true to his maverick nature. Among the reactions to his sabbatical are two of the seven deadly sins – envy and fear. Don responds quickly to both. He encourages the envious to venture forth in their own way and time. As for the fearful, "I believe that confronting your fear is like standing on the edge of a cliff. Once you take the first step, it's over."

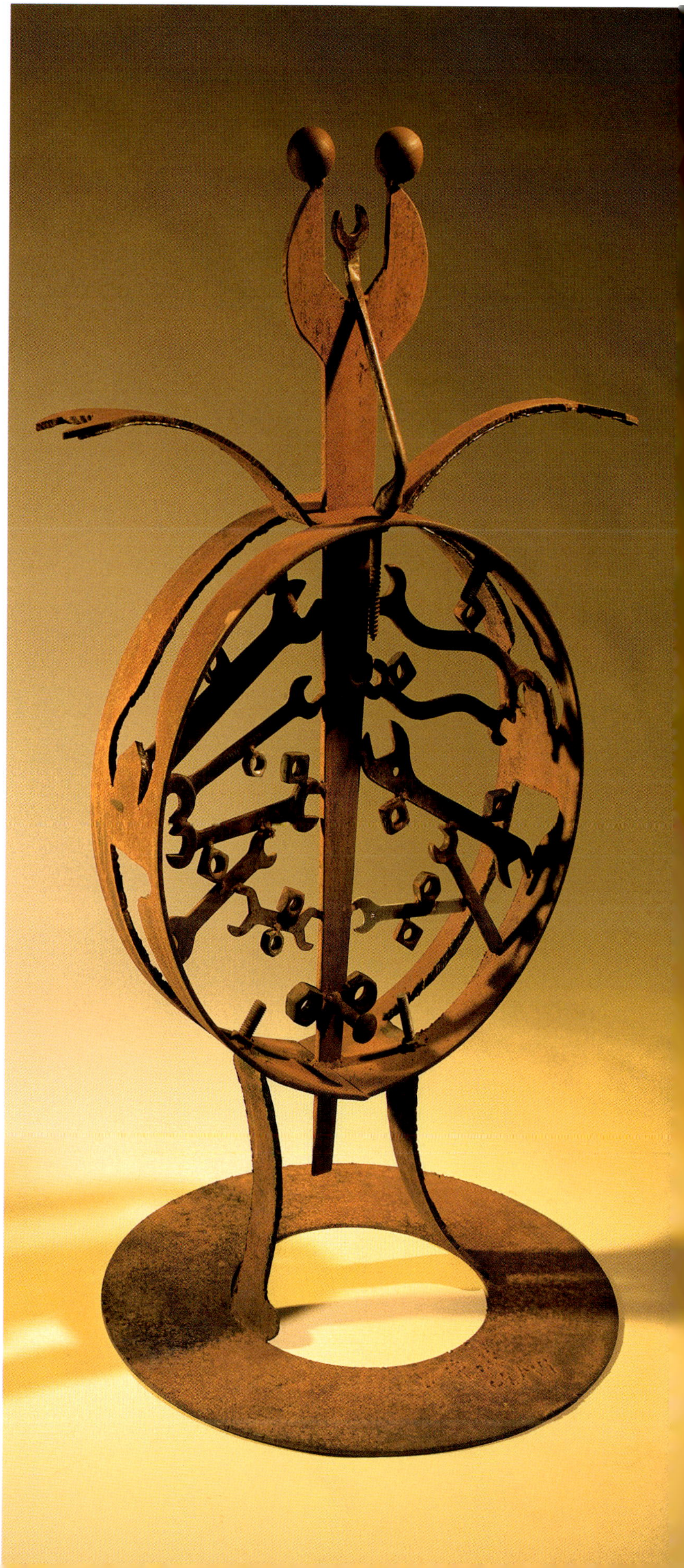

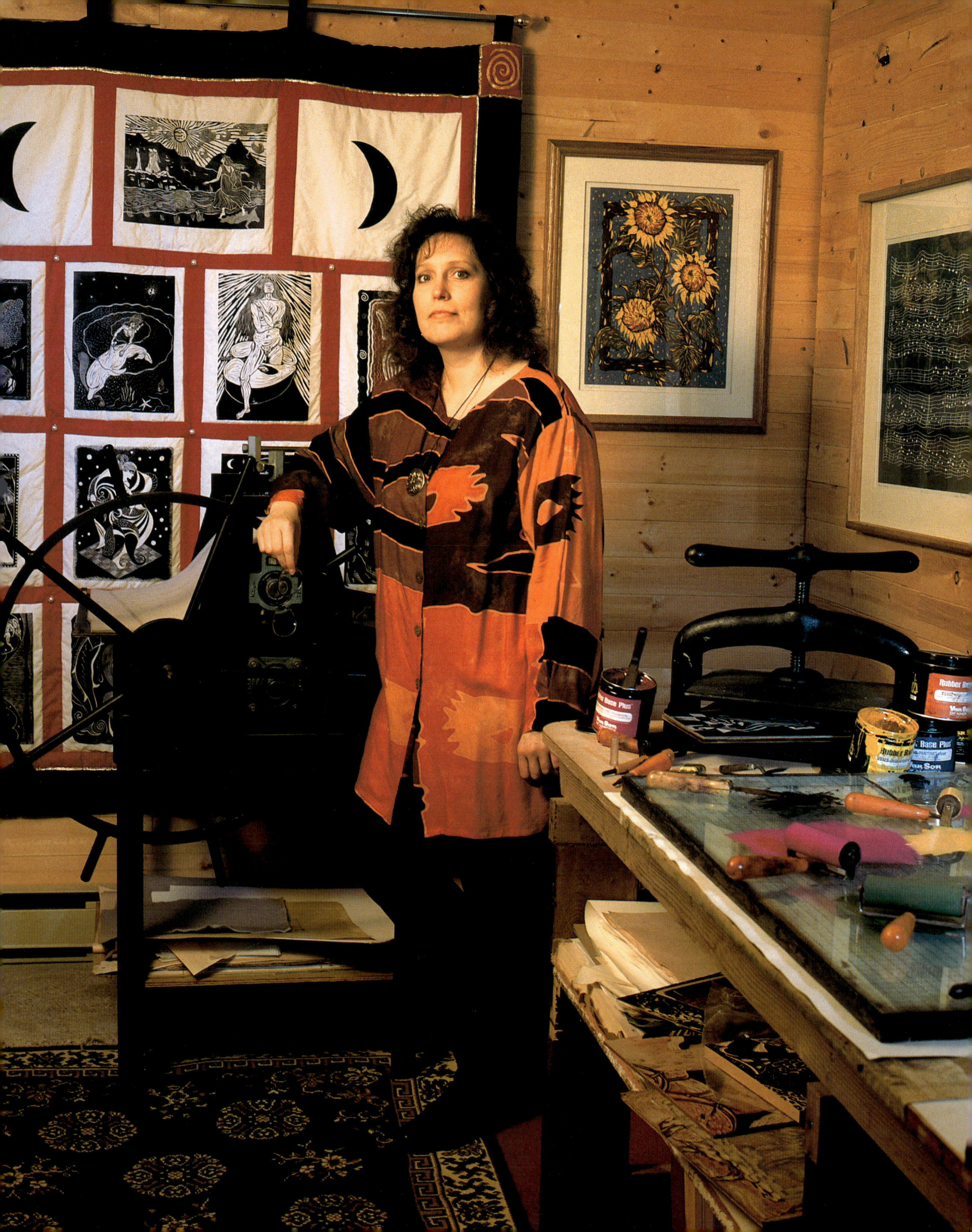
Base Plus
Base Plus
Van Son

There are many good and highly gifted mystics, but almost without exception they are unhappy. You might have been just such a one. But instead, God be praised, you are a craftsman; you have conquered your own world in which you can be lord and creator, instead of having remained an imperfect thinker. – Hermann Hesse

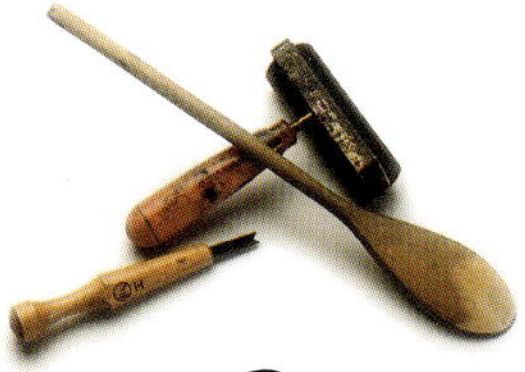

Inner Landscapes

Two visitors cross the threshold of Tapawingo, Janet Stahle-Fraser's studio on the outskirts of Baysville. A preliminary sweep of Janet's unique woodcuts, linocuts, etchings and stone lithographs halts them like deer in the headlights of a car. "Do you do Muskoka landscapes," they ask, finally.

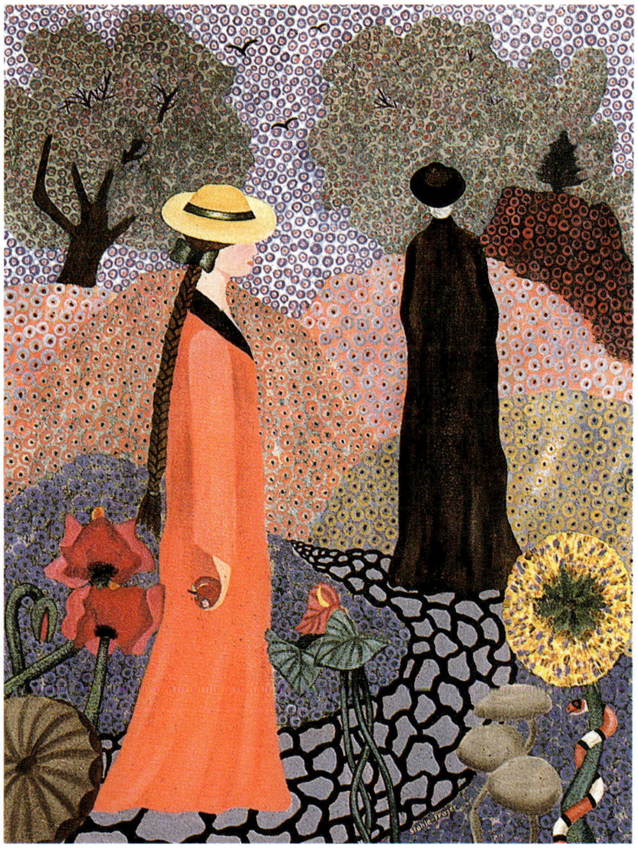

"No," Janet replies. "Not outer landscapes. I do inner landscapes."

Those curious to see these inner landscapes cross her pine log living room and enter an alcove where Janet displays her handmade prints. Subject matter varies, from dream-like abstractions to instantly recognizable cultural icons. Eventually, all eyes are drawn toward *A Woman's Book of Hours*. A white glove atop the hand-bound limited edition signals a ceremony through which readers enter the story within.

Completed during what Janet describes as a "deep winter" in 1995, the book consists of 13 limited-edition linocuts and hand-printed poems, each appearing in a unique calligraphic style. The poems and illustrations depict a woman's journey through the dark and desolate hours from midnight to six a.m., and her rebirth during the daylight hours of morning. No other piece of Janet's work expresses so elegantly her artistic eclecticism, nor captures so completely her inner landscapes.

Born in Brantford, Ontario and raised in nearby Elmira, Janet Stahle was the second of four children. At age 15, in a matter of months, she faced sorrows and losses most of us don't encounter until much later in life. A younger brother died in a car accident, her parents separated, another brother left with her father, and a sister married. These events triggered an inward journey that began as Janet's salvation and ultimately became her gift back to the world.

Janet describes herself as wild during high school. She cut classes and gave attitude, but still achieved high marks. "I was always asking questions. 'How does that work? Why are you doing it that way?' I had to know." At age 18, while browsing at the University Plaza Coles in Dundas, she thumbed through Immanuel Kant's *Critique of Pure Reason*. While the book made little sense to her at the time, she bought it and tucked it away. She finished her studies at Hamilton Collegiate Institute, excelling in the sciences and math.

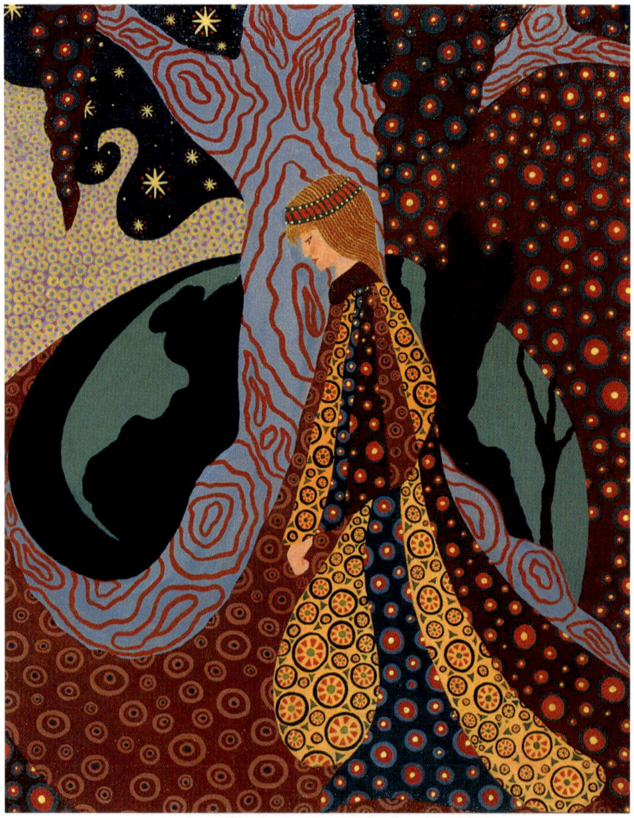

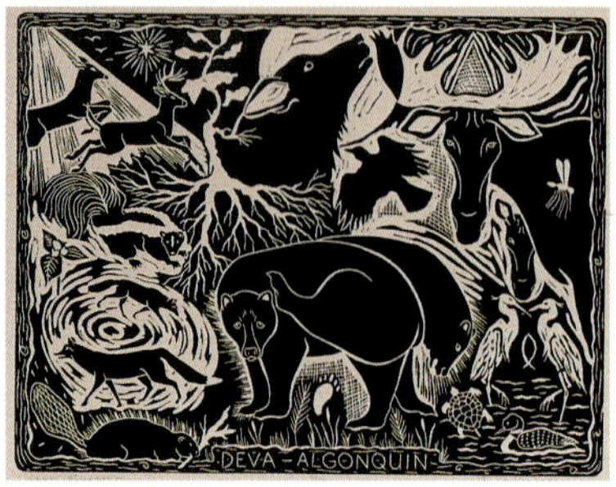

Fascinated by the science and mechanics of health, Janet entered the University of Guelph's Applied Human Nutrition program. She was soon disappointed, finding more similarities to home economics than science, and learning little about the complex workings of the human body that so intrigued her. In her second year, Janet did an about face, taking courses in drama, fine arts, psychology and philosophy. From her first philosophy course, she was hooked. Two years later, her undergraduate degree behind her, she began a Master's degree in philosophy.

Early into the first year of her Master's, a letter from a friend unsettled her: "I can think of no better way to screw up a life than doing a Master's in philosophy," the friend wrote. The observation instilled in Janet a desire for balance between understanding life's mysteries through observation and experiencing them through action. She continued pursuing her Master's, but part-time. With growing enthusiasm she also studied mixed media, sculpture, life drawing and anatomy. All the while, Janet supported herself by working full time.

"I've worked at more jobs than I care to remember," Janet says. Maybe 40 or 50, part- and full-time jobs during and following her studies. The jobs may not have been memorable, but many experiences were.

Snapshot: Janet as night clerk at Guelph's Royal Hotel, admiring photos of another woman's grandchildren. The woman is a stripper taking a break between performances in the hotel's lounge. Snapshot: Janet as McMaster University office worker, practising smoke rings at her desk. On her desk is a full ashtray and an empty package of wine-tipped cigars; in her heart, a renewed conviction that smoking sucks. Snapshot: Janet as French language supply teacher, struggling to maintain order with a one-word vocabulary: "oui." Another snapshot, this one the first in an ongoing album: seeking a physical outlet for her energy, Janet buys a bicycle from Dave Fraser, a friend of a friend. Many snapshots later: Janet and Dave, as they sign a wedding registry.

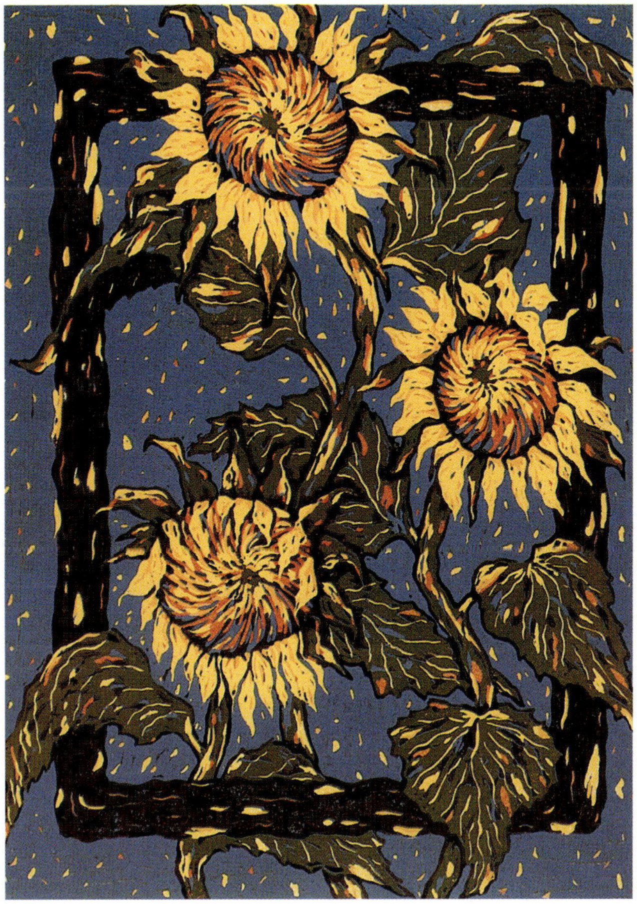

Shortly after marrying in 1980, Janet and Dave moved to Muskoka in search of a simpler life. Living in a basement apartment in her mother-in-law's home, they saved money and kept watch for land on which they could build a place of their own. Misfortune returned in 1983 when Dave, working on a construction site, fell from a second storey roof. At first, Dave's chances for survival were slim. Suffering a collapsed lung, crushed vertebrae and a cranial fracture, he lay in a coma for three weeks.

Eventually Dave's health returned and they soon began building a log home, naming it Tapawingo, a word used by Six Nations Indians for "Place of Joy." Janet and Dave's Tapawingo was ready for habitation in 1988.

It was not until the early 1990s that Janet began pursuing a full-time career in art. During the 1980s, she completed a series of short-term public relations contracts with the Ministry of Environment's Dorset Research Centre and the Muskoka District Health Unit, positions that enabled her to hone her photographic and writing skills. Fascinated by the interplay of light and dark in black and white photography, Janet experimented with high contrast toning, reticulated negatives and special paper to achieve unique visual and textural effects. Sales of her photography at craft shows provided the psychic income her day jobs lacked, but little support for the mortgage.

In the mid 1980s, Janet started taking a serious interest in printmaking. She acquired a second-hand Praga etching press from a local artist and enlisted her brother Buck to build a relief press for producing woodcuts and linocuts. A favourite piece of equipment, it's introduced to studio tour visitors as the "Buck-built." During the next 10 years, she studied various aspects of printmaking – lithography, etching, woodcuts, linocuts, bromoil and transfer photography, as well as multimedia, calligraphy and bookmaking – through the University of Waterloo, Canadore College and the Haliburton School of Fine Art.

With time, Janet gained recognition for her unusual prints. In 1991, the chairman of the Lake of Bays Artisans invited her to join their studio tour. "I don't have a studio," she replied, though flattered by the invitation. Looking around Janet's spacious front room, he shrugged: "What's the matter with this room?"

That same year, Janet finished her last public relations contract. Every May, she now converts her front room into the studio from which she manages a busy summer business. Then she spends autumn, winter and spring in her brightly lit downstairs workshop creating print works.

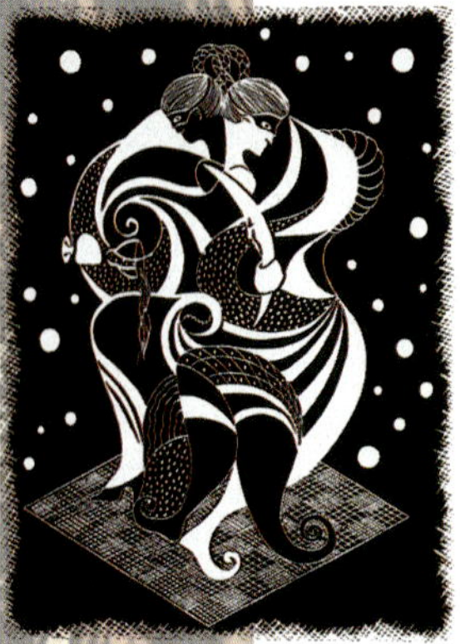

Besides exhibiting with Pentad, a group of five women artists, Janet has shown in numerous group exhibitions, including The McMichael Autumn Art Show, an annual event featuring over 50 juried artists at the McMichael Gallery[9] in Kleinburg, Ontario. In 1996, she joined the Muskoka Autumn Studio Tour.

"I can see now why I was never happy in any job. It just wasn't where I was supposed to be, and I denied that for many years." Today, Janet doesn't need to set aside quality time for herself. All day is quality time, time that corresponds with rhythms natural to her own flow.

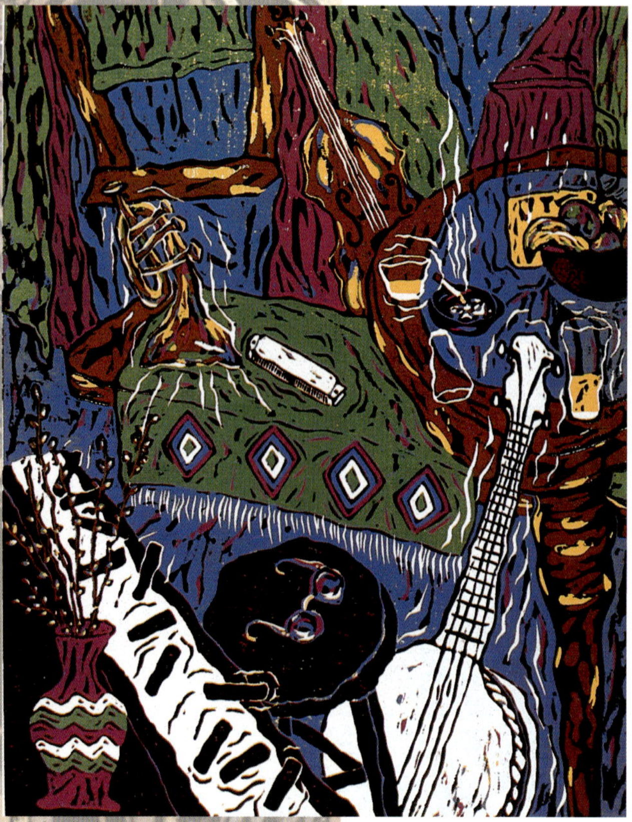

Mornings and afternoons, Janet concentrates on production. She works in silence, engaged in a meditative process that draws a rhythm from paint rollers hissing over her wood blocks, or bird songs filtering through the window. Evenings are reserved for creative thinking, when she designs, sketches, notes ideas in a journal and plans new projects. Summertime means early to bed and early to rise. In winter, the reverse takes hold, when she might become so immersed in a creative effort she'll work until 2:00 or 3:00 in the morning.

Asked what she thinks prevents others from pursuing work they love, Janet scarcely hesitates, thrice repeating a single word: fear. Has Janet ever felt that fear? "All the time."

Having faced the death of her brother and the near loss of her husband, Janet sees death as a powerful factor in her decision to pursue art as a career. "I know I'm going to die one day. And I finally decided I don't want to live one more day doing something I hate."

Living with less financial security has meant making material and lifestyle sacrifices. "Almost every penny of disposable income went toward equipment and material for my art, not

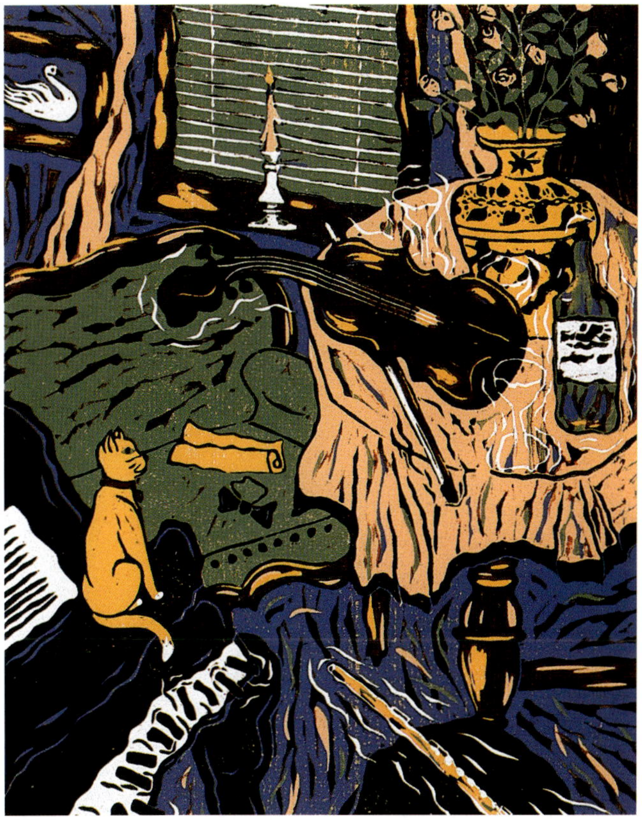

clothes or nights out." Would she go back to a traditional day job? "I suppose if things got bad enough and I needed to buy groceries... then again, it would have to be the absolute last resort."

Janet's love of philosophy continues to guide her life, 25 years after picking up *Critique of Pure Reason*. "I see philosophy as a tug on my ear to listen to life and my being. I'm still like a kid, always asking why, always reflecting on what life means and trying to bring that out in art." While her study of philosophy enables Janet to maintain a childlike curiosity about the purpose and meaning of life, it's her art that engages her fully in its playful dance.

A Woman's Book of Hours

Books of hours contain prayers or meditations for certain hours of the day, days of the week, months or seasons. In the Middle Ages, these books were hand-copied and illustrated by scribes. Woodcut illustrations began to appear in the late 15th century.

Janet Stahle-Fraser's book of hours contains 13 poems and linocuts that recount a woman's inner journey, beginning at midnight, the soul's darkest hour, and ending at noon, the height of day.

The book begins with "Call for Lunar Dancers," in which we confront darkness and disillusionment. Turning inward, we shed the trappings of the outer world and learn to trust our inner guide. As each hour of the clock chimes, we learn a new lesson. In the early light, we test our newfound strength and wisdom, achieved as we accept the cycle of creation and destruction through which all lives must pass. As we approach the noon hour, our disappearing shadow suggests a temporary surrender of the source of our power for both good and evil. And the cycle begins anew.

Each poem in *A Woman's Book of Hours* is hand-scribed in a distinct calligraphic style and illustrated with a hand-printed linocut. The pages are hand-sewn into handmade covers. Only 13 copies of the book exist. All are numbered.

The images in *A Woman's Book of Hours* also appear in an award-winning wall hanging. Janet fashioned the wall hanging in response to requests for readings from the book. Listeners can now follow both her words and images as she progresses through the hours.

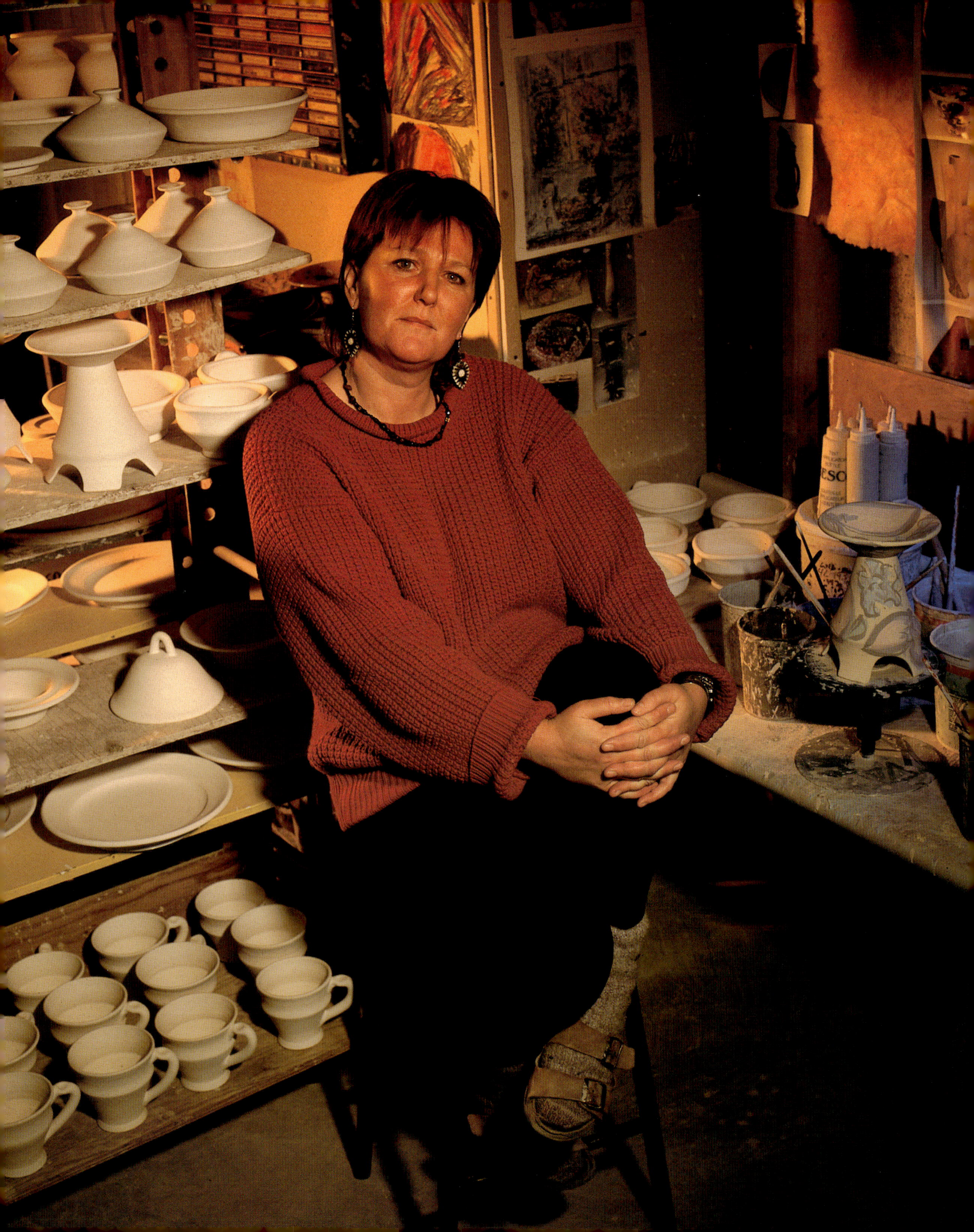

You do not have to be good. You do not have to walk on your knees for 100 miles through the desert repenting.
You only have to let the soft animal of your body love what it loves. – Mary Oliver

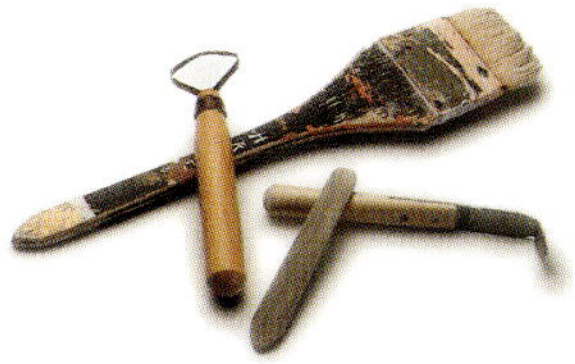

Permission to Play

Linda Wright is a potter. Making a living as a potter isn't easy, but "it's music to my ears when people say they start their day with my coffee mug or cereal bowl. To be able to connect with others and be part of their daily rituals is reward in itself."

Linda throws clay into functional forms – dinnerware, teapots, oil lamps, planters, bowls, jars, chip and dip platters. Not just a celebration of everyday life, Linda's work is also a celebration of colour. Spontaneous splashes of pure joy that jive and jitterbug on a shiny ceramic dance floor.

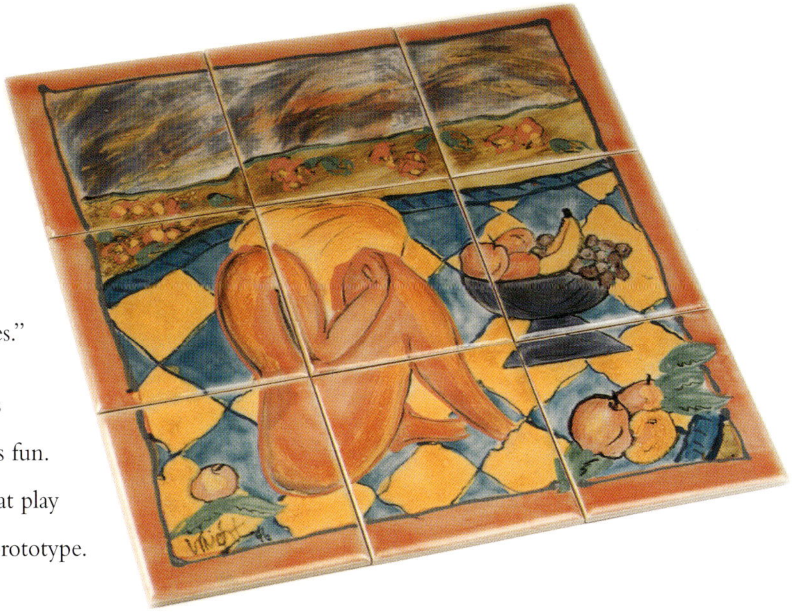

The walls of Linda's first studio, a basement in Hamilton, were sunshine yellow, her wheel, watermelon pink. You'd never guess from her first pieces. Colour slipped out tentatively. A dab here, a dab there. A lot of white glaze. "Everyone wanted earth tones. People would come to my booth at craft shows and comment on my colours. Then they would go next door and buy the brown ones."

One day in 1988, while preparing for a show, Linda let go. She was tired and had one mug left to glaze. Out came lots of colour. It was fun. Better still, it looked good. She decided to keep it as a reminder that play is good too, but that was the mug customers wanted. It became a prototype. Colourful studio. Colourful pottery. Colourful life.

Linda, Day 1: on April 6, 1952, Linda Wright is born in Edinburgh, Scotland. She's the first of two daughters, and her parents are proud. Except she's late. Had she arrived just a couple hours earlier, her father would have received a full year's tax rebate. "You were born late and you're still bloody late," he reminds her to this day.

Like most people who are naturally late, Linda doesn't stick to rigid plans. She prefers to go with the flow. She did, however, plan to have one child. She made that clear to her life partner, Andrew Gibson. Then the ultrasound showed she was carrying two.

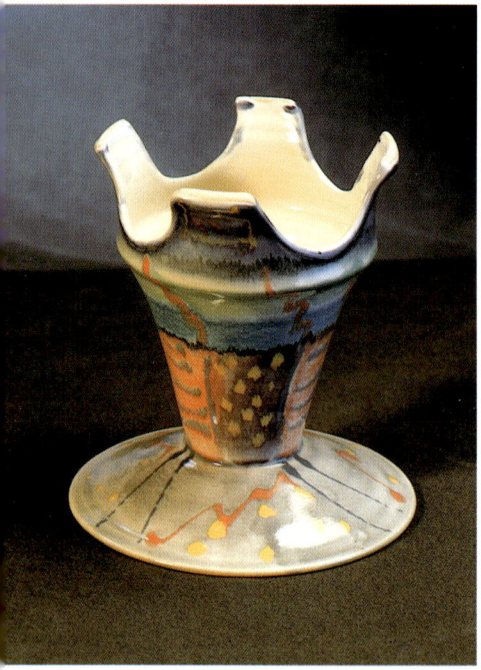

She had also planned for a birth in February, her quiet season. Twin daughters Morgan and Bronwyn entered the world on November 26, 1988, 10 weeks early and days before the year's biggest event, the One of a Kind show. Their arrival put everything on hold. Cancel the show. Cancel the Christmas orders. Write off the losses. Genetic revenge, Linda calls it. Some things you just can't plan. Others are definitely within your control.

Linda at 22: Crossing the Atlantic aboard a Boeing 747, she has a broken leg and a broken heart. She's leaving the known world – family, friends, work, community – and heading into the unknown. "All my friends were getting married, and I needed a break from the class structure in Scotland. Canada seemed like paradise. Canadians were lovely, outgoing and friendly. I liked their accents. People back home thought I was a big brave girl, but I had a return ticket in case things didn't work out." The big brave girl drank whisky to calm her nerves and cried all across the ocean.

She never used the return portion of her ticket. "The first year was torture, especially being displaced from my family. But I became a much stronger person. Here, no one knew me, I had no history, I was forced to find out and face who I was and what I wanted."

After graduating from McAdams Secretarial School in Edinburgh, she had worked as a secretary. "My first job

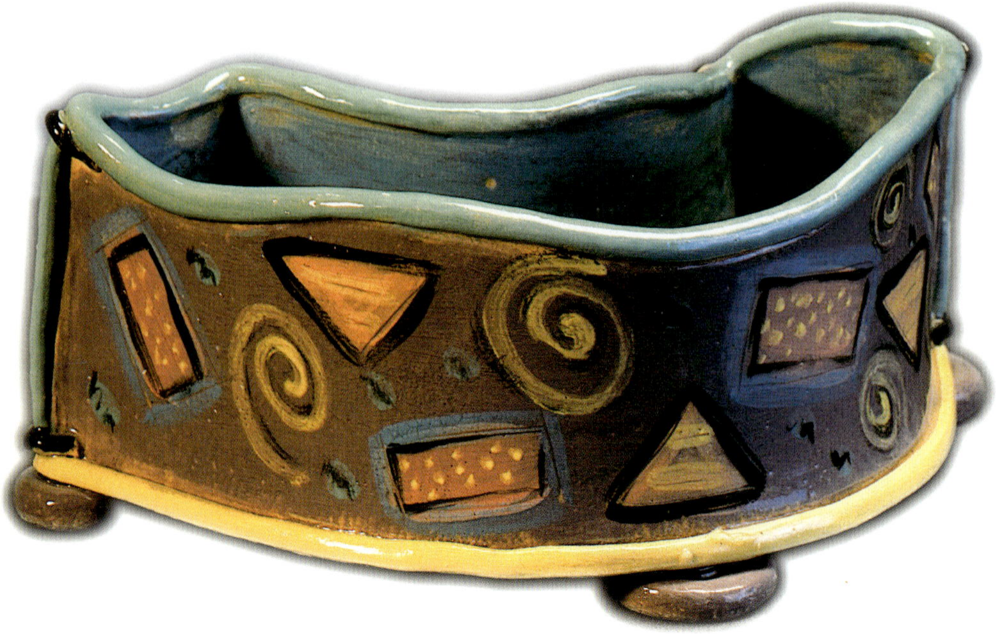

was assistant to the assistant to Mr. Guilmour, a serious Scotsman who wore a kilt. He used to point to his watch every morning when I arrived and scowl. Finally, he took me aside and said 'This is not worrrrking out Linda. You'rrrre always late and you'rrrre always making mistakes.' I was terrible at typing and shorthand, and couldn't spell. I really wanted to be a vet but had been told girls aren't smart enough to go to university."

Linda moved on to the University of Edinburgh, as secretary to a team of researchers. It turned out to be good training for Linda's first job in Canada, working for the Toronto General Hospital's Department of Psychiatry. After two years, she left to work for the assistant dean of University of Toronto's graduate school.

Surrounded by academics and students of all ages, she figured maybe she was smart enough to go to university. She began exploring a variety of subjects, including anthropology, English literature, and Greek mythology, for no other reason than a desire to learn.

Linda at 27: a women's studies course in 1979 opens her eyes to concepts of power and self-empowerment. "I was paralyzed by the thought of sleeping in my house alone, so I lived communally for many years. This course made me realize how much power I'd given up all those years, how controlled I was by fear."

Training in self-defense restored a sense of power. She then taught self-defense for the next five years, overcoming a phobia that had restricted her for most of her adult life. But it wasn't just a lesson in staying home alone. "I learned self-reliance. I learned how to take care of myself."

Conquer one fear, and others are that much easier to tackle. In 1980, she realized it was time for other changes. She had tired of pushing paper. "It was unsatisfying. There was nothing of me in it. I felt empty."

Evening courses in pottery had introduced her to the tactile rewards of clay. The turning point was a 2-day workshop in pottery with Les Manning, a potter who then was head of the ceramics department at the Banff School of Fine Arts.[10] "I soaked up information like a sponge, asked him all kinds of questions about how to go back to school, how to become a production potter."

Linda at 30: in 1982, she enters Sheridan College. "It felt like someone had given me the key to kindergarten so I could play for three years. I flourished. I finally had a means to express myself that made me feel at home. Writing papers and learning a potter's skills are both major struggles. But with pottery, I felt an instinctiveness about it, an ability to trust what I was doing at a much deeper level."

Linda spent her first summer apprenticing with Scott Barnum, a Dundas Valley potter. Scott invited Linda to replace him as committee member with the Ontario Pottery Association. There she met Andrew Gibson, at the time a ceramics technologist, today her partner in life and work.

That same summer, the couple camped on Andrew's property near Muskoka's Three Mile Lake. Linda loved the water, the trees, the rocks. Hated the bugs. As for winter, they were blissfully unaware of its glacial effect on water pipes and fingertips, and contemplated a move to the area. Like most wishful thoughts, it circled back each year around the same time – set aside, but never quite tossed out.

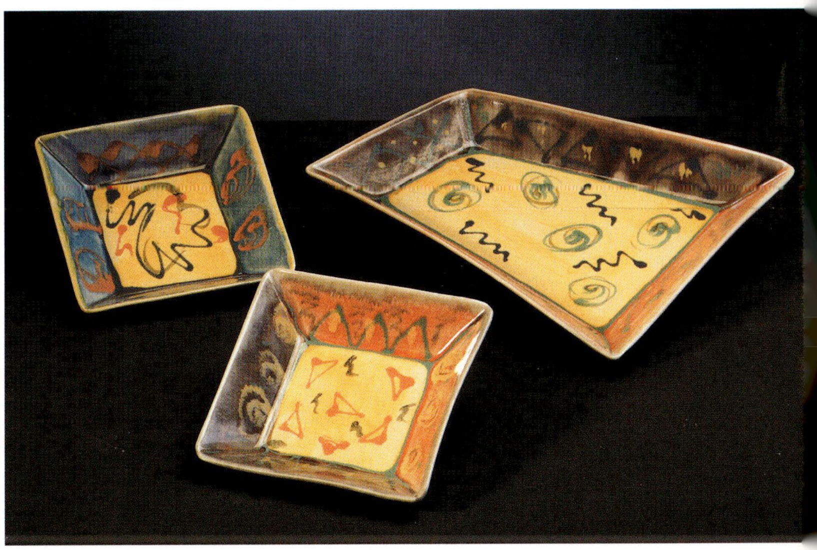

Three years later, a wide-eyed graduate, Linda was invited to take over Scott's studio while he went on sabbatical to Wales. The newly qualified potter was thrilled and daunted. She now had a fully equipped studio. She could even walk to work.

A dream fulfilled, at first glance. Then there's reality. "I had this idea in my head of teapot as metaphor, that I could be a creative artist and make these wonky one-of-a-kind objects. It was a big disappointment to learn that people wanted matching sets."

To supplement her income, Linda waitressed, then worked part-time as a secretary with a group of interior designers who supported her ambitions. "They encouraged me to do what I wanted and accommodated my need to prepare for shows."

When Scott returned, Linda and Andrew moved to Hamilton, where Andrew owned and managed a bookstore. No longer willing to accept make-do jobs, Linda assessed her resources. First challenge: the dark basement that was to become her studio. She lit its concrete walls with sunshine yellow. Next challenge: a wheel. She ordered one, then arrived at the manufacturer's with a bucket of paint, watermelon pink. Though startled by her request not to paint it the standard steel grey, he complied. Final challenge: finished pots and a means to sell them.

Linda limited herself to one or two lines of pottery that would sell well, then put her energies into promoting her work. "I hoofed it. I called shops to show my pottery, was my own door-to-door sales agent. It was scary – my stomach was always in a knot. But it paid off. I still have two or three stores I started with back then."

By the twins' birth in 1988, Linda had a healthy business base. The new parents decided they wanted to raise the girls in the country. House hunting outside Hamilton led them to a Viceroy home display. They were impressed with its clean, open, light-inviting atmosphere. They dusted off the idea of moving to Muskoka and began making plans in earnest.

Linda at 38: up goes the Northshore Pottery sign. "Unless I was prepared

Joy of Colour

"The most common response to my pottery is: 'It's so fun, so bright and cheerful.' Colour is essential to my pottery and to me.

"When I started out, I'm not sure I realized why colour had such appeal. I just remember struggling to find a style that was my own, one that I could call home. So many potters were into the dark, muted hues of brown, blue and green. I wanted to be different, so I guess I gravitated toward colour. Discovering majolica – a 15th century Italian glazing technique that uses several colours over a white glaze – was probably my main influence.

"Today, I have a better understanding of the role colour plays in our lives. It helps us to express ourselves, even if it's just by the way we dress or the way we decorate our homes.

"It's hard to feel dowdy and down in a bright red dress. But surround yourself with nothing but grey and eventually, you feel grey. Some colours make us feel joyful. A bright blue we associate with clear skies – it lifts you up. A warm yellow, we associate with the sun – it makes you glow."

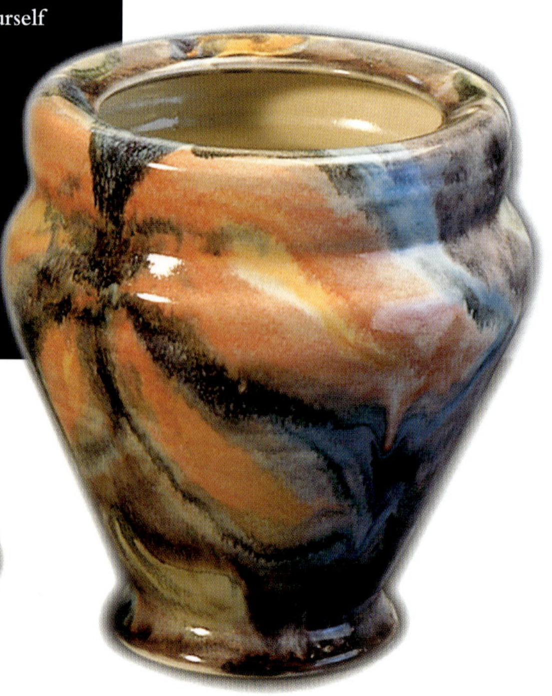

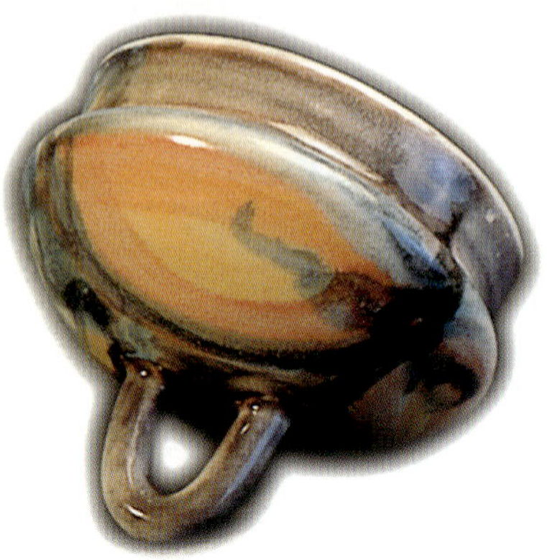

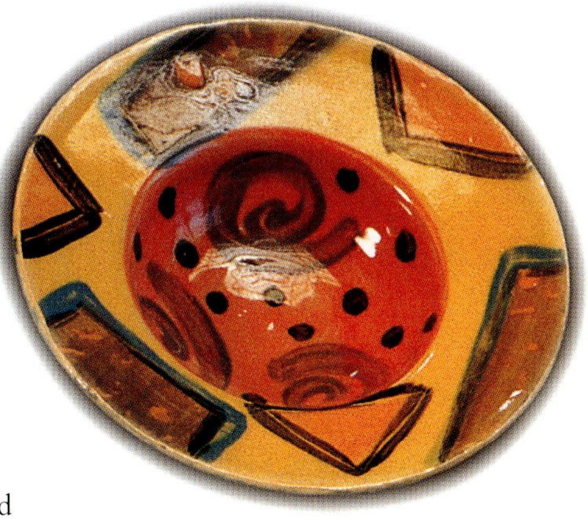

to work for someone else, there was no other way to make a living up here. So, I had to get serious about producing a lot of work. I became obsessed with getting things done. I got into a rhythm of throwing 60 mugs or bowls at a time. I had no time to myself. For a few years, I hardly changed my designs. I had two lines – one with two colours and one in black. I worked the craft show circuit and would literally cancel my life before a show. The good part was that I was making money. The bad part was that I had become a machine. I was miserable."

Slowly Linda learned to give herself permission to play. She still struggles to find that elusive balance between work and play, but is confident she's heading in the right direction. She keeps to the same demanding schedule of shows, an active participant in the Muskoka Arts and Crafts summer and winter shows, the Muskoka Autumn Studio Tour, and One of a Kind. For the last four years, however, Linda has taken time for herself and experiments regularly with new shapes, colours and forms. Her day starts with personal centring exercises in a journal, or a high-energy dance tape. She takes art classes to relax and release the creative energy that can get trapped by too much routine production. "I'm a lot happier now that I've given myself time to explore. I've developed an additional line of pottery, I do wonky items, and I don't care if they sell, though they usually do. I'm also a better mother."

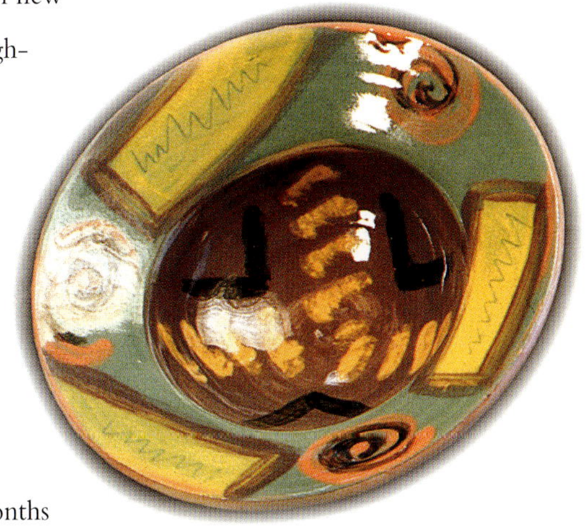

Case in point: Linda's twins, age eight, decide they will save up for a second-hand electric guitar. Linda refrains from speaking her motherly doubts out loud. At craft shows and through Linda's retail studio, they sell their own soap stone sculptures, charging an extra $1 to carve customers' initials. They offer clean-up services to Linda and neighbours. Two months later, they've earned enough to buy the guitar. Again, Linda refrains from cautioning them against getting their hopes up too high. What if the guitar's been sold? They return later that day, proudly bearing their purchase.

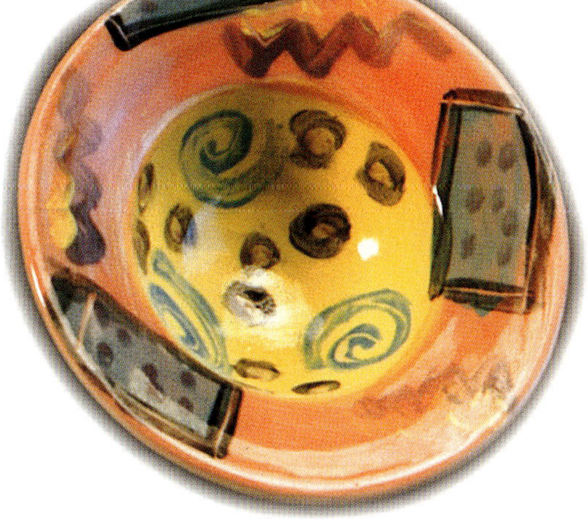

While the twins take turns strumming the guitar and croon the lyrics to their new song, "Sitting by the Side of the Road," Linda reflects: "As a kid, I always kept within those little paint-by-numbers lines so that my parents or teachers would praise me. Now, I try very hard to keep outside them and I encourage our girls to do the same. The trick in life is to give yourself the time and space to dig around and dream so that you can come up with what you want. Then you gotta do it. This is your life."

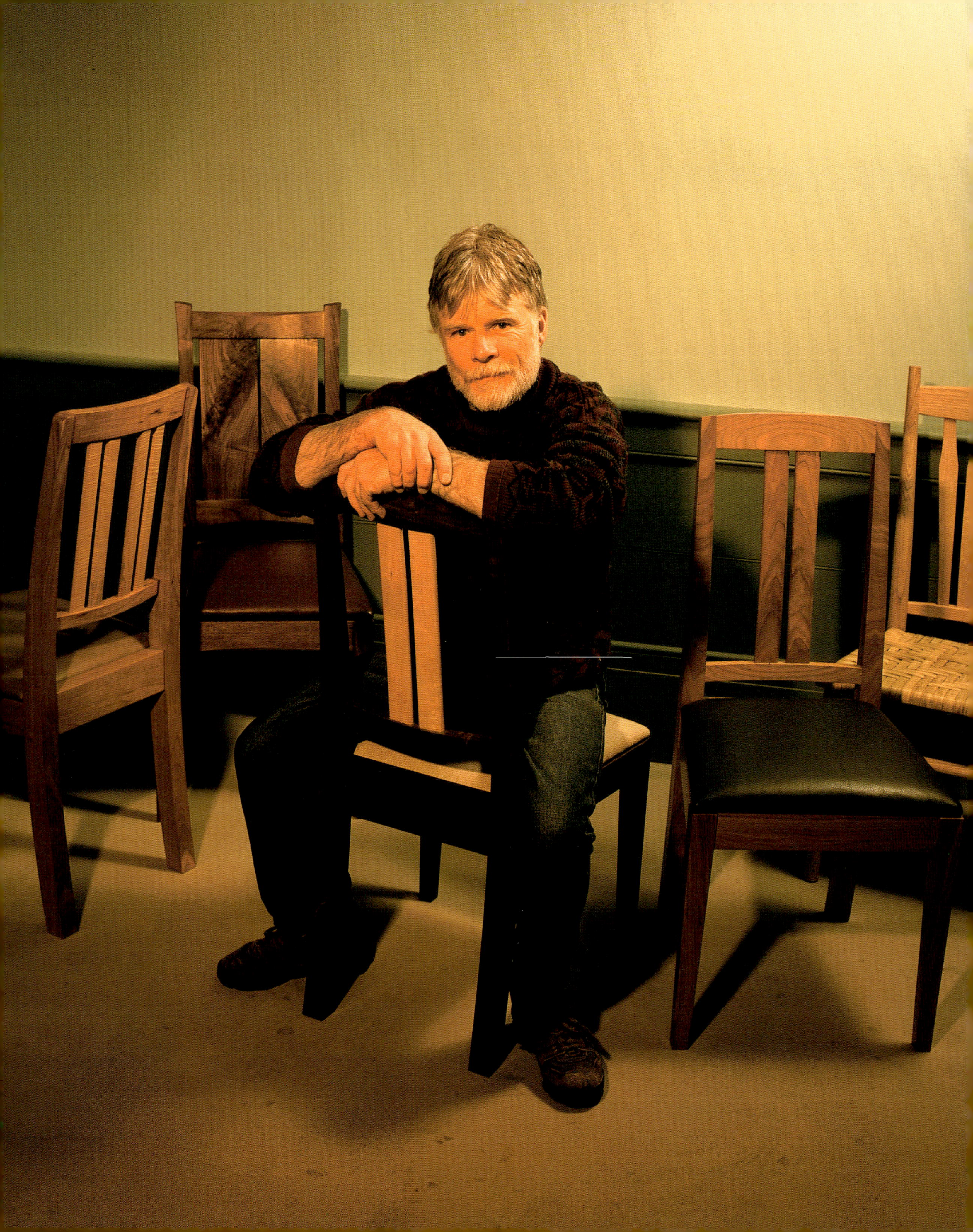

Each of us has the ability to act powerfully for change; together we can regain that ancient and sustaining harmony, in which human needs and the needs of all our companions on the planet are held in balance with the sacred, self-renewing processes of Earth. – David Suzuki

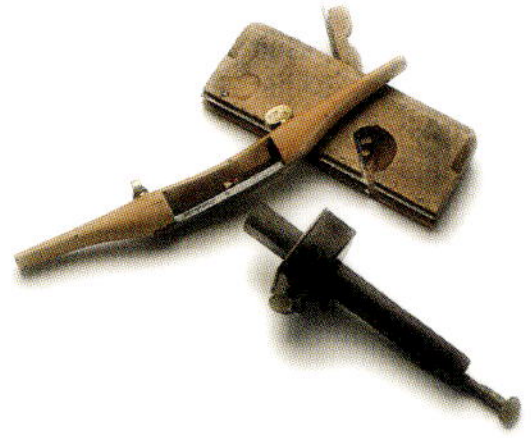

Restoring Nature – Legacy of a Cabinet Maker

Goodbyes echo in the covered porch of the 2-storey red-brick farm house. The screen door whines gently as it swings back into its frame, a car motor fades into the distance.

Stephen returns to the kitchen. As he clears the dregs of breakfast from the table, Joanne pops into his mind. She scurried out with an armload of papers she'd marked last evening.

Many years before, they had planned to enter teacher's college together. Stephen had been working for Ontario's Ministry of Natural Resources in Muskoka after graduating in wildlife biology from the University of Guelph. Hired as a nature interpreter, he was moved by government cutbacks into park maintenance. Cleaning up canoe routes in Georgian Bay was satisfying, outhouses less so. Thinking that teaching might be more challenging, he applied with Joanne to Queen's University in Kingston. Stephen's transcripts went astray and he wasn't accepted. Joanne was.

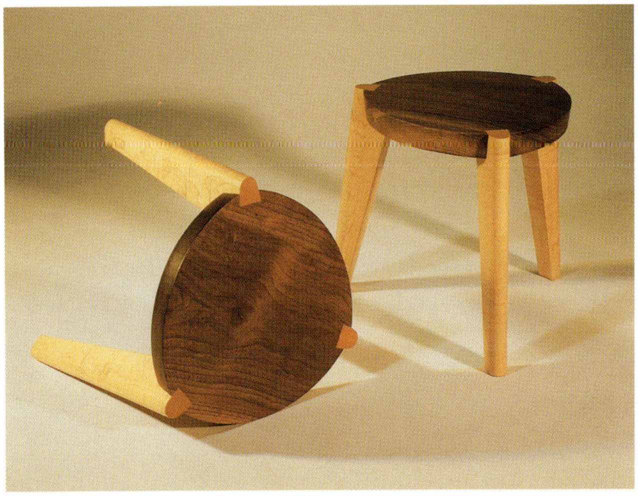

"Who knows, maybe I'd be a shop teacher today," Stephen sighs. He begins his tour of domestic duty, tidying the kids' bedrooms. Into the washing machine go Leah's basketball jersey, Celia's skating skirt, John's hockey sweater – remnants of yesterday's busy lives. "Laundry never ends for a family of five. At least the solar collectors I installed provide plenty of hot water." Cleaning and tidying, Stephen's mind wanders toward dinner. He settles on lamb with tomato, rosemary and feta, then reminds himself to remove the meat from the freezer.

Flashback to 1969, the year Stephen visited Greece. A lot of students were doing Europe on $3 a day. He did it on a buck and a half. Sleeping in ditches wasn't comfortable, but the learning compensated. Thanks to his mom, he already had an interest in the classics. But history, art and culture absorbed from books wane in comparison to wandering from gallery to gallery through the narrow streets of Florence, admiring La Pieta in St. Peter's Cathedral in Rome, and ordering retsina in a taverna below the Parthenon. In Yugoslavia and Turkey, Stephen realized he made more back home in one day – even at $1.50/hour minimum wage – than many made in an entire month. Money's not everything.

Stephen refills his coffee cup. It's 9:00 a.m. Time to go to work. A young pup leaps to the end of his tether cord when he sees his daily companion approach the side door.

Stephen had wanted an older dog who would snooze by his side all day, not chew the finish off newly installed doors. He was outnumbered four to one. "You like woodworking so much," he says patting Toby's head, "maybe I'll teach you to buff the furniture with your tail." Man and dog walk to his workshop a hundred yards away.

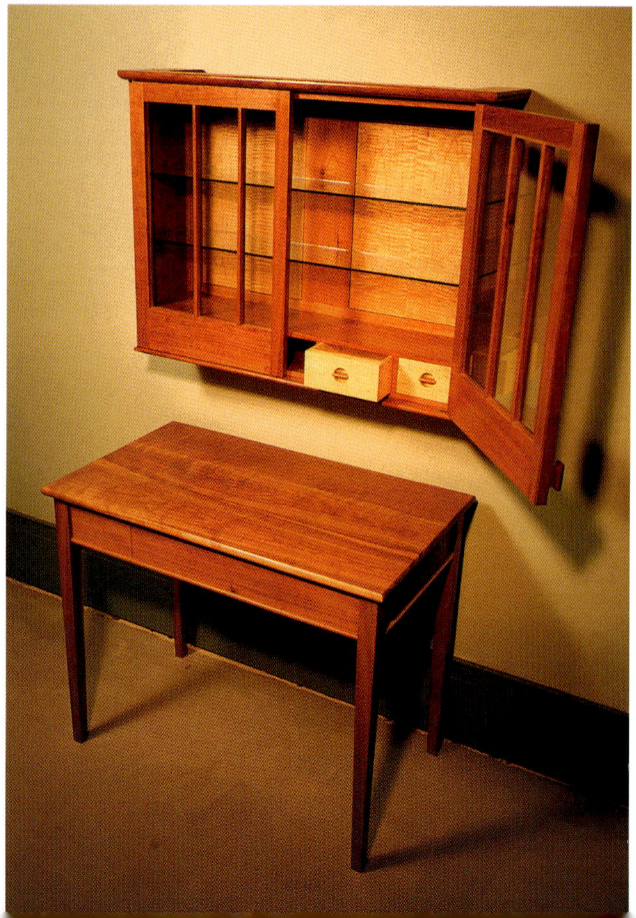

The workshop is chilly, so Stephen gathers kindling and wood, and stokes the stove. A card-carrying member of the environmental movement for over 25 years, he prefers to use a renewable resource as much as possible. "Toby, you think you'd be rewarded in this country for conserving fossil fuel. I heat my house and workshop with wood. But can I get insurance? It's so frustrating."

Before Toby joined the family, Stephen worked alone. He didn't always. For a while, he worked for a millwork manufacturer in St. Catharines that specialized in kitchen cabinetry, doors and stairs. He learned about production woodworking and equipment, but a year was all he could take. Tired of the noise, dust and crank-it-out mentality, he started his own company, Architectural Woodcraft. His brother Harry joined him shortly after. A growing reputation for good work led to commissions restoring grand homes, some dating back to the war of 1812. Stephen began to earn his reputation as a manic recycler. It broke his heart to see historic homes torn down. Such a waste.

Toby's bark returns Stephen to the moment. "Almost everything in this shop was saved from becoming landfill." Toby's eyes follow Stephen's to hazy 150-year old window panes in their original sashes, then up to white pine beams hewn from virgin timber.

His stationary equipment – jointers, planers, lathe, saws and sanders – takes up much of the floor space. On a workbench are antique moulding planes, bench planes and chisels. These days he works more with hand tools. They allow a more intimate understanding of the wood. Machines get you there faster, but embellishments like hand-cut dovetails or a carved drawer-pull lend to the work the hand of the maker. And the finishing is critical. That last 1000th of an inch makes such a difference.

A recently completed post and rung chair attracts the cabinet maker's attention. "What do you think, Toby? William Morris says that we should surround ourselves with beautiful things. I like to think that's why people buy my work. I love it when they run their hand over the surface of the wood and smile."

The chair is unadorned, well proportioned. The wood grain shines through the flawless finish.

Customers often ask him about his influences. "How do you summarize a life-long study of period forms from the 17th century to today's arts and crafts revival? 'Neo funky Shaker contemporary?'"

Stephen's interest in art and form began at an early age. By age eight, he was taking classes in drawing at the Hamilton Art Gallery. He also spent many hours with his father, an amazing home handyman, and two brothers in a basement full of tools. By age 12, he was carving "Tiki gods" with a Swiss army knife and drawing ratfinks on his buddies' gym shirts for $2 a pop.

In his late teens he began working for an electrical contractor in Muskoka. The work was hard but spending summers at the family cottage on Lake Joseph had its rewards. He learned a great deal about the building trades and funded his university education. He also met Joanne at a nearby resort, sealing a summer romance while canoeing in the Muskoka moonlight.

His year in Kingston while Joanne studied introduced him to Upper Canadian architecture and antique furniture. He examined them like bugs under the microscope, wanting to understand the aged wood down to its cell structure. He marvelled at work rendered not by machine, but by the hands and hand tools of a master craftsman.

When Stephen and Joanne moved to St. Catharines, they bought a run-down Victorian home. They had the pleasure of renovating

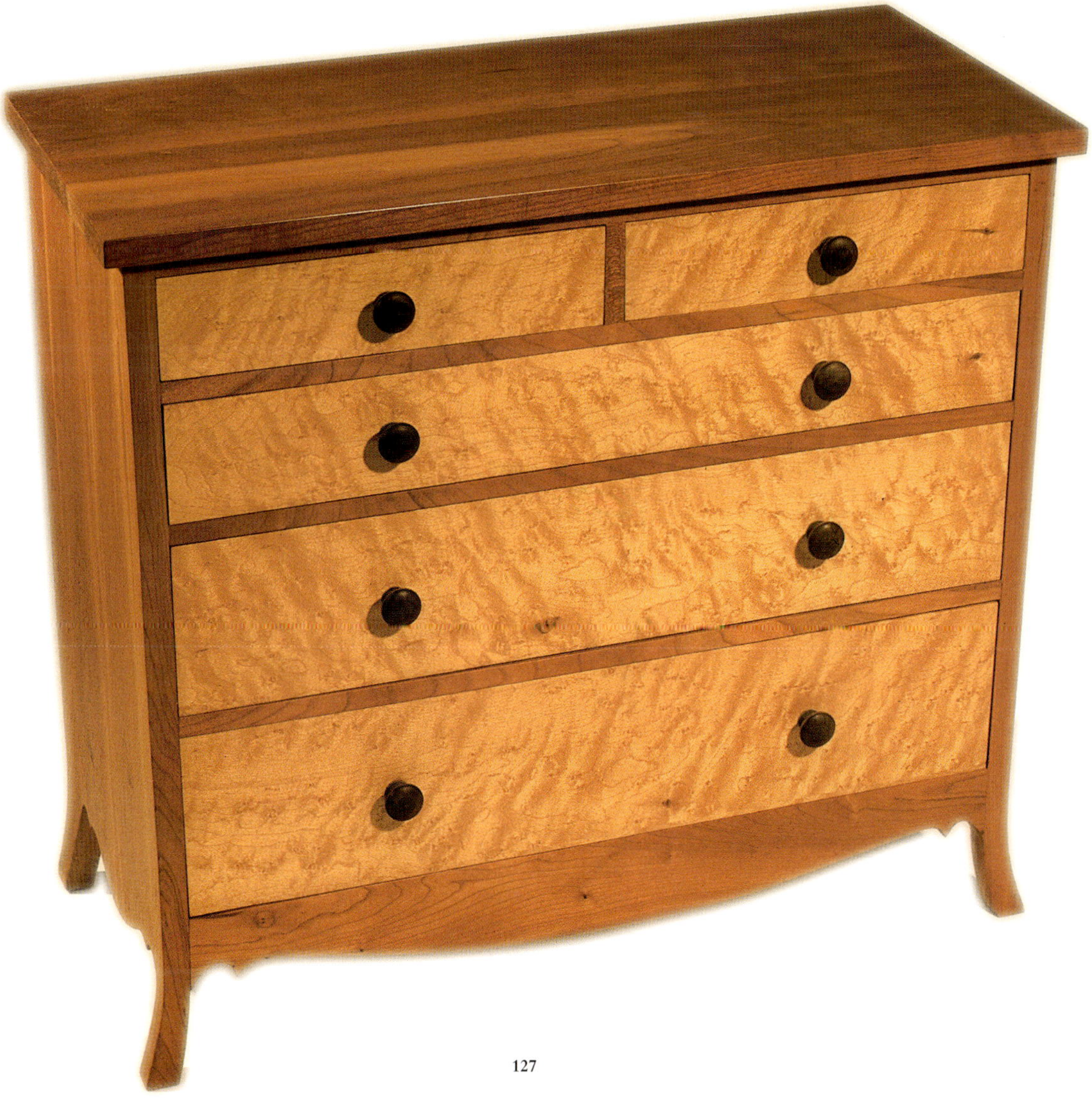

it, then furnishing it with their collection of antique rejects, all bought for a song, all restored to their original splendour.

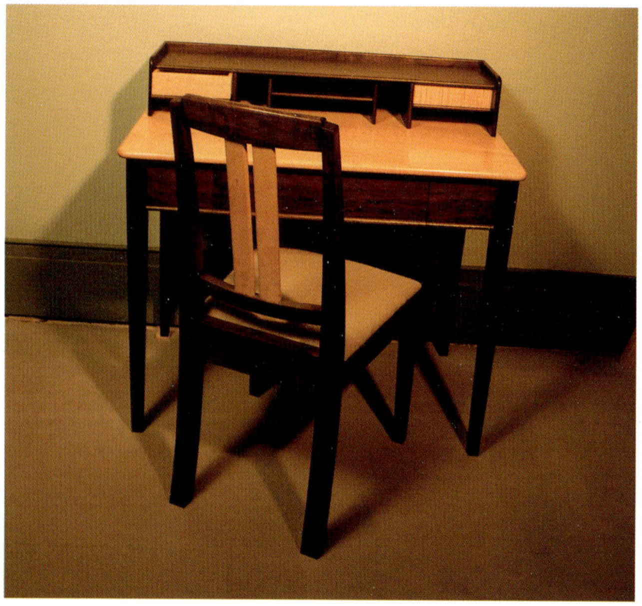

In 1985, Stephen, Joanne and their two young daughters left St. Catharines for Muskoka. They bought a wreck of a farmhouse on seven acres. Over the summer, Stephen and Joanne gutted the farmhouse. With the help of family and friends, they began renovating. In the midst of all these changes, their third child, John, arrived. No problem! They were young, energetic and had a dream: living in Muskoka and raising their children in a healthier environment.

As a family, the Spragues have always enjoyed environmentally friendly pursuits, such as cross-country skiing, sailing and canoeing. At least once a year they try to slip away on a wilderness canoe trip.

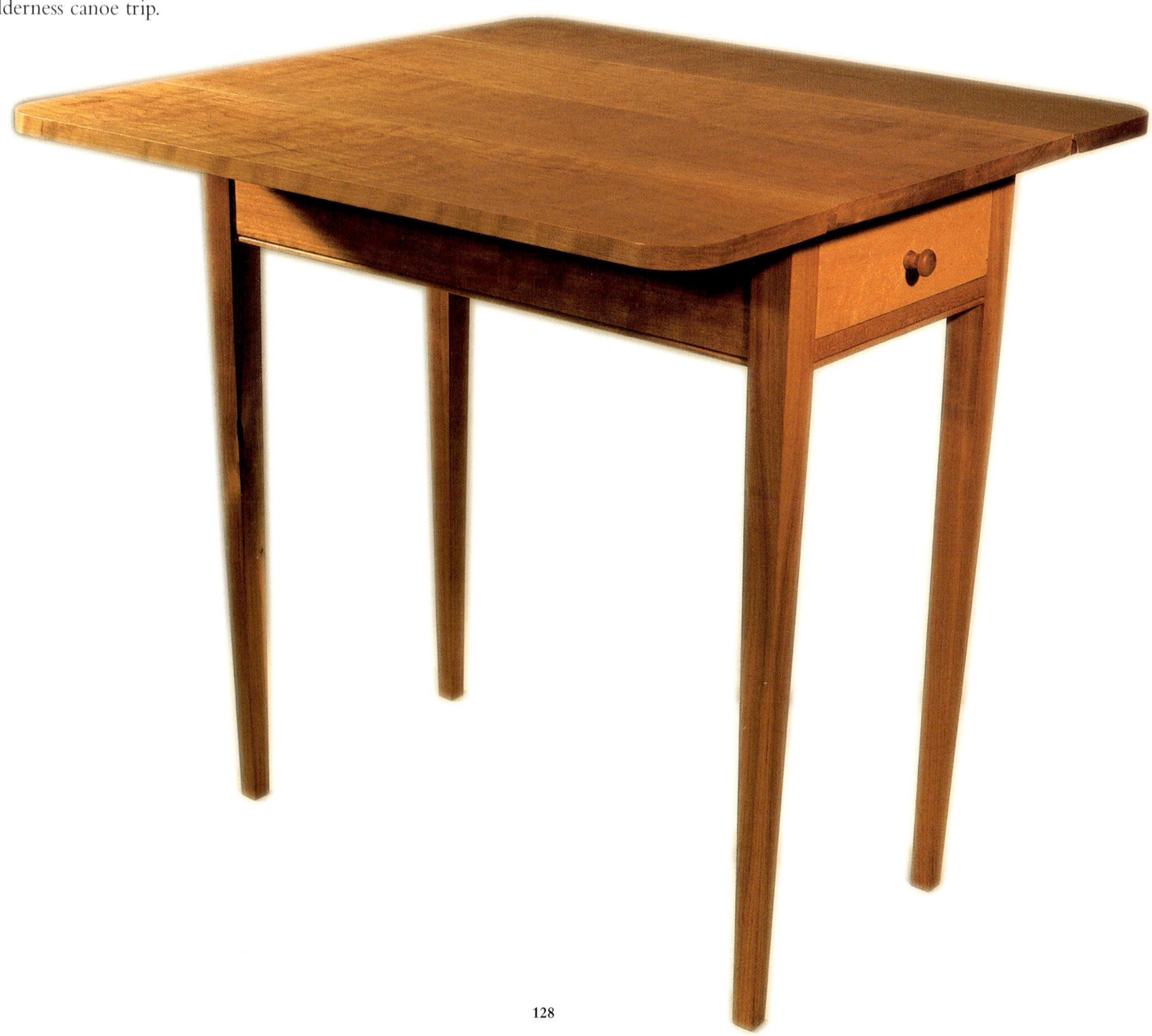

The kids have camped in Georgian Bay, Temagami, Manitoulin and the Gaspé Peninsula. They've canoed across lakes, up rivers and down rapids more scenic and exciting than anything in a theme park. "Our kids know where Canada's wonderland really is."

Stephen breaks for lunch, then heads into town on errands in his pick-up, manufactured the same year his 17-year old daughter was born. Back home, his afternoon's work ends with a walk in his arboretum. It's been a while since he's checked out his trees. The wagging of Toby's tail almost propels him off the ground.

After they had moved to Muskoka, Stephen began a living legacy in an old pasture: over 5,000 new trees, 23 different species – cedar and pine, maple and birch, oak and elm, it's a long list. He figures it's his chance to put back some of the natural resources he's used. Never mind that he's always selected material carefully, buying from local sawmills, harvesting wind-thrown trees, avoiding endangered species such as teak and rosewood.

As the afternoon light dims, man and dog turn back toward the house.

After dinner, the family pitches in to clear the dishes. Then Leah, Celia and John head upstairs to do their homework, Joanne settles into her marking and Stephen returns to his shop for the graveyard shift.

Stephen works for a few hours, then puts his shop to bed for the night. He inspects for today's oil soaked rag that could be tonight's fire hazard, damps down the stove, turns off the radio and lights. Outside, the air is crisp, the sky is clear. The Northern Lights dance above his head. The moon is full. Coyotes howl.

St. Catharines has urban sprawl. Stephen smiles. He has nature at his doorstep.

Muskoka Treescapes: What Stephen Sees

"As a youngster, I spent a lot of time wandering the Carolinian woodlands of the Dundas Valley. In comparison, Muskoka doesn't have as much diversity. White pine and hemlock once covered the area, and some magnificent stands remain. Spindly hardwoods came in after the old growth pines were felled 100 years ago.

"What you see really depends on the season. In winter, you can recognize trees by their shape. American elms have a magnificent spreading crown.

"In spring, it's the colour of leaf buds and flowers. Each species exhibits its own wash of green, yellow or red.

"During the summer we're on the water a lot, and reflections mirror more subtle variations. Hardwoods really stand out against conifers, and the colours are richer than in spring. Poplars are a silvery green, conifers a deep chrome. I tend to notice the incredible girth of trunks and roots, especially when I'm portaging with a canoe on my head. I'm also more aware of sounds, wind whispering through the foliage, birds singing high up in the canopy.

"People who talk of fall colours in Muskoka are mostly thinking of maples. But the colours continue long after the bus tours are gone. When maples are bare, poplars burst into a fiery yellow, tamarack needles warm to a vibrant gold, and beech and oaks are cast in a coppery bronze."

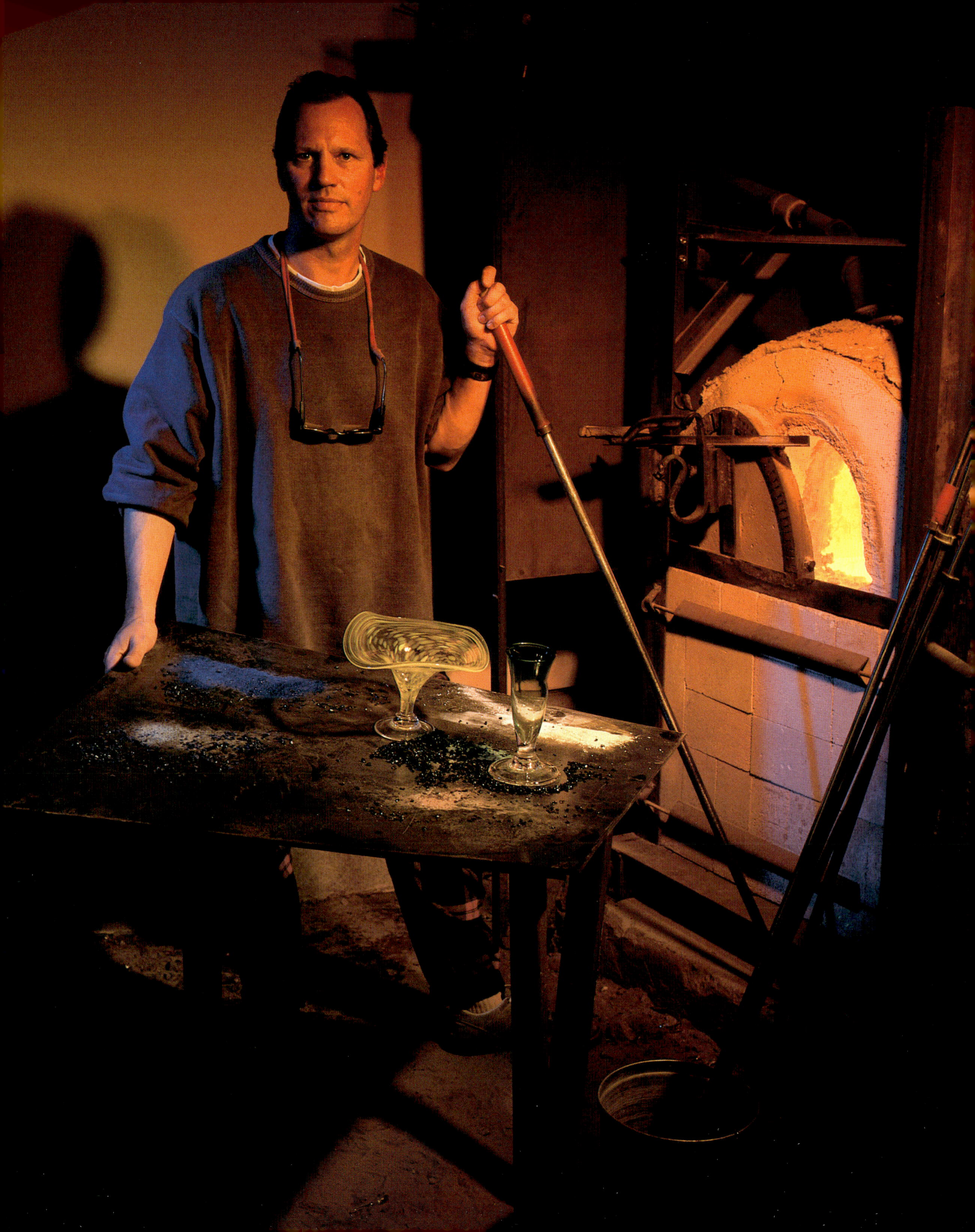

"Glass blowing is for me a medium of movement, a dance to an inner rhythm that extends far beyond the studio. I would like to think my glass reflects the spirit of that dance." — Simon Bisley

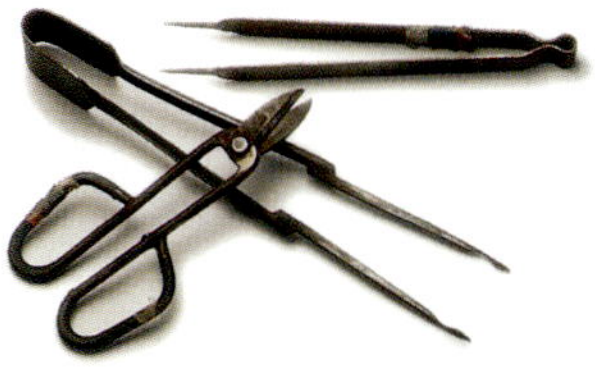

Dance to an Inner Rhythm

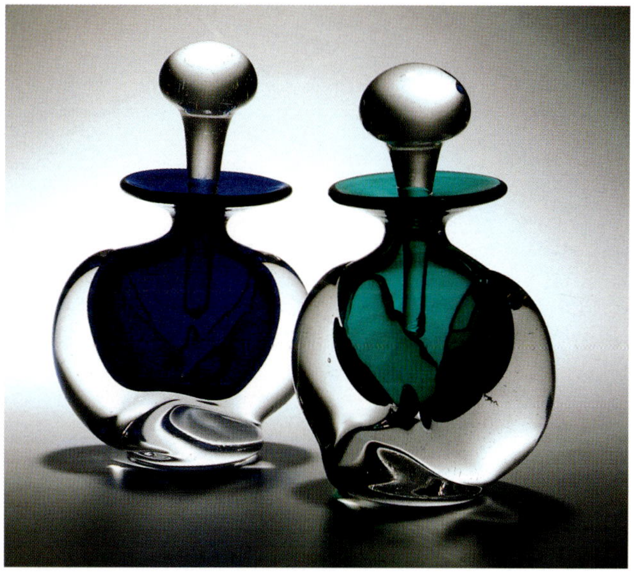

Nine months out of 12, Simon Bisley dances around his glass studio, music cranked, wearing sunglasses and shorts. The remaining three months, he takes it easy. At least, that's how Simon puts it.

Simon lets on that he doesn't take life too seriously. This is a man who motorcycled through Europe, the Middle East, the Indian subcontinent and Australia, who modelled menswear in the Himalayas, dug trenches in the Adelaide zoo, and decided to take up glass blowing after drinking a beer from a hand-blown glass. Yet this same man has dedicated himself to glass blowing for almost 15 years. Who is this man?

Try to pin him down, and he dazzles you with a smile instead. Or changes the subject completely. He's courteous, helpful, serious when required, but you quickly sense he's not interested in other people's rules.

Born in London, England in 1955, Simon was raised in Epsom, County Surrey. He can't recall any artistic leanings as a child. Too busy playing soccer? At 17, he joined the police cadets, which he likens to an Outward Bound experience. Where else can you get a steady diet of rock climbing, canoe trips and gliding lessons? "Even if you had to clean your boots and do military-like drills, the rest was a blast." Press him a little, and Simon concedes that he didn't know what he wanted to do with his life. The cadet corp was a good place to tread water.

At 19, Simon signed up for training to become a police officer. It was a logical step for a cadet and the son of a Scotland Yard detective. For the next six years, Simon tried on various uniformed and plain clothes roles, from bomb squad to murder investigator, from beat-bobby in Hampstead to diplomatic protection officer throughout London.

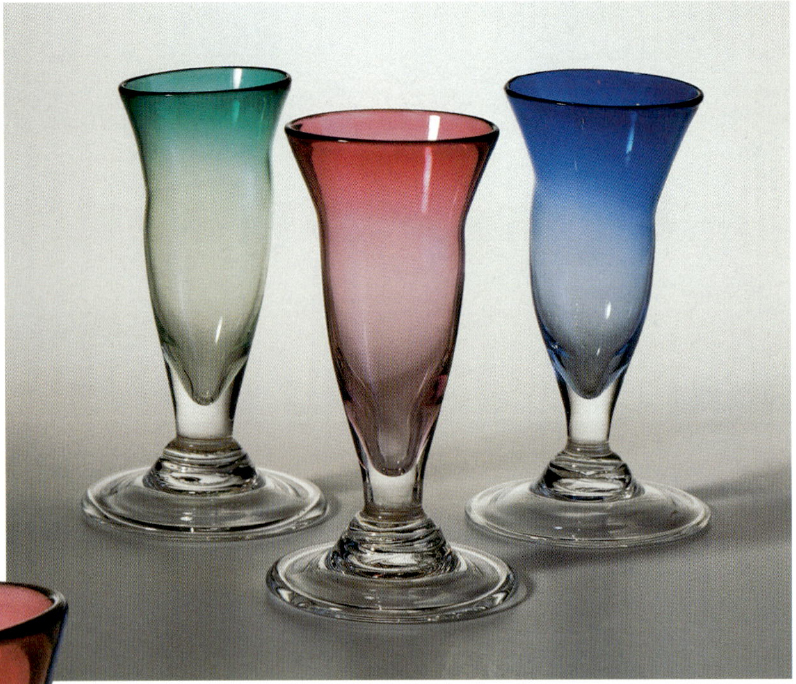

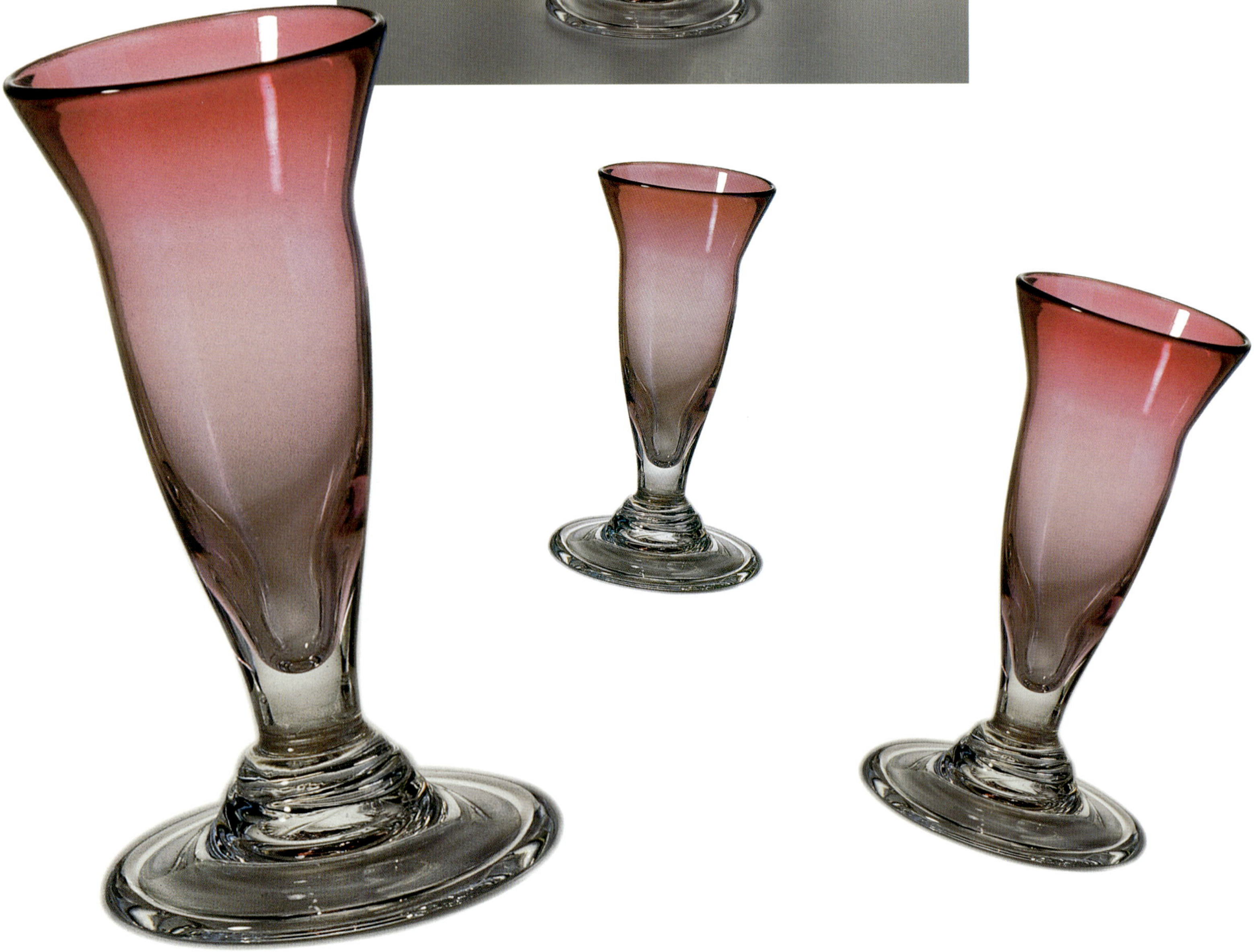

Life was fine, but somehow wanting. Reading an article about a motorcycle trip through Australia sparked an urge to travel. "I had itchy feet and decided to scratch them."

Simon gave himself a year to prepare. He saved whatever he could. He transferred into a position that would allow a clean leave-taking – no incomplete investigations or unfinished paperwork. He shed possessions. He bought a bike and taught himself how to ride it. Then he bought a bigger bike, a hefty BMW 750, practical and powerful. A week before leaving, he sat in a movie theatre watching Easy Rider and feeling the wind in his hair.

Striving for Imperfection

"Glass blowing is a craft, a skill to be learned. Once you know your medium, you can take more risks, push for that little bit extra.

"Perfection itself is unattainable, but you can strive for imperfection. It's the imperfections that can add interest and take you in new directions."

"It was scary in the beginning. It helped to be moving along with other travellers going in the same direction." From Belgium, he biked through Europe and into the Middle East. It was 1978. He arrived in Iran two days after the Shah had fled to the West. He arrived in southern Afghanistan as Soviet tanks started making incursions into the north. "It was the wildest country I'd been in. Huge mountains, tiny roads. Medieval. I got streetwise pretty fast. When you have only the clothes on your back, people judge what they see. You have to be strong and give out the message that you want to fit in, but don't try and put one over on me."

Moving on, Simon eventually wheeled into Goa, a former Portuguese protectorate on the Indian Ocean, known for its spectacular beaches and a footloose population of travellers. "Goa in those days wasn't as crazy as it had been in the '60s, and I was staying on the outlying beaches, which were quieter."

He remained in Goa for three months, picking up some of the language, eating in local hang-outs, getting around on public transit, and always, always meeting people. On any given day, 10 or 15 travellers from around the world would share plates of just-caught fish in garlic sauce, enjoy the sea breeze and laugh at each others' tales.

A travelling spirit can only sit for so long. From Goa, Simon headed off through India and Nepal, over to Thailand, through Malaysia to Singapore, and across to Australia. He took on odd jobs, working here and there for a year. Then he'd had enough. He sold the bike, and within two weeks was back in England. Two years had passed.

Before leaving England, Simon had intended to resume his job as a police officer. On his return, he decided against it, choosing to wait tables in a French restaurant, paint houses, jockey cars, whatever would make enough money to continue travelling. He left again, for Central and South America. "You can live and travel cheaply if you're not in a hurry. Trains can sometimes be three days late."

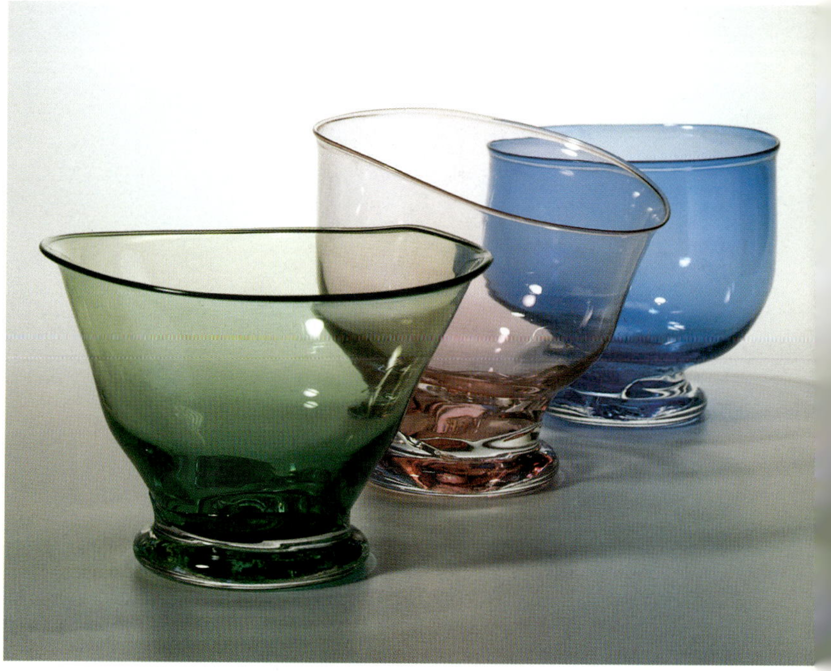

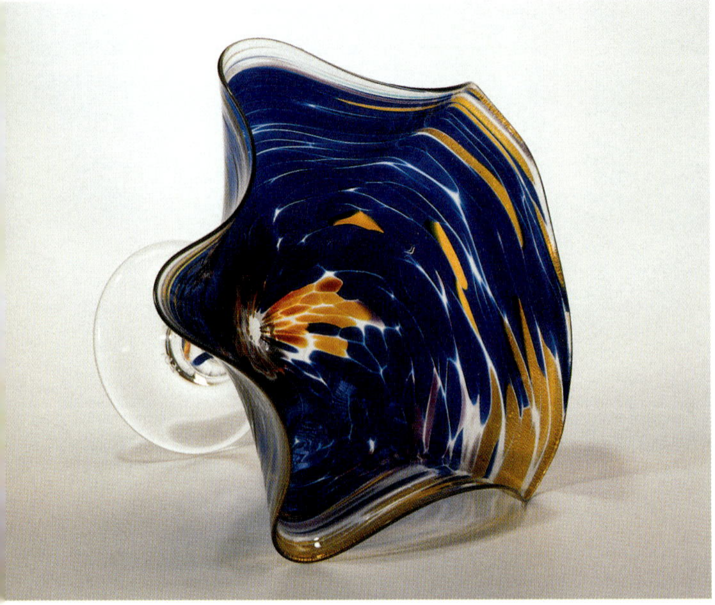

Adventures continued. In Costa Rica, he joined a gold panning expedition. Armed with machetes, pans and shovels, he waded up river in Wellington boots.

"Why are the toes cut out?" he asked.

"So the water will drain out after walking in deep water."

"Why bother wearing boots at all?"

"To protect your feet from the snakes."

After a year, Simon's money ran out. He rejoined his parents in England and helped renovate their new home near Bognor, in West Sussex. Between renovations and games of snooker, he bought a little boat and taught himself to sail.

After eight months, he headed off again. "I knew this would be my last big trip, and I wanted to go back to India and Nepal because I loved them so much." Trekking in the mountains, he cut trails across glaciers, crossed gorges on flimsy rope bridges, and woke up some mornings with a frozen beard.

At one point Simon met a photographer on assignment. "He wanted someone who could model a man's suit in the most obscure setting possible. I tried the suit on, and it fit. The photographs show me wearing a black business suit and shoes, tie and dress shirt, leaning casually against a Yak. Mountain peaks rise on either side of me, and the vista is so wide you can see the curvature of the earth."

At a teahouse in Ladakh, high in the Tibetan mountains, he met Karen Davis. A school teacher from Canada, she had made her way through Indonesia, the Philippines, Pakistan and India. The two travellers teamed up, continued to Kashmir, then returned together to England. They married and moved to Canada in 1984.

Karen resumed teaching while Simon weighed options. "I had considered going back into police work, but decided it's not good to return to the past. I realized I had a completely clean slate. I could do whatever I wanted, where I wanted. Social work was one possibility. Then one afternoon I had a few beers with a friend of a friend. We drank from glasses that he had hand blown.

"Glass blowing was something new and different for me. I hadn't really ever visited my artistic side, and I already fancied going back to college. It had been a while, and I wanted to see if my brain would still work." The next day Simon signed up at Sheridan College.

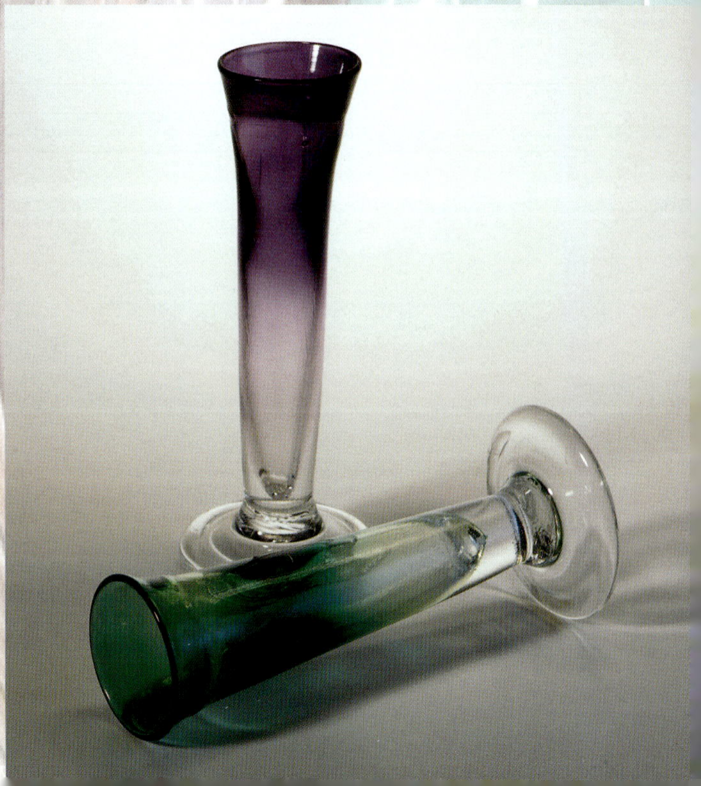

Blowing glass for the first time confirmed his choice of medium. "Glass is free, wild, loose. It's about fire and movement. If you make a mistake, you just go along with it and see where it leads. Beautiful things can come from happy accidents."

In year one, Simon hovered like a vulture over the work benches, observing the technique of third year students and waiting for someone to pack up early, eager for as little as 10 minutes at the glory hole. As a mature student, he had at least one advantage over the others: more practice in living with and without rules, and more experience in cutting through to what's essential. "What are you going on about, what's this deadline thing?"

In his three years at Sheridan Simon was less concerned with going by the book, more concerned with dancing to his own rhythm. He graduated with high honours in 1987. "If you're going to do something, acquit yourself well."

After working for two years with an established glass blower in Toronto, Simon was ready to go out on his own. Karen quit her job as a special education teacher with the North York Board of Education. Their firstborn, Kyle, was still an infant. Liam was yet to come. They bought 65 acres north of Milford Bay, arriving in Muskoka without guaranteed incomes, but with perspective on life from their travels.

In the mountains of Tibet, a country spiritually wealthy but materially impoverished, a Buddhist monk had told Simon and Karen, "You westerners are poor because you have no beliefs." They reminded themselves of this during tough times. "The cash flowed okay, just in the wrong direction. I called it just-in-time financing – the money would come in just in time to pay the bills."

On their travels they had learned the expression "shanti, shanti." Slowly, slowly, don't sweat it, it will all swing back. They also learned that the present is a gift, not something to be squandered by regretting the past or fearing the future.

Karen found work with the Muskoka Board of Education. Simon, with a manual in one hand and hammer in the other, built a hot glass studio. He gradually established a broad client base through craft shows and galleries, and the cash assumed a steady flow in a more appropriate direction.

When Simon was still a police officer, he testified in court against someone who had broken the law. "It was scary. When you arrest someone, you take away their liberty." Since that time, he has pursued liberty in his own life. He loves working with glass, but will continue only so long as it stimulates and challenges him. For Simon, while staying by what he values is critical, moving on is magical.

Simon cranks up the music in his studio and follows the impulse of the moment. "Hot glass on the end of your pipe is like a runny honey. It's fascinating. What starts as a fruit bowl evolves into a vase. First I make the piece, then come up with my concept." He has directions, not deadlines. He makes lists, but never looks at them again. Whatever he sets his mind to is as good as done.

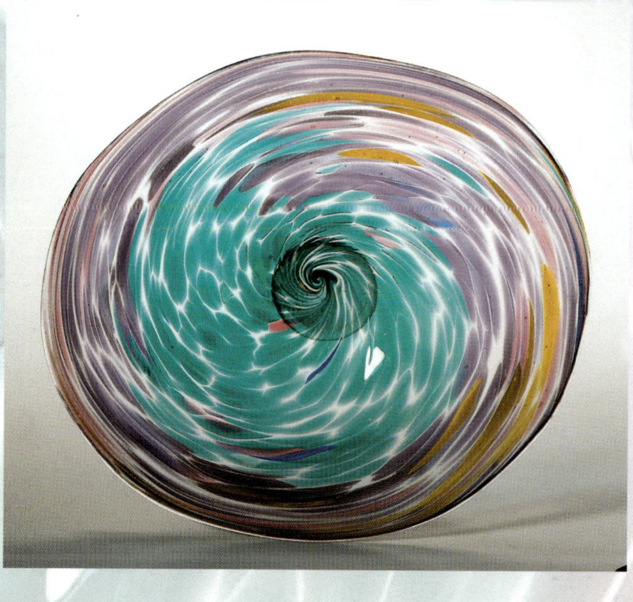

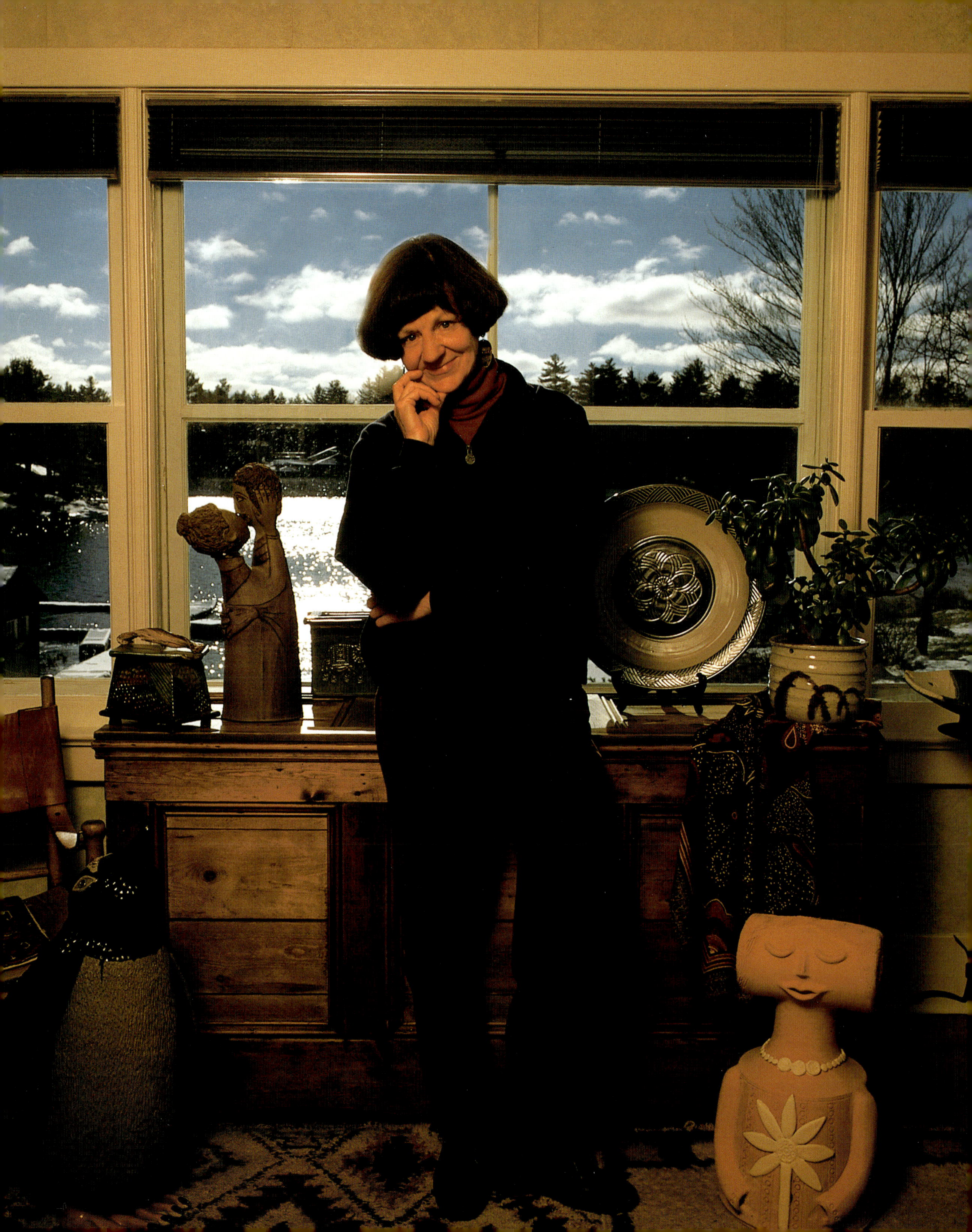

What we call the beginning is often the end. And to make an end is to make a beginning. The end is where we start from. – T.S. Eliot

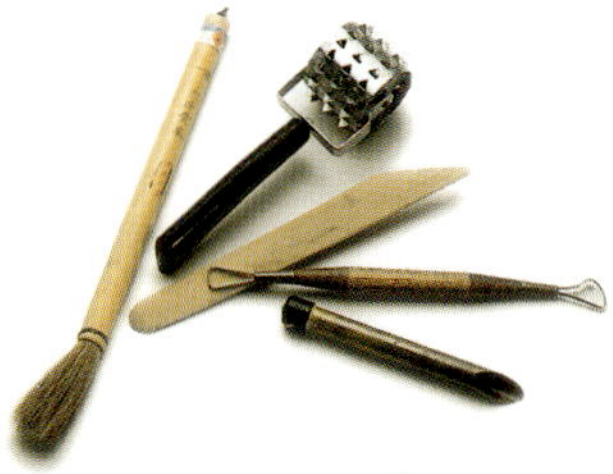

Clay in the Blood

On May 3, 1955, The Waterman, a Dutch ship out of Rotterdam, pulls into the Port of Halifax and docks at Pier 21. Mieke Soontiëns disembarks, in the company of her parents, five brothers and five sisters. After years of sitting around the dining room table to study the future, as writ on the pages of a world atlas, the Soontiëns had selected Canada.

One foot on the ship, the other on Canadian soil, Mieke makes the transition with all of youth's enthusiasm. "I was sad to leave my home country and friends, but very excited about a new beginning. My father always had wanderlust, and after all those evenings around the atlas, I guess I caught the bug."

Decades later, Mieke Martin Soontiëns, Muskoka resident since 1978, established potter and long-time member of the Muskoka Autumn Studio Tour, prepares for another adventure. With husband David Martin, she's carting potter's wheel, kiln and inventory to Nova Scotia's south shore.

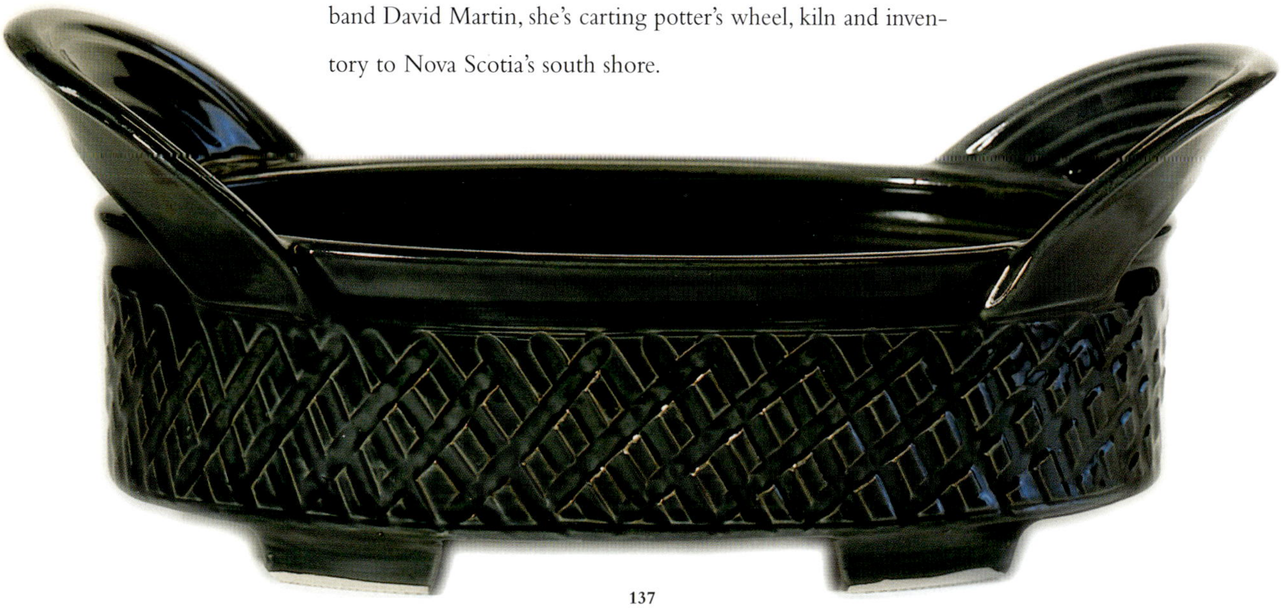

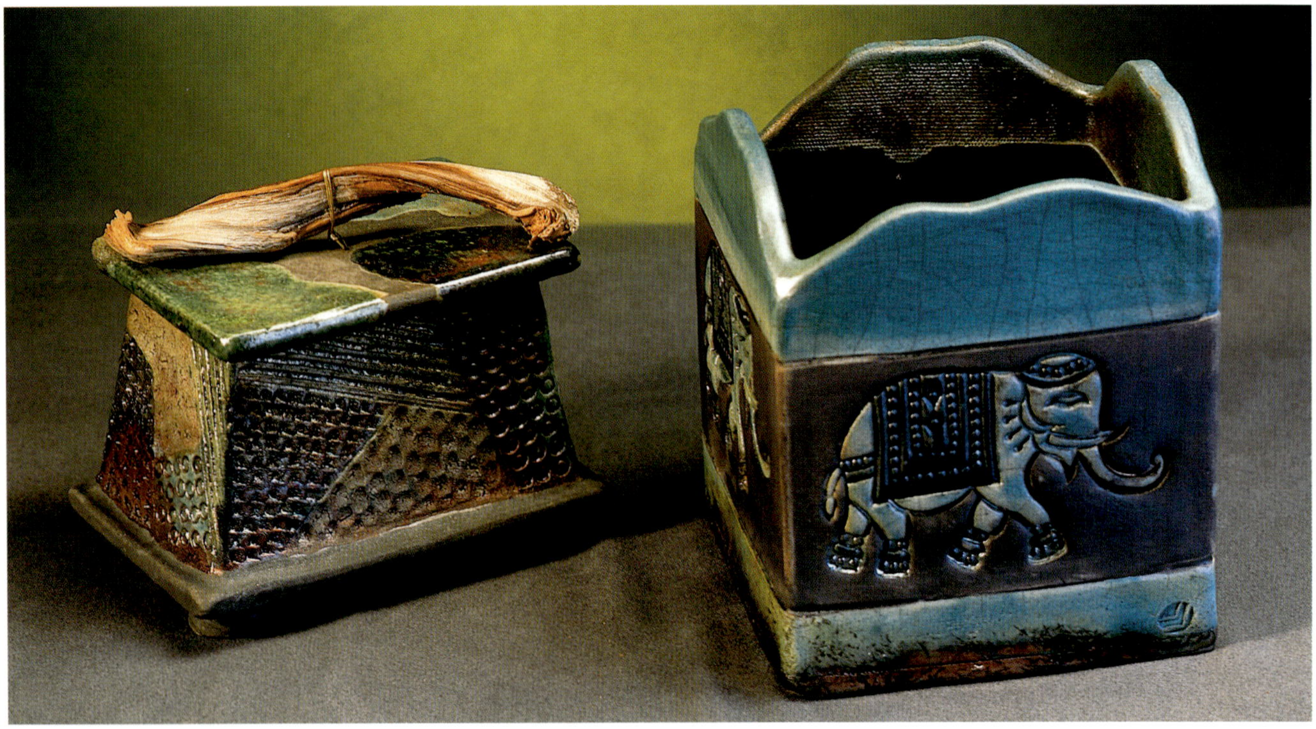

After sealing a box of books with packing tape, Mieke stands back to survey her progress. "So many books. I should leave some behind, but I hate to part with them. They're like old friends." Mieke can already picture their books lining the library of the new house. "It's going to be great," Mieke says as she reaches for another box.

Books are relatively easy to pack, memories less so. They resist order and sequence, spilling out randomly in various colours and moods. "After 20 years in Muskoka, it's difficult to leave it all behind. Very scary, too. But it's also exciting. I'm happy that I'll be closer to my family. I'll be building a new studio, so I can fix all the little problems I've lived with for so long, like tight spaces and inadequate shelving. All these years, I've looked at a wall while I throw pots on the wheel. In Nova Scotia, I'll have an ocean view, which I'm sure will encourage creativity."

Mieke's belongings have travelled far, from Moncton, New Brunswick to Sydney, Australia, from Paris to Saint John, Halifax, and on to Gravenhurst. For nearly 20 years she worked for Air Canada. She might still be with Air Canada if friends hadn't introduced her to David Martin. Two years later, as a newly married couple, they moved to Gravenhurst, Ontario.

David, a hotelier, had accepted a position as general manager with the Muskoka Sands Inn, leaving Mieke at a career crossroad. With no Air Canada location in driving distance of Gravenhurst, she decided to step away from the working world. "We spent the summer getting to know Muskoka, but after two months I was ready to do something useful, something I would enjoy." She signed up for a ceramics course at Georgian College in Barrie.

"I love the feel of clay. It's squishy. It feels good. I can't explain the attraction better than that. It's one of the oldest crafts. It's universal."

On all her travels, Mieke has always gravitated to ceramics and pottery, whether in museums or shops. "The more rustic pots with lots of texture were especially appealing to me. When I see a piece of old pottery in a museum, I inevitably start speculating about the people, what life was like back then, what was in their minds as they were building the piece."

A short time into the course at Georgian, Mieke decided, "This is it. I want to be a potter." What had begun as an interest, a means of being productive, flared into a three-year commitment. "I hadn't planned to become a potter, it just happened."

At the outset, Mieke strove for technical expertise. "It was important to me to learn the techniques well. I figured the artistic expression would come later."

Mastering the techniques was difficult. "It isn't easy discovering something new at the age of 40. I had to learn chemistry, how to work the potter's wheel, kiln technology. Instructors questioned why I bothered. But I loved it enough that I wanted to master it and knew that I would. I don't give in easily."

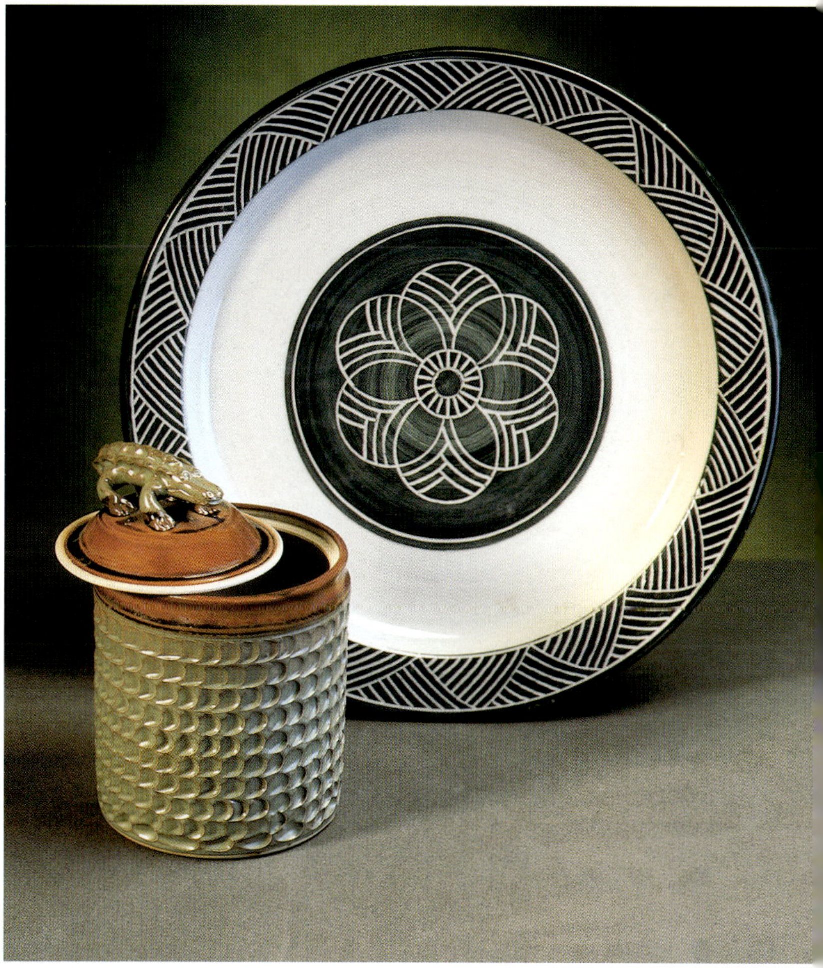

After finishing the course in 1981, Mieke opened a little studio on the grounds of the Muskoka Sands Inn. Technique remained paramount. "I concentrated on making good pots, good shapes, functional articles, not many one-of-a-kind objects. I was just interested in becoming a better potter and earning enough to keep myself in clay money."

Mieke's situation took a radical turn in 1984. A change of ownership at the Muskoka Sands Inn left David without a job and Mieke without a studio. The couple searched the area for real estate that would meet their needs. They purchased Pine Lake Cottages, on Highway 169 outside Gravenhurst. Pine Lake Pottery opened the following year. What had been a personal interest was now a contributing factor in their economic health and well-being.

Mieke's new studio was nestled far enough from the buzz of traffic to ensure peace and quiet, and close enough to the lake for inspiration and rejuvenation. Inside the studio, a former boat storage space, two small rooms served as gallery and studio. Just outside the studio, she created a garden sanctuary. There on warm summer days, she would sit on a bench in an ivy-entwined gazebo to etch geometric patterns on bowls or carve scales on fanciful fish platters.

The Origin of Inspiration

Inspiration comes in many forms, from many sources. In 1986, Mieke the artist studies a new garden laid out by Mieke the gardener. She approves the flow of colour and shape, the play of proportions and texture. But somehow it's incomplete. In a burst of insight and energy, she creates a series of outdoor sculptures – birdbaths, fountains and four garden ladies, christened *Spring, Summer, Autumn* and *Winter.* Customers, friends and colleagues respond enthusiastically.

"Once I started with sculptural pieces, I found inspiration everywhere." A series of penguins evolve from reading a biography of a sailor shipwrecked in Antarctica in 1738. After a trip to Kenya, lionesses and crocodiles creep onto her pots, curling and stretching. Masai warriors and maidens rear up as freestanding sculptures, lean and proud.

Along with inspiration comes new challenges. "It isn't always easy to work out the technical problems, to make my fingers create what I see in my mind, but I continue until I get it right. The learning never ends. That's what keeps it exciting."

Over the years, Mieke has achieved success with distinctive dinner and cookware. They're her mainstay, but increasingly she expresses herself in sculpture. Her travels across many continents are a continuous source of new designs, challenging her to explore through trial and error unfamiliar territory, from reproducing the texture of African crocodile leather to recreating a Tibetan prayer stone. She confronts occasional disasters with good cheer. "Like any medium, clay has its limitations. But I hate to give in to them. I sometimes go beyond what the clay will do. Through all the accidents, you learn.

"I get a lot of joy from what I do. I can do it at my own pace. I'm my own boss and don't have to do anything I don't want to do. Mind you, I work harder for myself than I would for anyone else."

Mieke continues to work 12-hour days in summer, seven days a week. In winter, she might cut back to 10 hours. "I'd love to have more time to work in my garden, work on more sculptural pieces, and make nice meals, but there are never enough hours in a day. I wake up in the morning and I go to bed at night with pottery on my mind. I dream in the middle of the night about ongoing projects. At this time, this is life, getting up, going down to my studio and creating something that at the end of the day I can say, 'I made that, that's me.'"

A part of Mieke now sits on display in cottages and homes across Canada and around the world. A visit to a Mövenpick restaurant in Toronto, Ottawa or Montreal may draw your eye instantly to her careful sgraffito patterns preserved in serving bowls and platters. Just lift up the bowl or platter. Her signature is there for all to see.

By the time the lupines bloom, Mieke and David will have unpacked their boxes, chests and trunks in the oceanfront bed and breakfast they purchased in Blandford, Nova Scotia.

Notes

1. Ontario College of Art & Design (OCAD)

The Ontario College of Art & Design (OCAD) is one of only four accredited, independent, art and design colleges in Canada, and is also the largest college devoted exclusively to the education of professional artists and designers. All of its resources – the students, faculty and staff, as well as the equipment and studios – are organized to create an environment that supports the personal, creative development of aspiring artists and designers.

2. Selwyn Dewdney

Selwyn Dewdney (1909-1979) spent most of his 70 years in a love affair with the north. He saw his first native rock paintings on a boyhood canoe trip to Blindfold Lake, near Kenora, and after an abundantly creative life as an artist, adventurer, writer and teacher, he took up the study of these mysterious images full time. This was 1957, when aboriginal rock art was almost unheard of in Canada. After years of canoeing through the fantastic jumble of rock-bound lakes and rivers that make up the Canadian Shield, Dewdney had a wealth of knowledge of what he realized was an ancient artistic tradition, scattered across the vastness of the north, from Saskatchewan to Quebec. He passed this gift on to his students. In 1973, he went on his last expedition to the north, to Frances Lake, Ontario, taking along a young archaeologist, Brian Leigh Molyneaux. In the following years, while his mentor worked on the masses of drawings, photographs and journals of his many expeditions, Molyneaux continued the relentless search for the north's artistic treasures.

3. Georgian College

The design and visual arts department of Georgian College features programs in advertising, fine arts, graphic design, interior design, jewellery and metals and product design. Design and visual arts programs are intended to foster creative ability and artistic discrimination in a variety of subject areas. Students are taught by faculty who are practising professional artists with a feel for current trends and technology. Georgian College is one of Ontario's 25 community colleges. Campuses are located in Barrie, Orillia and Owen Sound.

4. One of a Kind Canadian Craft Show

The One of a Kind Canadian Craft Show is the largest craft event in North America and draws more than 200,000 visitors each year. Since its launch in 1974, the show's primary objective has been to support and celebrate Canadian craft. Besides generating career-sustaining revenue for hundreds of exhibitors, the show presents a forum for meeting other artisans and establishing relationships with clients and retailers. One of a Kind takes place twice a year (spring and Christmas) at Toronto's Exhibition Place, home of the historic Canadian National Exhibition.

5. Haliburton School of Fine Arts

Established in 1967, the Haliburton School of Fine Arts quickly established a reputation for the depth and breadth of its programming. Set in the glorious Haliburton Highlands, the school attracts Canada's finest professional artists and craftspeople to teach weekend and week-long courses. These courses are offered in a wide range of media, including clay, fibre, fashion, wood, printmaking, painting, basketry, glass, photography, metal, design, colour, sculpture and painting, and at levels that attract beginners to advanced students.

6. Central Technical School

With the arts comprising the fourth largest employment group in Canada, high calibre visual art education is vital. The Art Centre at Central Technical School has been the focus of superior art training for three quarters of a century. An award winning building, (among the first in the country specifically designed and constructed as an art school) is a unique home for almost 60 courses in the visual arts discipline. Fifteen specialized studios and a large teaching staff, combined with a talented student body, foster a dynamic sharing environment. The curriculum stresses drawing and design as a sound framework; it favours broad yet intensive art exploration and encourages individual aptitude, potential and ambitions.

7. Muskoka Arts and Crafts Inc.

A community-based visual arts organization, Muskoka Arts and Crafts organizes exhibits and stages craft shows, workshops and other events year round. MAC offices are in the Chapel Gallery in Bracebridge. The gallery is a leading exhibit space for Muskoka artists.

8. Sheridan College

The School of Crafts and Design is the largest facility in Canada devoted to craft education. We offer intensive training in four studio areas: ceramics, furniture, textiles, and glass. Students can also undertake studies in design, drawing, photography, craft history, and communications.

Emphasis is placed on improving both creative design capabilities and technical skills. Students also learn about related areas from equipment maintenance to studio and small business management. Self-sufficiency, responsiveness to market needs, and a thorough appreciation of craft heritage and potential are stressed.

Throughout the program, students and faculty members discuss work both individually and as part of group discussions. Visiting craftspeople and artists add to the program with guest lectures and workshops. Field trips to galleries, studios, and special conferences are also common.

9. McMichael Gallery

Experience all that is Canadian at the McMichael in the charming village of Kleinburg, north or Toronto. Renowned for its collection of 20th-century Canadian art, the gallery features exhibitions by Group of Seven, First Nation, Inuit and contemporary Canadian artists. A sprawling complex of galleries features picture windows offering panoramic views of 100 acres of stunning woodland. The gallery shop specializes in one-of-a-kind sculpture, glass works, prints and collectors items.

10. The Banff Centre

When most people think of Banff, they think of the mountains. Artists, however, think of The Banff Centre: a place where they can draw inspiration and energy from each other as well as the setting. Since 1933, 41,000 artists from around the world have attended the centre's programs in theatre arts, music and sound, writing and publishing, aboriginal arts, and media and visual arts. Not only artists, but managers, conference guests and mountain community leaders have benefited from the centre's stimulating environment.

Les Manning headed The Banff Centre's ceramic program from 1972 until 1994. Now working out of his studio near Kingston, Ontario, he has played a key role in encouraging the development of Canada's ceramic community. As a vice-president of the Geneva-based International Academy of Ceramics, he continues to champion the work of Canadian ceramists on the world stage.

Mieke's final and 20th year in Muskoka coincides with the 20th anniversary celebration of the Muskoka Autumn Studio Tour. Not wanting to miss the event after 17 years as a member, she will return to display outdoor sculptures in Penny Varney's garden. No doubt, she'll stay on for the festivities of tour end. It will be her last chance to say goodbye and thank you to a community of friends who have been an enduring source of creative and professional support and inspiration.

For now, Mieke stands with one foot here, one foot there. On the threshold of a new beginning, Mieke's time in Muskoka may have come to an end, but her commitment to the art and business of throwing pots continues. "It's very gratifying to create something from beginning to end. I'll never retire. I have clay in my blood now."

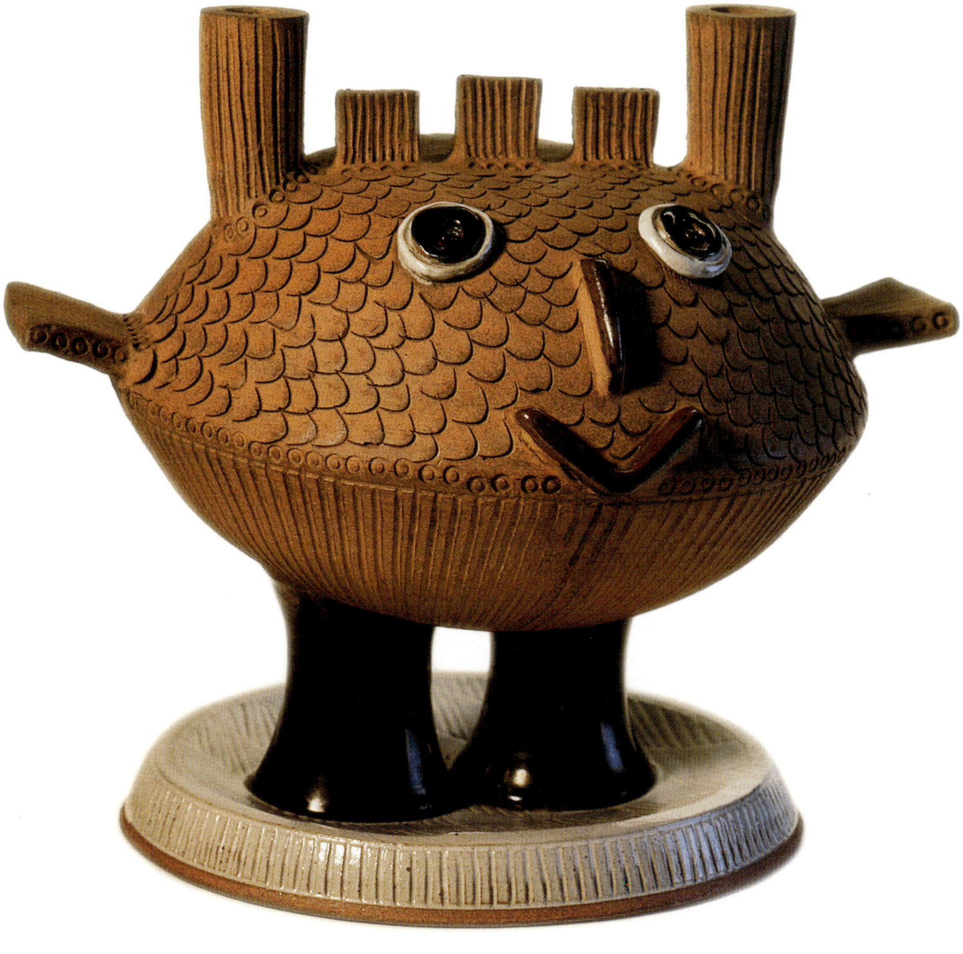

Muskoka Autumn Studio Tour Membership 1979-1998

Brian Ashby*	1980-1996; 1998
Kathy Ashby*	1983-1996; 1998
Gerhardt Balzerit	1981-1988
Janice Barnes	1982-1986; 1989-1996
Beth Barry	1989-1994
Lyette Beaulac	1984-1997
Simon Bisley*	1997-1998
Michael Cleary	1979-1986; 1987**
Wayne Church*	1979-1994; 1996-1998
Hilarey Cole	1979**
Aileen Cowan	1980**
Jim Drury	1990-1996
D.A. Dunford*	1982-1984**; 1985-1987; 1989-1998
Lorraine Eidlitz*	1992-1998
Marina Fricke	1984-1990
Doug Gatche	1987-1995
Robert Gause	1986-1991
Norm Golledge	1985-1988
Richard Green	1979-1983; 1984**; 1985-1988
Ken Hoeght	1980-1995
Merv Hopkins	1983-1990; 1992**; 1993-1994
Roma Hopkins	1983-1985; 1989-1990; 1992**; 1997
Linda Hrynyk*	1989-1998
Bill Hunnisett*	1980-1981; 1990-1998
Elizabeth Johnson*	1996-1998
Frank Johnston	1986-1995
Richard Karon	1979-1980
Charles Knapp*	1979-1998
June Knapp	1982-1985
Eric Lindgren*	1981-1998
Kathy Lindgren	1982-1989
Mieke Martin Soontiëns*	1981-1997; 1998**
Alex Matson	1987-1993
Lyle McIntyre	1979
Jeff Miller	1989-1995
Ed Novak*	1996-1998
John O'Byrne	1981-1984; 1986
Nancy Gray Ogle	1992-1994
Jon Partridge*	1979-1998
Don Pell*	1991-1998
Eyvind Petersen	1990
Paul Rainey	1979-1980; 1982
Will Ruch	1991-1993
Anne Schwartz Bünemann	1987-1989
Barbara Scott	1981-1985
Jamie Sherman	1987-1993; 1996
Stephen Sprague*	1996-1998
Janet Stahle-Fraser*	1996-1998
Stan Tait*	1994-1998
Bill Urban	1980
Richard Vail	1979-1987
Penny Varney*	1993-1998
Brenda Wainman Goulet*	1992-1998
Dirk Wehrmann*	1986-1991; 1997-1998
David Woolcox	1982-1989
Harold Wright	1984-1985; 1987; 1989-1990
Linda Wright*	1991-1998

*1998 Member **Guest Artist

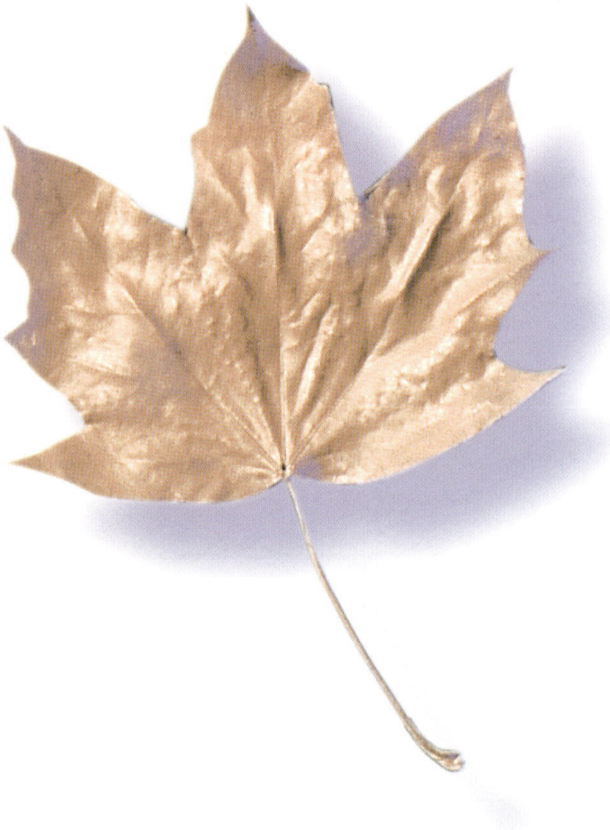